MicroFranchising

MicroFranchising

Creating Wealth at the Bottom of the Pyramid

Edited by

Jason S. Fairbourne, Stephen W. Gibson
and W. Gibb Dyer, Jr

Brigham Young University, USA

Edward Elgar
Cheltenham, UK • Northampton, MA, USA

Published by
Edward Elgar Publishing Limited
Glensanda House
Montpellier Parade
Cheltenham
Glos GL50 1UA
UK

Edward Elgar Publishing, Inc.
William Pratt House
9 Dewey Court
Northampton
Massachusetts 01060
USA

A catalogue record for this book
is available from the British Library

Library of Congress Cataloging in Publication Data

Microfranchising : creating wealth at the bottom of the pyramid / edited by Jason S. Fairbourne, Stephen W. Gibson and W. Gibb Dyer.
    p. cm.
  Includes bibliographical references and index.
1. Franchises (Retail trade) 2. Small business. 3. Poverty. 4. Poverty–Prevention.
I. Fairbourne, Jason S., 1973- II. Gibson, Stephen W. (Stephen Wallace), 1941-
III. Dyer, W. Gibb, 1954-
  HF5429.23.M53 2007
  381'.13–dc22   2006028683

ISBN 978 1 84720 108 9 (cased)

Printed and bound in Great Britain by MPG Books Ltd, Bodmin, Cornwall

Contents

PART III CONCLUSION

Figures

Tables

Boxes

ix

Contributors

Neil Blumenthal is Director of Programs at the Scojo Foundation, is responsible for worldwide programmatic implementation, including expansion, training, and monitoring and evaluation. Neil has several years of experience working abroad and began his association with Scojo Foundation as a consultant in El Salvador. Before joining Scojo, he worked with the International Crisis Group and studied at the Institute for International Mediation and Conflict Resolution in The Hague, Netherlands. He received his Bachelor of Arts in International Relations and History from Tufts University.

Lisa Jones Christensen is an Assistant Professor in the Entrepreneurship Department at the University of North Carolina at Chapel Hill, where she teaches Sustainable Enterprise and courses related to innovation and entrepreneurship in developing economies. She earned an MBA and an MA in International Development from Brigham Young University, and her BA from the University of California at Berkeley.

Jason S. Fairbourne is a Visiting Research Associate Professor at Brigham Young University's Center for Economic Self-reliance. He is the Director of the MicroFranchise Development Initiative and teaches graduate and undergraduate MicroFranchise Consulting Classes. Jason earned a BS in Sociology from UVSC, earning the Behavioral Science Outstanding Student of the Year award. He then earned an MSc in Development Management from the London School of Economics and Political Science, focusing his research on international political economy, Africa's informal economy, poverty, and development management. Jason has written several pieces on microfranchising. Jason co-authored the *MicroFranchise Handbook*, outlining various microenterprises that are being replicated around the world. He is editor and author of the *MicroFranchise Toolkit*, a guide to assisting organizations in systematizing and replicating microfranchises. He also authored the article "MicroFranchising: New Innovative Tool for Economic Development". Jason has presented at various conferences and MicroFranchise Learning Labs and has consulted various organizations in establishing microfranchises.

Naoko Felder-Kuzu is Advisory Board Member of BlueOrchard Finance SA. Since 1988 she has been living in Zurich, Switzerland, working in the financial industry, holding several senior positions in the area of asset management.

Michelle Fertig received an MBA from Columbia Business School, where she focused on General Management. Michelle currently works for Deloitte in the Strategy and Operations Group and lives in NYC.

W. Gibb Dyer, Jr is the O. Leslie Stone Professor of Entrepreneurship and the Academic Director of the Center for Economic Self-reliance in the Marriott School of Management at Brigham Young University. He received his BS and MBA degrees from Brigham Young University and his PhD in management philosophy from the Massachusetts Institute of Technology. He has also served as a visiting professor at IESE (Instituto de Estudios Superiores de la Empresa) in Barcelona, Spain and in 2005 was a visiting scholar at the University of Bath in England. He publishes widely on the topics of family business, entrepreneurship, organizational culture, and on managing change in organizations, and his articles have appeared in many of the top journals in his field. Because of his innovative approach to teaching, Dr Dyer was awarded the 1990 Leavy Award for Excellence in Private Enterprise Education by the Freedoms Foundation at Valley Forge. Professor Dyer has consulted with numerous organizations and is a recognized authority on organizational change, family business, and entrepreneurship. He has been quoted in publications such as *Fortune, The Wall Street Journal, The New York Times*, and *Nation's Business*. At Brigham Young University, he has previously served as Chair of the Department of Organizational Behavior, Director of the Masters Program in Organizational Behavior, and on the University Council on Faculty Rank and Status. He and his wife, Theresa, are the parents of seven children—six daughters and one son.

Stephen W. Gibson is Senior Entrepreneur-in-Residence, Center for Entrepreneurship, and a teaching professor at Brigham Young University Marriott Business School. In 1999, he and his wife, Bette, founded the Academy for Creating Enterprise, in Cebu. This is a non-profit venture, which has taught 865 Fililpino young adults how to start and grow microenterprises. Hundreds of families have worked themselves out of poverty after attending the Academy. He is also the founder of UtahAngels.org, which has invested $18 million in US-based start-ups since 1998. He has started nine businesses, including Barclays Oxygen Homecare with eight offices in six states. Barclays was sold to a national company shortly after being listed as an *Inc.* magazine company. Currently, he teaches, writes and mentors both at BYU and in the Philippines. His primary interests include microfranchising, entrepreneurship, and international development. In

2001 he was named BYU Hawaii Executive of the Year. The Academy was recognized in June 2006 by the Cebu Chamber of Commerce for its contribution in helping alleviate poverty among Filipino young adults and their families. He has written and co-edited a four-volume series entitled *Where There Are No Jobs*. His latest co-edited book, *The MicroFranchise Toolkit*, was published in April 2007. He has also written three other books, including, *Success Beyond the Bottom Line*. He lives with his wife in Provo, Utah.

John Hatch is Founder and Director of Research, FINCA International.

Michael Henriques is the Director of the Job Creation and Enterprise Development Department, ILO, Geneva.

Matthias Herr is an enterprise development specialist, currently working on an ILO project in Sri Lanka.

Molly Hoyt is a partner at Origo Inc., a firm that helps companies working in emerging markets achieve multiple sources of value—financial, social, and environmental. Before Origo, Molly was Director of Partner Programs for Vodafone, where she helped bring hundreds of small to medium-size software companies into partnership with Vodafone around the world. Molly has worked in corporate strategy and marketing roles for a variety of information and communication companies, including Hewlett Packard, Airtouch Communications, and Openwave. Molly has an MBA in International Business from the University of Notre Dame.

Eliot Jamison is a partner at Origo (www.origoinc.com), a research and consulting firm that helps foundations, companies and non-profits become more effective as businesses and as vehicles for social change. At Origo, Eliot manages the consulting business and has a particular focus on projects related to financial and organizational structuring. Before joining Origo, Eliot worked in investment banking for Merrill Lynch and at the private equity investment firm Bessemer Partners. Eliot has a BA from Columbia University in economics and philosophy and an MBA from the University of California at Berkeley Haas School of Business.

Farouk Jiwa is the Director of Business Development & Partnerships at CARE Enterprise Partners, a division of CARE Canada. Farouk is also the Co-founder and Director of Honey Care Africa. He is an Aga Khan Foundation Scholar as well as a Sauvé Scholar (McGill University) and holds a Masters in Environmental Studies from York University, a Postgraduate Diploma in Business & Environment from the Schulich Business School.

Jordan Kassalow co-founded Scojo Vision LLC in 1999. In 2001, he and his partner designated 5 percent of the company's profits to fund the Scojo Foundation, a social enterprise that trains entrepreneurs in developing countries to give basic eye exams and sell low-cost reading glasses in their communities. Dr Kassalow is also a practicing optometrist and senior partner at Drs Farkas, Kassalow, Resnick, PC. Before founding Scojo, he created the Global Health Policy program at the Council on Foreign Relations. He earned a BA from the University of Vermont, and graduated Beta Sigma Kappa from the New England College of Optometry. Dr Kassalow is a 2005 Henry Crown Fellow at the Aspen Institute and a Draper Richards Fellow.

Graham Macmillan is Director of Scojo Foundation. He has had previous experience managing international development programs, most recently with Helen Keller International as Director of Business Development for the ChildSight program. Graham Macmillan serves on the Board of Directors of the FISH Hospitality Program and is a member of the MicroFranchise Development Initiative at Brigham Young University's Marriott School of Management. He received his Bachelor of Arts in International Studies and History from Colby College and his Master of Science in Management of International Public Service Organizations from New York University's Robert F. Wagner School for Public Service.

Kirk Magleby is a Board member of Ascend Alliance.

Herc Tzaras graduated with an MBA from the Columbia Business School in 2006 and is currently working as a consultant for international aid organizations.

Jennifer (Reck) Van Kirk received her MBA from the University of North Carolina at Chapel Hill and currently works for RTI International. Her main projects include working with the Jordan Overseas Investment Network in the United States (JOIN US), which will develop linkages between companies in Jordan and the United States to promote a sustainable trade and investment relationship.

Brad Wood received a BA in Political Science and an MS in Instructional Technology from Utah State University. After working in the tech sector in Washington DC, Brad returned to school to get his MBA from the University of North Carolina at Chapel Hill where he emphasized Real Estate Development and Sustainable Enterprise. Brad currently works as the Project Manager for Cherokee Investment Partner's Mainstream GreenHome.

Warner Woodworth is a Social Entrepreneur and Professor of Organizational Leadership and Strategy in the Marriott School, Brigham Young University. Warner has also founded over a dozen NGOs.

Foreword

As Secretary General of the United Nations, Kofi Annan once stated before a meeting of high-level business representatives: "open markets offer the only realistic hope of pulling billions of people in developing countries out of abject poverty, while sustaining prosperity in the industrialized world." Annan is among those who recognize that the noble efforts of NGOs and charity organizations are not nearly enough to raise the world's poor out of poverty. Long-term solutions are more likely to arise from enterprise creation and market development.

It is my view that business—more than either government or civil society—is uniquely equipped to lead us toward a sustainable world in the years ahead. And that means a world without abject poverty. The need for sustainable economic development at the base of the pyramid (BOP) is clear. What is needed are viable solutions and ways to implement them. This book presents microfranchising as just such a possible solution.

As a Professor of Management at Cornell's Johnson Graduate School of Management, my expertise lies in the implications of environment and sustainability for corporate and competitive strategy. I explain in my book *Capitalism at the Crossroads* (2005) that it is helpful to think of world markets as being of three varieties: developed, emerging, and traditional. While corporations currently focus their efforts almost exclusively on the developed and emerging markets, the vast majority of humanity—some four billion people—live in traditional markets.

Business models for the traditional market must leverage local talent, create employment opportunities, and build capacity in the community. This book shows how microfranchising can be a tool for poverty alleviation that achieves these three objectives and more. By building small, replicable businesses that are adapted to the local culture, microfranchising is a way to provide the poor with valuable goods and services. Even more importantly, however, it also provides a new business model that facilitates local entrepreneurs in launching business ventures that employ local people, and establishes feasible platforms for multinational corporations wishing to work at the BOP.

Microfranchising is not a handout; rather, it is a handover mechanism or tool. The opportunity of running a proven business model is handed over to willing and able individuals who would otherwise be forced to learn through the painful and often very traumatic start-up, fail and start again cycle prevailing in the informal economy. With the capital available either through microcredit institutions or other types of NGOs (or the MNC partner) and the guidance, training, and direction of a microfranchisor, talented but inexperienced and untrained individuals can bridge the gap between the informal and formal economies in ways that were previously nearly impossible.

As many have noted, the market is not an invention of capitalism—it has existed for millennia; indeed, the market appears to be part of the human social DNA. As one who believes that business is the most powerful force for positive change on the planet today, I recommend this book to all business people, government leaders, and others who have a genuine interest in building a sustainable global society. The co-editors and authors in this book are at the forefront of a poverty alleviation movement that could be as promising as microcredit was in the early 1970s.

Stuart L. Hart
SC Johnson Chair of Sustainable Global Enterprise
Professor of Management, Johnson Graduate School of Management
Cornell University

Acknowledgments

This book was conceptualized and developed through the sponsorship of the Academy for Creating Enterprise and Brigham Young University's Center for Economic Self-Reliance, under the direction of the MicroFranchise Development Initiative. We express our gratitude to these groups for their ongoing support of the microfranchise movement.

We are grateful to those that have labored and shared their expertise on the various subjects addressed in this book. These authors include: Michael Henriques, Mathias Herr, John Hatch, Warner Woodworth, Kirk Magleby, Eliot Jamison, Molly Hoyt, Naoko Felder-Kuzu, Lisa Jones Christensen, Jennifer (Reck) Van Kirk, Brad Wood, Michelle Fertig, Herc Tzaras, Jordan Kassalow, Graham Macmillan, Neil Blumenthal, and Farouk Jiwa. We would also like to thank Matt Campbell who provided research and editorial assistance on several of the case studies.

We would like to give a special thanks to all of those who assisted in organizing and who attended the MicroFranchise Learning Labs. The discussions were very interactive and have led to the further development of the microfranchising concept. We would also like to offer a special thanks to the institutions that hosted these learning labs: Brigham Young University, the Millennium Challenge Corporation, and Stanford's Reuters Digital Vision Program. We are particularly grateful to our editor at Edward Elgar Publishing, Alan Sturmer, for his interest in this topic and his ongoing support and counsel.

Finally, we would like to thank our families, friends, and colleagues who have provided support throughout the process.

1. Why Microfranchising is needed now: introduction and book overview

Jason S. Fairbourne

> There is no doubt that the free market, as now organized, does not provide solutions to all social ills. It provides neither economic opportunities nor access to health and education for the poor and elderly.[1]

We live in a unique period of time in which people living in developed nations, such as the United States, enjoy technological advancements that have surpassed previous generations' wildest imaginations and are experiencing a standard of living that was unfathomable half a century ago. Simultaneously, many more are suffering from the tribulations of poverty.

Our world continues to develop technologically at an exponential rate. When learning of new technological innovations, my wife reflects on Penny from the late 1980s cartoon *Inspector Gadget*. In this futuristic cartoon Penny had a notebook that she would use to contact Inspector Gadget and access information from a vast database. Two decades later we call it a Blackberry. I personally own an iPod that has 60 GB of memory; plays movies, songs, audio books, and games; and is smaller than the basic calculator I possessed in high school. This amount of memory is remarkable considering I recently bought my parents a new computer, which replaced their ten-year-old IBM that had less than 1 GB of memory.

Other advancements, such as the Internet, have allowed us to communicate with people around the world as if they were in the cubicle next door. The Internet has also provided anyone who can use a keyboard access to unlimited information, just like Penny. All of these advancements, plus many others, have led to the flattening of our world[2] and allowed the most fortunate to live copious lifestyles.

Regardless of our ingenuity and unsurpassed standard of living, when considering international income levels and poverty, the world is anything but flat. Nearly four billion people still live in poverty, resulting in the deaths of 30 000 children each day. In 2003, 10.6 million of these children died before they reached the age of five.

Numerous similar statistics exist. However, I have found it is hard to explain, and for some to truly understand, the intricacies of poverty solely through mind-boggling statistics. I say this not because I believe that we humans are a callous bunch, or cannot comprehend figures, but simply because I believe that we are emotional beings. We have heard the statistics year after year, yet we allow continents such as Africa to continue to grow poorer.

A girl from my community was kidnapped a few years ago; they found her miraculously over a year later. In the interim, thousands scoured the local mountains searching for her and the story was broadcast around the world, millions knew that she was missing, and had followed the story. Roughly a year after the reunion with the girl and her family, I was living in London and mentioned to a colleague that I was from Utah. He said, "Oh, I know about Utah. That is where Elizabeth Smart was kidnapped. She was on the news every night in Wales." Joseph Stalin and his infamous comment that "a million deaths is a statistic, one death is a tragedy" immediately came to mind. I thought to myself, the true tragedy that this person and millions of others do not see on their televisions is the 30 000 children who die each day from starvation, malnutrition, malaria, TB, diarrhea, and many other preventable diseases. They are no different from Elizabeth Smart, except for the fact that many of those deaths could have been prevented for a few dollars.

However, statistics do impact some of us. Scott Hillstrom read the previous statistic and woke up one day conjuring up the image of 30 000 dead children a day being piled on his front yard. The image was mortifying, and he decided to do something about it. He now has 64 health shops in Kenya providing essential medicines to poor people who previously had no access to medicines. He made a difference. Scott created a business system that delivered health care services to the rural areas of Kenya. He systematized the operation and replicated it 64 times.

The replication of business systems at the grassroots micro level with the intent to alleviate poverty is what we have termed microfranchising. It mirrors franchising except on a smaller scale, with intents to benefit those at the bottom of the pyramid rather than merely elevate the wealthy. Scott Hillstrom's HealthStores are considered microfranchises; they are systematized businesses that are replicated. The underlying intent of a microfranchise is to alleviate poverty through the creation and provision of sound, proven businesses that will in turn increase the earning potential of the microfranchisee. Microfranchises are independently owned and operated; thus, they create income for the individual owner and the owner's employees, while simultaneously providing needed goods and services at an affordable price.

Microfranchising is needed now more than ever. Poverty is ubiquitous throughout the developing world with little signs of diminishing. Market globalization is spreading across the world but leaving many behind while income inequality continues to increase. There have been many attempts to alleviate poverty over the years; some tools have experienced more success than others. More recently there has been a movement for market-based theories of development, particularly Stuart Hart's[3] and C.K. Prahalad's[4] work concerning the base of the pyramid (BOP). This introduction provides an overview of poverty and why microfranchising is needed, briefly describes some of the major methods previously deployed to assist people in need, and highlights the following chapters of this book.

POVERTY

Currently more than eight million people die around the world each year because they are too poor to stay alive.[5]

Both portraying and understanding poverty with its associated destructive implications is indeed a challenge. I have spent a fair amount of time in developing countries, I have lived in mud houses, and I still find defining or describing poverty difficult. The most effective method that I have found is to share personal accounts of this appalling scourge, appalling because absolute poverty can be eradicated.

My first international experience took me to East Asia where I found myself assisting young homeless children in Katmandu; my heart went out to them. But not until a few years later, while living in a rural village in Kenya, did I actually begin to understand what poverty truly is. I was retuning to my *boma* (home) when a neighbor approached me with a lost, troubled look in her eyes. She rushed me to her *boma* where I was handed a small child who lay limp, bending backward over my arms. The child was shaking violently, her eyes were rolled back in the head, and a white substance permeated the mouth. My medical knowledge was limited to my trusty bible *Where There Is No Doctor* (Werner, Thuman and Maxwell, 2006), a book that details symptoms and treatments for primary sicknesses that affect those in developing nations. However, to my credit, I had seen many cases of malaria while in Kenya and spotted it immediately. My first question was how long had the child been in her current state. The answer was a shocking 18 hours. Stunned, I asked the woman what she had done over the last 18 hours to assist her child; I was hoping she would say she visited the clinic, a 45-minute walk down the street.

Unfortunately, she replied that her husband had been searching for the bush doctor to cast the demons out all day and had not returned. I did not want to go against the wishes of her husband, but I knew the child was in the late stages of malaria, so I asked the woman if she would like to visit a medical clinic. She responded yes and I put the woman and child on the back of my motorcycle and was at the clinic in less than five minutes. The clinic was closed, but we found the doctor who lived adjacent to the clinic. She diagnosed the child with malaria and further warned the child would not live long without immediate treatment. For a ten-cent (subsidized) treatment the child was walking three days later.

For the few minutes that I held the child, I empathized with her. I felt the child's pains, struggles, and confusion. As if the young girl was telepathing the question "why?" I asked myself the same question. The face of the young innocent child is still vivid in my mind and I still ask "why?" The child had done nothing to deserve her predicament, except be born into a poor family in Sub-Saharan Africa.

The concept of poverty has many faces, can be approached in many ways, and is difficult to measure. In order to avoid the poverty debates concerning various concepts, I will use the World Bank's definition, which includes many aspects of poverty:

> Poverty is hunger . . . lack of shelter . . . being sick and not being able to see a doctor. Poverty is not being able to go to school and not knowing how to read. Poverty is not having a job, is fear for the future, living one day at a time. Poverty is losing a child to illness brought about by unclean water. Poverty is powerlessness, lack of representation and freedom.
>
> Poverty has many faces, changing from place to place and across time, and has been described in many ways. Most often, poverty is a situation people want to escape.[6]

The developing world is plagued with chronic poverty, which is perpetuated through wars, AIDS, natural cataclysms, corruption, and many other complex variables. Africa and South Asia are the most poverty-stricken regions in the world, with the "lowest levels of per capita income."[7] A 2004 article in *The Economist* highlighted the frailty of the developing world, paying specific attention to the precariousness of Africa. Half of Africa's population lives on less than 65 cents a day; furthermore, Africa, as a whole, is the only continent to grow poorer in the last 25 years.[8]

Poverty is a vicious cycle that spirals out of control as each detrimental variable builds upon a previous one. Education, lack of hope, government, globalization, trade laws, population growth, lack of access to credit, natural disasters, lack of employment, war, disease, and many other variables combine to hold people in poverty. These variables are so inter-related that one does not supersede the other. For example, an impoverished family is struggling to survive by growing their own food and selling whatever they can to pay for school fees. Life is not easy, but they are surviving and they have hope for a better future for their educated children. Slowly the rains become fewer and fewer until it is official that their region is suffering from a drought. At first they have no surplus to sell, so their children are pulled from school. Then they are unable to produce enough food to survive, so they pack up and move to an urban center to find employment. Ultimately they lose hope for their children's future, they have abandoned their land, and years later, just as they are getting back on their feet, a coup forms to overthrow the government, starting a civil war. There are many examples and relationships among these variables, but the important thing to remember is they are inter-related.

One of the primary problems with development theories is everyone seems to have *the* solution to end poverty. Unfortunately, there is no silver bullet to ending poverty, there are merely tools that, if used properly and in conjunction with each other, can alleviate and end poverty.

MARKET GLOBALIZATION

There is no doubt poverty is present throughout the world, most of all in the developing world. With the onset of market globalization, people living in poverty have little choice but to turn to the market and create businesses to survive. They operate microenterprises in the informal economy, and they are innovative and persistent. But as much as we should admire their resolution to work hard and improve their lives, they remain very poor. Simply put, market economies as they are currently structured do not work for the poor. People operating within informal economies manage to eke out a hand-to-mouth subsistence living but do not have the know-how, skills, or capital needed to be successful business owners. In essence, they are forced entrepreneurs.

Amartya Sen[9] argues that increasing a person's capabilities is how development should be addressed; the right to work and earn a sufficient wage is a prudent method to the actualization of one's capabilities. Thus, according to Sen, the market is an important tool for increasing the standard of living of millions of people around the world. He is right that markets have indeed been successful, primarily in Asian countries and particularly in China; however, I must note that China's market is managed by a strong government. In other continents, such as Africa, weak states cannot govern the market effectively, and the poor suffer as a result. Even in China, recent studies show that income inequality is increasing rapidly.[10]

Globalization as defined by Joseph Stiglitz[11] is:

> The closer integration of the countries and peoples of the world which has been brought about by the enormous reduction in the cost of transportation and communication, the breaking down of artificial barriers to the flows of goods and services, capital, knowledge, and (to a lesser extent) people across borders.

Market capitalism is currently the prevailing ideology and development strategy and has been since the Bretton Woods conference in 1944, where the International Monetary Fund (IMF) and the International Bank for Reconstruction and Development (IBRD, which is commonly known as the World Bank) were formed. Market globalization is currently a buzz topic with advocates at each end of the debate fervently arguing their perspectives. The reality is that market globalization has had both successes and failures. One benefit of the general adoption of market ideology is it has provided a space for people to operate and earn a living. However, most do so informally, using the market merely as a survival mechanism. Additionally, one primary failure of the market globalization is that the income gap between the poor and the wealthy continues to increase. Thus, the poor are not the primary beneficiaries of market globalization as it is currently structured.

A few interesting statistics[12] show that:

1. Twenty percent of the population in developed nations consume 86 percent of the world's goods.
2. In 1960, 20 percent of the world's people in the richest countries had 30 times the income of the poorest 20 percent—in 1997, 74 times as much.
3. The combined wealth of the world's 200 richest people hit $1 trillion in 1999; the combined income of the 582 million people living in the 43 least developed countries is $146 billion.
4. An analysis of long-term trends shows the distance between the richest and poorest countries was roughly:
   - 3 to 1 in 1820;
   - 11 to 1 in 1913;
   - 35 to 1 in 1950;
   - 44 to 1 in 1973;
   - 72 to 1 in 1992.

Figure 1.1 shows the distribution of world GDP for 1989.

Furthermore, the prevailing theory is that the cost of goods and services decrease as market globalization spreads, trade barriers are lessened and access to goods and services increases. This is indeed what we experience in developing nations. However, developing countries have not benefited as we have. Goods and services often cost more to the poor than they do to

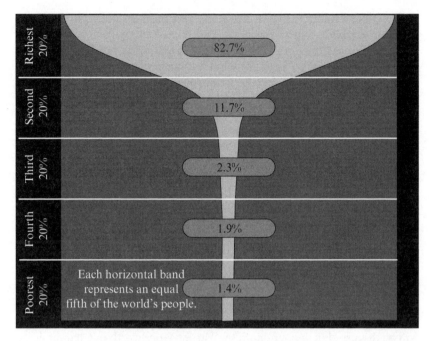

Source: United Nations Development Programme 1992, Human Development Report 1992 (New York: Oxford University Press for the United Nations Development Programme).[13]

Figure 1.1 *Distribution of world GDP, 1989 (percentage of total, with quintiles of population ranked by income)*

wealthy consumers in developed nations and more than they cost middle-class citizens in their own countries. A report to the Secretary General of the United Nations[14] illustrates this point: "In Mumbai, slum-dwellers in Dharavi pay 1.2 times more for rice, 10 times more for medicines, and 3.5 times more for water than do middle class people living at the other end of the city on Bhulabhai Road." All in all markets alone are not the panacea to eliminating poverty. However, they are part of the solution.

The market has successes as well. Currently, the market, primarily the informal market, provides employment opportunities and provides goods and services that weak markets cannot. For example, in developing countries, 63 percent of health care expenditures are in the private sector, as opposed to 33 percent spent in developed countries.[15] The downside is, as previously mentioned, the products come at a high price.

Many tools have been implemented to assist those operating within informal markets: from business development services (BDS) intended to assist existing microenterprises grow and develop their business to the tool of microfinance, which scales easily and provides access to capital to grow or establish a new business. The microfinance tool has arguably made the largest impact on poor people operating in market economies. Furthermore, there is a great potential for partnership between microfranchising and microfinance. In fact, we are already seeing partnerships being forged. Here are a few examples. BRAC, a large microfinance institution (MFI) in Bangladesh, has village health workers, called *Shastho Shebikas*, who have been trained to treat basic health ailments, record health information, and refer patients to health centers, in addition to selling essential health commodities to earn a profit. BRAC has replicated these health shops across Bangladesh and is currently partnering with the Scojo Foundation (see the case study in Part II) to add eyeglasses to its product offering. Grameen has been operating a village phone program where their borrowers sell phone time for years. SKS Microfinance is launching a franchise division and FINCA is in discussions with Honey Care Africa. The MicroFranchise Development Initiative at Brigham Young University is partnering with Freedom from Hunger to create a microfranchise that delivers health services to the poor in Ghana while providing a business for microcredit borrowers. These developing partnerships are not surprising, and I expect the trend to continue. Additional economic development tools will be discussed in greater depth by Warner Woodworth in Chapter 4.

C.K. Prahalad and Stuart Hart have been leading the way with the BOP movement, demonstrating that businesses can alleviate poverty through profits. They argue there is a large untapped market at the base of the pyramid, and if companies will restructure their delivery systems to provide goods and services at an affordable price, they can serve the poor while earning profits. The underlying theory is to sell products to billions of people at smaller margins instead of selling to millions of people at higher margins. The result of this action is a win-win situation for the poor and for investors. I believe it is indeed a good idea. However, the question remains: how do large companies restructure themselves to profit off of volume and penetrate a market with little to no infrastructure? This book proposes a new tool to assist the forced entrepreneur to create employment and to provide a method for MNCs to get their goods and services to the market, all in a sustainable manner through a concept called microfranchising.

MICROFRANCHISING: THE NEW TOOL

Besides the fact that the average US franchise costs roughly $250 000[15] and microfranchises range from $25 to 25 000,[17] the "micro" in microfranchising stands for more than mini or small. "Micro" is essential to microfranchising and in this sense has a social connotation that refers to grassroots bottom-up initiatives, poverty alleviation, benevolence, base of the pyramid, and the like. The term micro has been built up by the success of microfinance. Microfinance is, in its simplest form, the provision of capital to a person who lacks access to a formal financial institution. Microfinance has been extremely successful in reaching over 200 million people, while for the most part being economically sustainable. With all things considered, "micro" also represents sustainability. Thus, microfranchising can be thought of as poverty alleviating, social, grassroots, BOP, benevolent, and barefoot franchising.

The franchise in microfranchise represents replication to scale. This involves systematizing an operation, paying close attention to each and every aspect of a business until it is a turn-key operation, then replicating it to scale. Franchising embodies the concept of granting the right, privilege, or access to a proven business system. There is much to be learned from traditional franchises, which can be applied to microfranchising.

The marriage of the two terms makes up microfranchising, which is indeed very different from both microfinance and from franchising. For example, in traditional franchising, the purpose for establishing a franchise is to grow one's business quickly in order to increase profits. In microfranchising, the focus is more on the microfranchisee and how he/she benefits from buying into a proven systematized business. A microfranchise is established to assist the poor in creating a sustainable income through owning and operating their own business. The reduction of risk, provision of specific training, ongoing mentoring, and reduction of creative burden are all benefits to the microfranchisee. Microfranchises above all are established as a poverty-alleviation tool:

> Microfranchising addresses three core problems that prevent people from becoming economically self-reliant. (1) The lack of skills needed to grow a successful business. (2) The lack of jobs in developing countries. (3) The lack of goods and services available to the poor.
>
> Microfranchising provides a solution to these core problems by first, providing those who do not possess an entrepreneurial skill set with a business blueprint that, if followed, will lead to greater individual economic success. Thus, it is not necessary to have an entrepreneurial spirit in order to be a successful microfranchisee. In fact, a true entrepreneur would not be a good candidate as a microfranchisee. Second, microfranchises are often larger than traditional microenterprises; thus, creating jobs for those who do not have managerial skills and would be better suited as an employee or technician. Third, microfranchising provides multinational corporations (MNCs) with an effective method of delivery for their goods and services to the BOP at an equitable price.[18]

There are three key underlying financial structures that underpin the various business models (microfranchise business models will be discussed in Chapter 7). The three key underlying financial structures are as follows: social microfranchising, sustainable microfranchising, and for-profit micro-franchising. A microfranchise may begin operations in any one of these models and shift to another and ultimately end up as an amalgamation of multiple models.

Social Microfranchising

The objective of social microfranchising is first and foremost to provide goods and services at an affordable price and secondly to create jobs at the BOP. Social microfranchising operates off of a financial model that is not focused on sustainability. Therefore, a social microfranchise does not mind subsidizing product costs in order to reach its objective. One obvious draw-back of the model is that a continuous flow of funds into the project is needed. The benefit is that it is easier for the microfranchisee to earn higher income when the products cost him/her less. Also, the lower costs are passed on to the consumer. This model is commonly used by pharmacies in developing countries.

Sustainable Microfranchising

Sustainable microfranchising approaches the business model from an objective to create profit for the microfranchisee and enough surplus profit to sustain the microfranchisor. Any additional profit is used to either create more franchises or to assist the existing microfranchisees in increasing their profits through initiatives such as additional training and marketing. This model seeks a triple bottom line, which is: (1) creating profit for the microfranchisee; (2) financial sustainability; and (3) the provision of goods and services at an equitable cost.

For-profit Microfranchising

For-profit microfranchising is very similar to sustainable franchising with one added variable, which is to create enough profit for the microfranchisor to return profit to investors. The obvious downside is the potential for exploitation when a franchise system is not fully developed and is strug-gling financially. This model requires much higher start-up capital in order to scale quickly and become profitable enough to repay investors. Even within the sustainable microfranchise model, sustainability may not occur until the franchise system has grown to a sustainable point; that is to say, a microfranchise in any model may not be sustainable until it has a certain number of franchisees operating franchises that pay royalties. Thus, the start-up capital must be significant enough to launch enough microfranchises to generate profit for investors. This model works best with multinational corporations and the like (see the Vodacom case study in Part II of this book). People and organizations that pursue this model but lack the financial and technical capacity to see it through, run the risk of losing sight of the social aspect and placing an undue amount of emphasis on repaying investors. This is my primary concern with this model.

All three models contain "micro" and thus have a social objective. However, it is obvious that varying degrees of benevolent motives exist. Ultimately there is a fine balance between meeting financial objectives to reach sustainability and assisting the poor simultaneously. I believe this will be the ultimate challenge for microfranchisors as microfranchises continue to be launched. Various microfranchise business structures are emerging, with some adopting NGO status, others private, and some an amalgamation of the two, as is seen with Honey Care Africa (see Chapter 8).

Markets are indeed extremely important to the poor, just as they are to those who have benefited from them in developed countries. Markets are where people earn a living and survive; thus, markets must be made to work for the poor. Markets can be very harmful to the poor if they are exploitative. I believe microfranchising offers a path to increase success for those operating in developing and often informal markets without exploiting those at the bottom. Microfranchising is needed now more than ever; in fact, it may not have worked 20 years ago. Microfinance has paved the way and established a strong platform for new microeconomic development tools including microfranchising. However, it must be noted that markets are not *the* solution; they are merely part of the solution to the poverty conundrum. Governments are equally important; strong governments are imperative to govern markets. Microfranchising is a grassroots, bottom-up approach to increasing the success of people operating within emerging or developing markets. With market globalization and income inequality increasing, the deployment of microfranchising as a method of making markets work for the poor has great potential to create wealth at the base of the pyramid, allowing people to reach a state of economic self-reliance.

BOOK OVERVIEW

The following chapters were specifically written for this book; thus, there is more continuity and flow to this book than a typical edited publication that compiles essays and articles from various sources. The editors have selected key authoritative individuals to author chapters related to their field of expertise. The book is broken into three parts. Part I deals with theories of microfranchising and its potential to be a valuable poverty alleviation tool. Part II focuses on microfranchise business models, provides four case studies and discusses how to finance microfranchises, followed by the conclusion in Part III.

Part I: Microfranchise Theory

In Chapter 2, Stephen W. Gibson addresses the core microfranchising issues. Microfranchising is a new burgeoning poverty alleviation tool that is gaining much traction. However, considering the novelty of the concept, Chapter 2 is crucial in establishing a firm foundation concerning what microfranchising is and how it works.

Michael Henriques and Matthias Herr discuss the relationship between microfranchising and the informal sector in Chapter 3. They highlight various concepts surrounding the informal economy and how microfranchising can be a valuable tool not only to create employment but also to create sustainable businesses that move people out of informality and into formal institutions with the associated rights and privileges.

Microfranchising is a new tool, but there are many other tools that have been developed to assist those in the informal economy and lift people out of poverty. Warner Woodworth, in Chapter 4, addresses the current economic development tools and their corresponding advantages and disadvantages.

John Hatch, author of Chapter 5, outlines the benefits of microfranchising to the microcredit industry and how microcredit can assist microfranchising. He discusses the strengths and deficiencies of both microfinance and microfranchising; he concludes that the combination is more effective than either initiative as a stand-alone development tool.

Eliot Jamison and Molly Hoyt, tackle the issue of MNCs, the base of the pyramid, and microfranchising in Chapter 6. They begin the journey with corporate interest in emerging markets, MNCs' social responsibility, financial opportunity, and the need for innovation. This discussion leads Jamison and Hoyt into Hart and Prahalad's BOP literature and identifies cases of MNCs that have taken on the challenge of reaching the BOP. Jamison and Hoyt expound on the following three concepts: microfranchising as a distribution channel, microfranchises as a supply base, and microfranchising as an enterprise development strategy.

Part II: Microfranchising in Practice

Part II highlights various microfranchising models and provides pertinent case studies designed to enhance readers' understanding of how microfranchising applies to development. Kirk Magleby identifies 15 microfranchise business models in Chapter 7; he provides brief examples that exist in both developed and developing countries. The complexity of the models varies greatly—from a business-in-a-box to a business format microfranchise.

Chapters 8 through 11 examine four microfranchises in depth: Honey Care Africa, HealthStores, Vodacom, and Scojo. Honey Care Africa trains people to be beekeepers, provides them with the necessary equipment, and trains them to own and operate the microfranchise. HealthStores also operates in East Africa; it is located in Kenya and has a network of 64 health stores that provide essential medicines. Vodacom is an MNC that has utilized the microfranchising model to create impressive revenue. It has over 4000 microfranchises that sell phone services to people in rural villages in South Africa. Scojo is in operation in South America and in East Asia (India and Bangladesh) where it trains women to perform basic eye examinations and provides them with a backpack with eyeglasses, other complimentary products, and necessary tools to operate the business efficiently.

Naoko Felder-Kuzu, in Chapter 12, examines the idea that some microfinance funds, plus new funds, can be adjusted to support microfranchising. These microfranchise funds can be equally rewarding for both the franchise organizations and the franchisee. She addresses the key question as to how microfranchising can be funded.

Chapter 13 in Part III, written by W. Gibb Dyer, Jr, summarizes the opportun-ities associated with microfranchising, the barriers that will be faced, and future questions that need to be addressed.

CONCLUSION

This book is intended to highlight a new and innovative poverty-alleviation tool designed to create wealth at the base of the pyramid, and perhaps, spur some thought similar to Scott Hillstrom's that is followed by action. I propose we prove Stalin wrong; that the appalling poverty statistics do indeed have meaning, and that 30 000 children dying each day means something. The true tragedy will be if absolute poverty does not become a statistic of the past. If people have access to income that leads to economic self-reliance, they will be able to provide the basic necessities for their children. They will be able to educate them, immunize them, feed them properly, and put an end to the horrifying poverty statistics.

Considering that markets have failures and do not always work for the poor and considering the proliferation of market globalization, microfranchises are needed now more than ever. Microfranchising is an essential tool that helps people be more successful working in market economies. Microfranchising has an important role to play in the poverty-alleviation movement; with the potential to have a lasting impact on the developing world. Microfranchising offers a sustainable method to deliver goods and services to the poor at an affordable price, through a social business format that increases income and reduces costs simultaneously; thus, creating wealth at the bottom of the pyramid.

NOTES

1. Yunus, Muhammad (1997), *Banker to the Poor: Micro-lending and the Battle Against World Poverty*, United States of America: Public Affairs.
2. Friedman, Thomas L. (2005), *The World is Flat: A Brief History of the Twenty-first Century*, United States of America: Farrar, Straus and Giroux.
3. Hart, Stuart L. (2005), *Capitalism at the Crossroads: The Unlimited Business Opportunities in Solving the World's Most Difficult Problems*, United States of America: Pearson Education, Inc.
4. Prahalad, C.K. (2005), *Fortune at the Bottom of the Pyramid: Eradicating Poverty Through Profits*, United States of America: Pearson Education, Inc.
5. Sachs, Jeffrey (2005), *The End of Poverty: Economic Possibilities for Our Time*, United States of America: The Penguin Press.
6. Understanding Poverty (2006), The World Bank Group, 11 June 2006, accessed at www.worldbank.org/WBSITE/EXTERNAL/TOPICS/EXTPOVERTY/0,,contentMDK :20153855~menuPK:373757~pagePK:148956~piPK:216618~theSitePK:336992,00.html.
7. Sen, Amartya (1999), *Development as Freedom*, United States of America: Anchor Books, and simultaneously in Canada: Random House of Canada Limited, p. 99.
8. The *Economist* (2004), "How to Make Africa Smile: A Survey of Sub-Saharan Africa", 17–23 January.
9. Sen, Amartya (1999), *Development as Freedom*, United States of America: Anchor Books, and simultaneously in Canada: Random House of Canada Limited.
10. *The Economist* (2006), "A Survey of China", 25–31 March.
11. Stiglitz, Joseph E. (2002), *Globalization and Its Discontents*, New York: W.W. Norton & Company, Inc.
12. Shah, Anup, Poverty Facts and Stats, 3 April 2006. Global Issues That Affect Everyone, 11 June 2006, accessed at www.Globalissues.org/TradeRelated/Facts.asp.
13. Robert Hunter Wade (2001), 'The Rising Inequality of World Income Distribution', *Finance and Development*, **38**:(4), December 2001.
14. Commision on the Private Sector and Development (2004), "Unleashing entrepreneurship: making business work for the poor", report to the Secretary General of the United Nations.
15. Ibid.
16. Quick Franchise, Franchising, Facts & Statistics. 1999–2006. AZFranchises.com, 11 June 2006, accessed at www.azfranchises.com/franchisefacts.htm.
17. Fairbourne, Jason and Stephen W. Gibson (2005), *Where There Are No Jobs*, vol. 4.
18. Fairbourne, Jason (2006), "MicroFranchise development initiative: progressive thinking for creating economic self-reliance", *Advances in Economic Self-reliance*, forthcoming.

PART I

Microfranchise theory

2. Microfranchising: the next step on the development ladder

Stephen W. Gibson

After months of stressful job searching, Ricardo finally found a job at a clothing-production factory in Manila. Ricardo was so relieved to have a steady job that he learned his duties in just two days and always worked extra hard to please his supervisor. But his efforts were rewarded with what felt like a slap in the face: just three short months after being hired, Ricardo learned that he no longer had a job because the plant was moving to China to take advantage of cheaper labor. Ricardo's brother-in-law suggested that Ricardo begin selling burgers, so Ricardo opened up a burger stand as the family's sole source of income. He had high hopes about what he could accomplish. Opening his stand near a hospital with high foot traffic, Ricardo was able to sell 25 burgers – his whole inventory – on the first day. He was overjoyed because his sales revenue for that single day was more than twice what he brought home each day from the clothing factory.

Despite his excellent first day on the job, Ricardo's success during his first month of operations was quite varied. On some days, business was so good that he sold his entire supply of meat and buns; on other days, his meat patties would begin to spoil in the hot sun. Sometimes, his friends would stop by and ask for a free meal; Ricardo always obliged because he was grateful for their support. But sometimes, he gave away so much that he wouldn't have enough capital the next day to buy his needed meat and buns. Because Ricardo wasn't disciplined in how he ran his business, he soon became concerned that he might not be able to realize his dreams of supporting his family on the income provided by his burger stand.

Even though he continues to work 12-hour days and really enjoys running his business, Ricardo constantly struggles to stay ahead of his personal and business expenses and is perpetually just one or two working days away from hunger. Often, he wishes he were back at his old job where he never had to worry about anything but showing up on time.

Each day, he notices larger, more established food vendors in the marketplace that seem to be successful. He watches the actions of the owners (who seem much busier than he), but he doesn't know what they are doing differently to be successful. And in reality, he doesn't have much time to think about how to improve his business because he has to work so hard to just stay afloat. And so he continues watching . . . and waiting for his lucky day when his burger stand will become what he hopes it can be.

THE NEED FOR MICROFRANCHISING

Sadly, Ricardo's story is fairly descriptive of "normal life" for the majority of people living in developing nations. In those countries, local economies are very simple and are often built upon and sustained by the activity of millions of people like Ricardo—a group of impoverished people sometimes referred to as "necessity entrepreneurs."[1] These entrepreneurs don't create microenterprises because they are particularly interested in being in business for themselves; they are usually forced to set up small retail stores, stalls, and tables in order to survive—in order to have something to feed their families each day.

These hard-working necessity entrepreneurs are not in the minority. In fact, "the majority of the world's poor are not employed in factories; they are self-employed—as peasant farmers, rural peddlers, urban hawkers, and small producers, usually involved in agriculture and small trade in the world's vast 'informal economy.' "[2] This finding is supported by data from individual countries; in the Philippines, for example, Imelda Madarang, Director of the Philippine Center for Entrepreneurship, estimates that approximately 93 percent of all businesses are microenterprises run by necessity entrepreneurs.[3]

Most microentrepreneurs start buying and selling small items because no jobs are available for them[4] or because they lack the ability to recognize or take advantage of real opportunities when they do exist. This lack of available employment opportunities is often due to the absence of employers nearby, the person's lack of education or preparation, or the person's lack of political or social connections. Whatever the reason, many poor, uneducated people become necessity entrepreneurs simply because they have no other choice.

These hand-to-mouth livelihood businesses are inherently unstable. The meager daily income of necessity entrepreneurs rises and falls based on dozens of factors that are generally out of their control. They are victimized by price wars, government intervention, give-away relief programs, loan sharks, crooked law officers, civil unrest, national disasters, and numerous other external forces. They also suffer from the poverty penalty, meaning that they generally must pay higher prices for basic goods (e.g., credit, medication, food, shampoo) simply because they buy in smaller quantities.[5] Living as they do, necessity entrepreneurs seldom have enough time, knowledge, or capital to think about growing their microenterprises. They simply live from day to day, hoping to fight off any forces that could rob them and their families of a small meal at the end of the day.

Because running a sidewalk business is so stressful, most necessity entrepreneurs see their situation as hopeless – and, therefore, temporary. They plan to operate their microenterprise only as long as they have to. Early on, they hold high hopes of escaping their business and way of life by getting a job, winning a lottery, moving to the big city, marrying into money, emigrating to the West, or raising well-educated children who will support them in their old age. But as time passes and the operators see themselves still doing the same thing day in and day out, most lose hope all together.

While they are waiting for a "real job" or a "better break," these necessity entrepreneurs experience varying levels of success with their temporary businesses. People with some business experience are usually able to make a small amount of profit each day, but people who have no money to invest in a good product or who have no training in sales or business struggle to make ends meet. Only a very few make enough money to build a stable financial foundation for their struggling family or contribute to the growth of their local economies.

Herein lies the problem: vibrant economies cannot be built solely on the backs of microenterprises because these businesses are part of the informal economy and generate very little revenue, profit, or personal income for the business operator. Businesses that operate in the informal economy – as opposed to the more stable formal economy – don't have business licenses, don't keep accounting records, pay no taxes, and essentially operate in a recognized but gray or informal market.

In order for these temporary, informal microenterprises to move into the formal economy and begin generating profits that can contribute to the vitality of the local economy and to the self-reliance of the business owner, the microenterprises must grow to a point where they can provide beyond just a day-to-day subsistence. They must generate sufficient revenue to facilitate reinvestment of profits in the business, and they must increase in size so that business owners can break out of their poverty and begin enjoying a life of self-reliance that comes only with a consistent income and the acquisition of assets that increase in value.

HISTORY OF DEVELOPMENT WORK

For decades, people and organizations from modern nations have recognized that the significant changes that must take place in the Third World won't happen without outside help. And if these changes do take place without outside influences, they will likely take years, during which the grind of trauma, disappointment, and starvation can take a huge toll on the poor. Recognizing the hopelessness of the situation in which the world's poor find themselves,[6] tens of thousands of relief organizations have sped up their economic-growth efforts with the goal of helping people from some of the world's poorest countries and villages escape the grasp of poverty.

In the beginning, governments granted foreign aid to struggling countries with the express purpose of paying for food, medicine, and shelter provisions to be provided to the poor of those nations. Due to systematic abuses of these resources by people in positions of power in the receiving countries, much of the granted aid never made it to the people who needed it most.

In an attempt to remedy this problem, churches and religious charities became heavily involved in meeting the needs of people living in poverty around the world. They motivated volunteers to collect resources and give humanitarian services to people in dire need. These humanitarian efforts were desperately needed, but they were generally not successful at eradicating poverty – they just relieved its devastating effects for a very short period.

The history of outside relief efforts demonstrates that "[f]oreign aid can help but, like windfall wealth, can also hurt. It can discourage effort and plant a crippling sense of incapacity."[7] While these well-intentioned groups undoubtedly provide temporary relief for the sufferers, they often produce unwanted side-effects that end up hurting the local economies. For example, as they give out used clothing, they end up hurting local microentrepreneurs whose livelihoods depend upon selling used clothing. Similar relief efforts bring about other unintended consequences when the local economies are upset by free medicines, free dental care, free eye glasses, and other humanitarian efforts.[8]

Microcredit Organizations

In their search for a more permanent solution to poverty – one that "come[s] from within"[9] – groups of dedicated development workers led by social entrepreneurs (people like Muhammad Yunus, founder of Grameen Bank; John Hatch of FINCA; and Fazle Hasan Abed of BRAC) began acting on their beliefs that what the poor need to lift themselves out of poverty is not a handout, but a small amount of credit and some well-organized encouragement. These organizations pioneered new efforts to eliminate poverty by providing small microcredit loans so poor people could start microenterprises (or buy more merchandise for their already-operating stands) and begin generating or increasing income for their families.

The conceptual framework of microcredit has revolutionized development work. Although the microcredit industry was once made up of only a small handful of organization, the Microcredit Summit Campaign estimates that as of December 2004, a total of 3164 microcredit institutions were actively engaged in loaning money to and working with more than 92 million clients.[10] Some estimates reach as high as 125 million.

Many microcredit organizations distribute their funds through peer groups of five people, usually all women, who live close to each other and act as a support system for each other in the development of their microenterprises and the repayment of their loans. One secret to these groups' success is the fact that the loan is issued not to individuals but to the group of five as a single unit. The social pressure and sense of camaraderie created by this group organization has led to very high repayment rates – usually between 95 and 99 percent[11] – and often a gradual elimination of poverty from the lives of the loan recipients.

The results of various microcredit organizations and activities around the world have been very encouraging and have transformed millions of lives. Indeed, microcredit has proven to be an effective tool for helping women help themselves and their families. Alex Counts, President of Grameen Foundation USA and author of *Give Us Credit* (1996), comments on the effectiveness of microcredit programs by stating, "Among women who had been borrowing from Grameen for eight or more years, 46 percent had crossed above the poverty line and had accumulated enough assets to be unlikely to fall back below it. Others were making great progress."[12] Microcredit success stories are not limited only to Grameen Bank's work – hundreds of other microcredit organizations experience similar successes as they use microcredit to infuse hope and resources into individual families.

Although many microenterprises that were started with microcredit loans have prospered and transformed lifestyles for the people who run them, they seldom move beyond the ability to provide a somewhat meager income for the borrower. In 1998, a group of university students interviewed microcredit borrowers about the status and size of their microenterprises. Of 381 interviewees, only a very small percentage had grown their microenterprises to the point where they had hired a non-family employee; only one had a non-cottage business, several employees, and multiple locations in multiple villages. Although the rest of the interviewees had improved their standard of living, they were still very small by comparison.[13]

Although microcredit is doing much good, it is clearly not the sole solution to the world's poverty problems. Jeffrey D. Sachs describes the path from poverty to self-reliance as the "ladder of development."[14] In *The End of Poverty* (2005), Sachs defines three degrees of poverty into which all of the world's poor fall: extreme poverty, moderate poverty, and relative

poverty.[15] Those who live in "extreme poverty" cannot meet their basic survival needs; they are chronically hungry. "Moderate poverty" describes
those who can meet their basic needs, but just barely. The "relative poverty"
label is applied to those whose household income falls below a given pro-
portion of the average national income. These people generally lack quality
health care, education, and other prerequisites for upward social mobility.
While different types of development work are suited to each degree of
poverty, no single framework can meet the needs of every group.

Many believe that microcredit works best when it targets people who are
economically active (e.g., gainfully employed or involved in a promising
business-related activity), not those in extreme poverty with no promising
opportunities to progress, even with significant help.[16] By helping these
people, microcredit essentially rescues countries that have previously been
on the ground – unable to even start climbing the ladder. In other words,
microcredit's role in economic development is to help "the poorest countries . . . get a foot on the ladder."[17]

The Next Step

Microcredit leaders such as John Hatch[18] and Muhammad Yunus[19] have
recently begun turning their attention to what some believe is the next step
on the development ladder: microfranchising. (Although Yunus does not
describe his efforts as microfranchising, his group of enterprising
"Grameen phone ladies" is essentially an embodiment of this unique business method. Under its microfranchise-like structure, GrameenPhone provides financing and sells airtime to village residents in Bangladesh who
lease a cell phone and sell airtime to their neighbors. As of 2003,
GrameenPhone had 850 000 cellular phone subscribers, and 24 000 of those
were operated by Grameen phone ladies.)[20] The microfranchising method
of development is recognized by many as the most innovative and fastest
way to transform temporary, informal microenterprises (many of which
started as a result of microcredit loans) into legitimate, stable businesses.

Commenting on the GrameenPhone model, Alex Counts writes this
about franchising and Muhammad Yunus: "The genius of Muhammad
Yunus' work is not that he figured out how to empower poor people with
loans, but that he was able to develop a model that he could replicate more
than a thousand times while maintaining control over the quality of the
enterprise. . . . It takes an entirely different set of skills to start a pilot
project than it does to successfully 'franchise' it. Pilot projects reach hundreds of poor people; franchises touch millions."[21] Before we can understand microfranchising, let's begin with a discussion on franchising – the
model upon which microfranchising is based.

FRANCHISING

Franchising is a form of business whose purpose is to distribute products or services. Two groups of people are involved in a franchise system: (1) the *franchisor* who develops a product or service and essentially rents out the rights to the business name and system, and (2) the *franchisee* who pays fees and royalties for the right to operate under the franchisor's business name and according to the franchisor's specific business pattern and plan.[22,23]

Franchising has become the most popular system for growing a business in the United States and is currently a multi-billion dollar industry. In the United States, franchising "accounts for more than $1 trillion in sales annually and employs more than 8 million people, or 1 in every 7 adults. . . . A new franchised outlet is opened every 8 minutes of each business day, totaling more than 180 franchised outlets a day."[24]

The franchise model is unique in the business world because of the mutually beneficial relationship between the franchisor and the franchisees. Franchise USA™ Business Advisors explain that the franchisor and franchisees support each other because both parties "have a strong vested interest in the success of the brand and keeping their customers happy."[25] The franchisor does more than just sell a business idea and a turn-key system[26] to franchisees: the franchisor provides initial and ongoing training and support, develops new products and advertising campaigns to attract customers to franchisees' establishments, and sometimes offers bulk purchasing programs to help franchisees take advantage of bulk discounts.[27] Franchisees help the franchisor by providing feedback on the success of new promotions or products, increasing brand awareness by providing good customer service at each location, and paying royalties based on the franchise's sales.

Independent business owners usually turn to the franchise business model when they want to expand their business and replicate their successful processes but lack access to the capital necessary to fund that immediate growth and don't want to incur debt. Franchising facilitates rapid growth, makes money for the franchisor, and gives the franchisor a reasonable level of protection that the franchises will all be operated the way that that the franchisor wants. Potential franchisees buy into franchises because the franchise system increases their chances of being successful in a short amount of time. Franchising brings three distinct advantages to those who become franchisees rather than embarking on independent business ventures: reduced risk, proven systems and professional advertising, and branding methods.

Reduced Risk

The franchising model has been so successful in the developed world because it eliminates many of the risks involved in starting a business. "Born entrepreneurs" – people who possess the creativity, business acumen, and resources to start a new company – develop the business plan, the systems, and the products and then sell their ideas to franchisees who might lack entrepreneurial vision and skills but are qualified by their determination to follow a complete business blueprint. These franchisees purchase the rights to open a franchise of the business (an exact duplicate of the original business) and then operate that franchise just as the franchisor wants it to be run. They benefit greatly from having a system already in place; they simply put into action the plans that the franchisor developed.

Survey research done by the International Franchise Association suggests that franchises have much lower failure rates than independent small businesses.[28] The Association's research indicates that while 80 percent of small businesses in the United States fail within five years, only 8 percent of franchises fail over the same length of time.[29] Others quote less favorable statistics, yet the facts remain, the odds of success go up considerably while following the franchise model of business development and replication.

Buying a well-established franchise cuts down on the business failure rate because of the defining characteristic of the franchise model: the franchisor has already been through the painful process of discovering the majority of the problems with the business and has addressed those issues one by one in his or her own operation before starting to franchise. When franchisees buy a franchise, they buy an already-tested business. They buy a blueprint or a pattern and all of the accompanying systems that walk the new franchise owner step by step along the process that leads to success for that particular type of business. Simply put, people who buy a franchise have a much easier time mastering their business than people who start a business from scratch.

Proven Systems

If the franchisor has established a truly reliable business model, all of the franchisees who purchase rights to do business in the franchise's name get the benefits of the proven systems that are already operating successfully. The franchisees don't have to develop their systems, operations and employee manuals, and strategic plans from scratch – they essentially "climb on board a moving entity."[30] The time and mental anguish franchisees save by not having to develop systems on their own enables them to put their full energy into operations from the day they open their business.

Professional Advertising

In addition to starting a business with reduced risk and reliable systems, franchisees may also receive the benefit of national exposure due to large-scale, professional advertising efforts sponsored by the franchisor. Spinelli, Rosenberg, and Birley (2004) explain that "[a] franchisor generally spends the money needed to produce highly professional production materials and distributes them on a local level to franchisees. This separates the franchise from its mom-and-pop competitors in the community."[31] Julie's Bakeshops, based in Cebu, now has more than 500 locations and a strong brand identity throughout the Philippines based on national advertising and strong branding.

MICROFRANCHISING

Microfranchising is a relatively new development tool that is constantly evolving, as practitioners, academics, and impoverished people work together to create an economic development model that is both sustainable and replicable. It pairs talented microentrepreneurs who have a desire to expand their business (but who generally lack the managerial skills and capital to do so) with people who lack entrepreneurial skills but want to be involved in a self-employment venture. Through microfranchising, these two parties are brought together in a mutually beneficial relationship in which the microentrepreneurs (microfranchisors) expand their businesses by providing operational and ownership opportunities for people with little capital or business experience (microfranchisees).

In order for microfranchising to be successful, the business that is to be replicated must have established itself as a profitable model that is worthy of replication – and ready for the challenges replication entails. It must be well developed and must rely on proven market need, tested price points, selling strategies, established suppliers, and documented operational systems.

Microfranchising – though very different from franchising in its size and scale – can be as powerful a business model and economic accelerator in the developing world as franchising is in the developed world. The prefix "micro" should not be taken to mean that these businesses are not fully developed entities, that they aren't professional organizations, or that the franchisors or franchisees have small aspirations for their businesses. Just the opposite is true. They are simply called "micro" because replicating them requires relatively little capital. Further, they can be scaled to provide products and services to large populations in developing countries where the economies themselves are quite "micro" when compared with the well-established economies of the United States and Europe. Basically, microfranchising requires only a micro investment for replication.

Microfranchises bring stability and strength to fragmented markets worldwide by providing products and services in all sectors of the economy. Microfranchisors own cellular phone franchises, fast-food outlets, pharmacies, pizza parlors, water-distribution businesses, and many other shops and outlets that meet the varied basic needs of local peoples and economies.

Many of today's most established microfranchise systems were established by prominent non-governmental organizations (NGOs). Examples include Grameen Bank's well-organized "phone ladies" in Bangladesh; the Scojo Foundation's eye-care microfranchises in El Salvador and Guatemala; and the National Pharmaceutical Foundation's 380 Health Plus social franchisees serving the rural poor with low-cost medicines in the Philippines.[32] Hundreds of other microfranchise systems are currently under development, even though many of the owners and operators might not be aware of the label "microfranchise" or of the unique progress they are making.

HOW MICROFRANCHISING WORKS

Fashioned after the manner of franchising, microfranchising involves a major shift in perspective on the part of the microenterprise-owner-turned-microfranchisor and on the part of the necessity entrepreneur who would love to be involved in a real business opportunity. Microfranchising is all about making a better business (one that is worthy of being replicated) – not about making a better product or service. In short, while a microfranchisor may stay in the business of selling products, he or she shifts the major focus of his or her business efforts from selling products to creating and selling microfranchises that sell products and create wealth for the microfranchisees. His or her customers become the microfranchisees, not just the general public that buys his or her retail products.[33]

Microfranchising involves all the same components as traditional franchising: microfranchisors, microfranchisees, and similar business-expansion methods. However, while traditional franchisors are usually entrepreneurs who recruit investors and expand their operations individually, microfranchising occurs through more varied models and methods.

Microfranchising Models

Generally, microfranchising relationships are initiated by franchisors who are either independent business people, non-governmental organizations (NGOs), or multi-national corporations (MNCs).

Independent microenterprise owners as microfranchisors

Sometimes however, an independent microentrepreneur will accumulate enough business expertise, clientele, and capital to expand into multiple locations. This expansion usually happens in one of two ways: the business owner can independently open up a second location (currently the most popular method of expansion), or he or she can franchise his/her business and sell franchise rights to others (who then become microfranchisees). If the microentrepreneur turns to microfranchising, he/she becomes a microfranchisor. Then, each time he/she sells a new franchise, he/she gains another location (which helps the business increase its market share); a consistent, paying customer (the microfranchisee); royalty fees and franchise fees; and the opportunity to build a brand and to expand the franchise's product-distribution channel.

NGOs as three types of franchisors

Although some microenterprise owners can become microfranchisors without any outside assistance, most need substantial financial aid and business training. The change from microentrepreneur to microfranchisor can be accelerated (and implemented without all the accompanying financial and emotional pain) when well-funded NGOs get involved in this development process.

Microfranchise relationships are often initiated by NGOs that recognize the potential for helping the poor by teaching them how to build an income-generating venture for themselves. From the perspective of NGOs, microfranchising is all about helping struggling necessity entrepreneurs by giving them another alternative – that is, building a larger business in order to help make their families self-reliant.

Progressive NGOs are attracted to the growing microfranchising effort because a relatively small investment in a single microfranchising business can help dozens of families reap significant economic benefits. If an NGO can either find or create a proven business model, develop appropriate systems to guide that business, and then replicate that business, the NGO can bring the resulting economic benefits to many people in a fast and cost-effective way.

NGOs typically assume their franchisor role in one of three ways: (1) create a business from scratch and replicate it independently; (2) invest in a struggling microenterprise that has potential for growth and help that business become a microfranchise network; or (3) utilize a microequity method such as the BOOT Model:

NGOs as business creators   One way for NGOs to participate as franchisors is to create a very promising microenterprise; establish systems, protocols, and training that increase the likelihood of successful replication;

and then franchise it at a very reasonable cost to interested parties—as in the Grameen phone ladies.

The Academy for Creating Enterprise, an NGO based in Cebu, the Philippines, is an active equity partner with the Cellular City and Xpress Repair franchise based in General Santos. Both US-based NGO founders and local NGO officers serve on the board of directors and take an active part in the strategy for replicating the operations to more than 33 locations. Plans are to ramp up this microfranchise to more than 50 locations in next 12 months.

Yehu Microfinance in Kenya, with its 8000 microcredit borrowers, also illustrates how this creation process can work. The NGO founders saw that coconut trees are one of Kenya's most abundant natural resources and that the readily available coconuts from the trees can be made into a nutrient-rich organic oil used for cooking and skin care. Yehu Microfinance created a for-profit organization to build a model factory that could employ local villagers to process the oil, which could be sold locally or exported to higher-end markets. Plans are now in the works to establish microfranchises with oil presses in various villages so the more advanced Yehu borrowers can eventually become microfranchisees and own their own oil-pressing factories. The master franchisor will be responsible for creating the manufacturing system, training the microfranchisees, and marketing the product.

NGOs as investors in already-operating microenterprise   Instead of creating a business to franchise, an NGO may want to create a microfranchise network in an area in which the NGO is already working; thus, the NGO will likely already know microenterprise owners who have good business ideas but whose businesses are struggling. In these situations, instead of building and franchising a brand new business, the NGO will often invest in one of these already-operating microenterprises. When this happens, the NGO purchases or invests in an established and promising microenterprise (perhaps one that is in trouble), strengthens it to the point where it is a viable business, and then replicates it.

The Academy for Creating Enterprise, an educational NGO operating in the Philippines, recently invested in a struggling business owned by one of its graduates. Following Toots Gomez's microenterprise training at the Academy, his entrepreneurial skills had enabled him to open three drug store locations in a very short time, but his lack of managerial skills and lack of systems soon put him more than $20 000 in debt. He had a solid business plan, was targeting a specific niche (generic drugs), worked with good suppliers, and had loyal customers. But he had grown the business too quickly and couldn't afford the 10 percent monthly interest payments (of $2000 each) he was making in his over-leveraged state.

As an NGO interested in microfranchising, the Academy saw the perfect opportunity to help Toots ward off business failure while also creating microfranchise opportunities for other struggling drug store owners. The Academy partnered with Toots; it provided him low-interest loans and helped him create, document, and stabilize his systems. Once the business had a solid foundation, the NGO replicated Toots's business and began selling franchises to other small drug stores that were struggling to survive (thus turning them into microfranchises of Toots's main business). Once the franchise network was established, the Academy acted as the franchisor for all of the microfranchisees so that the owners could buy products for less, keep their prices low, and (with larger margins) increase their take-home income.

NGOs as BOOT Model franchisors   Another innovation and a most promising way to bring microfranchising benefits to microentrepreneurs is to use the BOOT Model (also referred to as microequity or a sliding scale of ownership). Using the BOOT Model, well-funded NGOs (or possibly MNCs) build, own, operate, and then gradually transfer ownership of a microfranchise to an operating manager who has been selected and tutored by the franchisor. The BOOT Model is an excellent method for getting a necessity entrepreneur or inexperienced person into a business and then coaching that person until the person is able to operate and eventually own (by means of purchasing it) either a majority or all of the business.

The BOOT Model requires only a relatively small investment on the part of the franchising NGO or MNC, but it requires a good deal of time in order to be successful. So as long as the franchisor doesn't need to turn a large profit immediately and is willing to invest time and effort in the microfranchisees, this approach can work very well.

Under this model, the NGO/franchisor has substantial upfront responsibility and assumes the costs for the establishment of the microfranchise. The NGO/franchisor finds the location, builds the outlet, buys the inventory, and hires an operator who has potential to learn and operate the business. The franchisor and operator enter into a unique sweat-equity agreement that facilitates the eventual and gradual transfer of ownership from the franchisor to the franchisee. Simply put, the more time and energy the operator invests in the business and the more profits the operator generates for the franchising organization, the greater the share of the business the operator can purchase. The goal is for the ownership to actually be transferred to the operator who purchases the business with his or her portion of the profits (see Figure 2.1).

Ideally, the franchisor mentors the operator for 6–12 months before beginning the gradual transfer of any ownership to the operator; and the

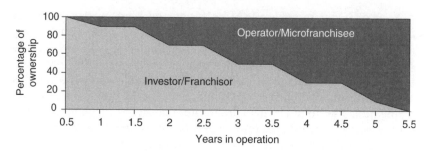

Figure 2.1   Ownership-transfer process using the BOOT Model

franchisor transfers ownership only as the operator purchases it and becomes financially invested in the business. The operator earns a regular salary throughout his or her involvement in the business, and once the NGO's start-up costs have been recovered, the operator also begins earning money as part of a profit-sharing program. The purpose of the program is to enable the operator to accrue extra funds by which he or she can begin purchasing partial ownership once the NGO decides the operator is ready to assume those responsibilities. That "waiting period" gives the franchising organization time to evaluate the operator's skills and potential for success. If the operator proves him or her self qualified in that time, he or she should be able to start purchasing portions of the microfranchise. If he or she is not qualified, the franchisor can begin to look for another operator.

Two microfranchise establishments in the Philippines illustrate how the BOOT Model works. InkPatrol USA was established using the BOOT Model. The original store was built by the Academy for Creating Enterprise. The US-based NGO originally invested $4000 in the creation of the ink cartridge-refilling business and then transferred ownership to a local NGO. Under the management of its executive director, the local NGO built, operated, and owned the first store. The NGO hired several graduates from the Academy to work in the store, first as interns and then as employees.

After a year, the NGO stopped directly managing the store and began transferring those responsibilities to an alumni of the Academy, naming him or her as operator/manager. While the ownership and oversight still resided with the local NGO, the operator became the manager of daily operations. With that promotion, the sponsoring NGO and the operator entered into a microequity agreement whereby the operator could eventually own the franchise by purchasing it gradually with part of his or her salary and percentage of the profits from the InkPatrol USA operation. Thus, the employee-turned-operator was eventually "BOOT"ed out of employment and was on his or her own as the majority owner. Once he assumes full ownership of the business, he or she will began paying franchise royalties to the sponsoring NGO.

The Academy for Creating Enterprise is currently engaged in a further morphing of the BOOT Model. Cellular City Franchise Corporation, a Filipino-owned franchise network, has 34 franchises scattered throughout the two major southern islands of the Philippines. While the franchises are all doing well for their owners, the franchisor has developed an expansion model that complements the original franchises but with much larger margins than selling phones and accessories. Called Xpress Repairs, the new microfranchises will be located (bundled) inside of the current Cellular City franchises and are being rolled out as BOOT Model ventures.

Xpress Repairs is being launched as a BOOT rather than a more conventional microfranchise because, although the majority of Cellular City microfranchisees are doing well financially compared with most microenterprise operators in the Philippines, it just does not have the $2500 necessary to launch the new microfranchise. By participating in the BOOT Model launch, the Xpress Repairs operators don't have to acquire all of their purchasing capital at once – they can work up to ownership of a microfranchise a little bit at a time, at their own pace.

Under the BOOT Model, the Cellular City franchisor will have the responsibility of training the Xpress Repairs technicians and managers. The Xpress Repairs outlets will be located within the footprint of the Cellular City franchisee's store, yet run as a separate business (this arrangement is probably unique to the Xpress Repairs franchise but could be replicated by other franchises as well). Xpress Repairs operators will pay rent to the Cellular City franchisee from the very beginning of the operation. A percentage of the profits will be set aside for the first 18 months to enable either the Xpress Repairs operator or the original Cellular City microfranchisee to eventually begin purchasing the operation.

At the end of the 18-month period, a portion of ownership will transfer to either the technician/operator of the Xpress Repairs outlets or to the original Cellular City franchisee, depending on cash flow issues as well as the interest of all parties.

Implementation of BOOT Model microfranchises Although implementation of the BOOT Model is still in its infancy in the Philippines, it will likely grow quickly as pioneering NGOs and microfranchisors demonstrate how effective the model is at taking poor, untrained people and transforming them into prospering microfranchise operators and owners. Eventually, this model will probably gain enough popularity and visibility that US-based donors will actually become large-scale investors, and some will also assume the role of mentor to help launch new BOOT Model microfranchise ventures.

MNCs as franchisors

Although NGOs have been involved in microfranchising for some time, multi-national corporations have just recently become involved in microfranchising efforts. Recognizing that profits can be made in markets other than those in the developed world – and that the four or five billion people who find themselves at the base of the economic pyramid have basic needs that are not being met – powerful businesses are expanding their efforts into these new markets at the "base of the pyramid." In his ground-breaking book, *The Fortune at the Bottom of the Pyramid*, C.K. Prahalad (2004) extolls the value of having microentrepreneurs partner with MNCs. He says, "MNCs and small-scale enterprises and entrepreneurs can co-create a market, and the BOP [bottom of the pyramid] consumers can benefit not only by the quality and choice of products and services available to them, but also by building local entrepreneurship."[34]

Microfranchising is quickly emerging as a leading method of getting businesses' distribution channels down to the lowest economic level. The relationship between profit-making motivations on the part of MNCs and poverty-elimination motivations by socially minded NGOs has proven to be good for both parties – and for the direct beneficiaries of their joint efforts.

Scojo Vision, a New York-based MNC, illustrates how MNCs that get involved in microfranchising can produce meaningful development benefits for communities around the world while also gaining distribution networks for some of their products. In 2001, Scojo Vision, an eye glasses manufacturer, formed Scojo Foundation to distribute low-cost reading glasses to impoverished people in El Salvador and Guatemala (and recently in India).[35] Scojo established a microfranchising network to facilitate the distribution of the much-needed glasses. The MNC now has hundreds (soon to be thousands) of "vision advisors" who act as independent microfranchisees, providing Scojo's products to needy populations.

BENEFITS OF MICROFRANCHISING

The benefits of microfranchising can be tremendous, and they are shared by everyone who is involved in microfranchising efforts. The relationships formed between enterprising franchisors and hard-working microfranchisees are so mutually beneficial that individual efforts almost always produce benefits for all involved in a given microfranchising endeavor or network.

Benefits to all Parties

The biggest benefit of microfranchising was alluded to earlier in this chapter: microfranchising brings development practitioners and residents of Third World countries closer to achieving the ever sought-after and ever elusive goal of economic development that is self-sustaining. In order to be truly sustainable, development efforts must do more than just temporarily relieve suffering or temporarily provide hope. They must be able to *permanently* relieve suffering and provide hope (see Figure 2.2). Microfranchising fulfills these two mandates by creating something of value (a microfranchise) that can change lives in the present time and improve the overall quality of life for future generations. By helping poor people acquire legal ownership of an asset, a formally recognized business, microfranchising is truly a more sustainable form of development that is bringing life to local economies and lasting hope to poor families. It also provides a model for multi-generational development for family assets.

Microfranchising can bring benefits not only to new generations, but also to new groups of people—specifically, those in rural areas who have previously had very few opportunities for upward social mobility. As many Third World countries begin to develop in a traditional sense, the development is

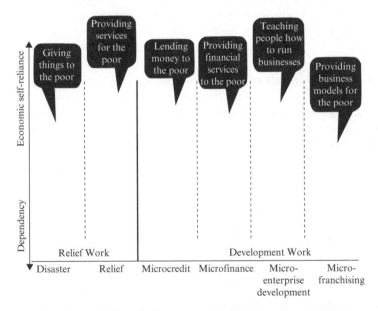

Figure 2.2   The spectrum of relief vs. economic development

usually confined to the cities—where factories are built, where mass trans-portation systems exist, and where cheap labor can be found. This phe-nomenon causes a large population shift (often referred to as urban migration) and huge problems for small towns and outlying cities. As poor people throughout the countries see that jobs are being created in the large cities, able-bodied workers migrate from the rural areas to the big cities to look for jobs. As they leave their rural homes and their families behind, they weaken the rural economies and place an even heavier burden on the people who remain.

Microfranchising addresses a portion of this migration problem because it works not only in large cities but also in very remote locations. Even the smallest village has its share of microcredit borrowers and/or microentre-preneurs. If development organizations are willing to invest in microfran-chising networks and to take those networks to the rural areas, the flow of people from the villages to the cities can be stemmed and people can begin flourishing wherever they live.

Benefits to Microfranchisees

Clearly, the objective of microfranchising is to enable and empower poor people to raise their standard of living and gain a greater degree of financial stability. Existing microfranchising networks are achieving this goal daily, providing business benefits and personal benefits to each new microfranchisee:

Business benefits

Whenever a microfranchisee establishes a business relationship with a fran-chisor, his or her business opportunities are literally transformed. Instead of being perpetually engaged in a struggle for existence as a necessity entre-preneur, microfranchisees gain a proven business model with tested and well-developed systems. These fundamental improvements result in numer-ous business benefits:

Business-placement support   Microfranchisees buy into a microfranchise system because by doing so, they buy into an established model and can rely on the franchisor to make many of the usual preliminary business decisions. In a microfranchising model, the franchisor helps with site selec-tion, measuring traffic patterns, negotiating the terms of the lease for the storefront, and establishing an effective store layout for optimum display of merchandise. Microfranchisees get the benefit of a lighter load because the franchisor takes care of a myriad of small decisions.

Tested operational guidelines   Another business benefit that microfranchisees gain is the stability provided by rules and regulations incorporated into the operation they buy. These checklists and operational guidelines help structure the daily activities of the microfranchisee and help the microfranchisee gauge his or her progress. For example, the franchisor provides daily, weekly, and monthly "to-do checklists"; performance standards and expectations; templates for income statements and balance sheets that help record business activity; pricing guidelines; standard hours and operating procedures; and other guidelines that teach the microfranchisees what to focus on in order to be successful.[36]

Established suppliers   Microfranchising also gives the microfranchisee an immediate source of suppliers, thus reducing the time associated with shopping around for suppliers and negotiating low rates and credit terms. The franchisor often facilitates the flow of supplies to the microfranchisees by acting as a go-between between suppliers and the microfranchisee. Because the franchisor may well be supplying goods to dozens of microfranchises, it can buy in bulk (taking advantage of pricing economies of scale that individual microfranchisees could never obtain on their own) and pass the savings on to each microfranchisee.

Access to government loans   Another way in which microfranchising brings economic benefits to microfranchisees is by giving them increased access to capital. In many Third World countries, the government is the largest source of capital for businesses, but government funds are available only for businesses that the government recognizes as stable and secure. Because microenterprises usually operate in the informal economy, many governments refuse to loan money to operators of these enterprises. However, when microentrepreneurs are bound together in a microfranchising relationship, the governments recognize them as being more established and as having a greater potential for success. So microfranchisees are more likely to receive capital loans than individual business owners are.[37]

Built-in support systems   When a microfranchisee enters into a microfranchising relationship with a franchisor, the financial success of the franchisor is tied directly to the financial success of the microfranchisees; thus, the franchisor has a significant vested interest in seeing that all microfranchisees get the support that they need. Kirk Magleby, a pioneer in microfranchise thinking, calls this a symbiotic relationship.[38] This interdependent and mutually beneficial relationship ensures that every microfranchisee automatically gets initial business-development help, a mentor, and a network of supportive peers:

- Business-development help. Before microfranchisees even open their doors for business, they usually receive intense training from the franchisor. This training includes a detailed discussion of norms or standards for certain expenses categories (e.g., salaries, rent, utilities, and costs of supplies) and benchmarks for what the store's daily and weekly income should be. This initial training should establish the microfranchisees on a sure path toward success.
- Mentor. In order to provide much-needed support, the franchisor designates a mentor/coach for each microfranchisee (each franchisor representative is usually assigned to 15 or 20 microfranchisees). The job of the mentor/coach is to work with the microfranchisee on a frequent and ongoing basis to encourage and consult the microfranchisee through all of his or her major business decisions. The franchisor representative advises on topics such as operations and finances, teaches the operator to practice critical rules of thumb for microenterprise success,[39] and monitors the microfranchise's progress.
- Network of peers. Microfranchisees can also take advantage of relationships with other microfranchisees within the franchisor's network. These peer-group relationships enable microfranchisees to learn from and teach each other as they discover what does and does not work in their respective businesses.

Personal benefits

In addition to all of the business benefits microfranchisees receive from this unique business model, they also receive significant personal benefits:

Asset development and inter-generational transfer   Microfranchising enables poor people to build something of value (the ongoing business) that can not only support their family's immediate needs but can also be passed on to future generations. The increased development of the business with each new generation establishes a pattern of increased financial stability and standing over time. The microfranchise can become an asset that can be borrowed against in times of family emergencies, which tend to drain working capital from a traditional microenterprise.[40]

Protection of rule of law   In Third World countries where the rule of law is often trumped by the rule of the wealthy, having a legally established business also serves as a protection against the whims of landowners, government officials, and others who might seek to take away other people's personal assets for their own financial gain. When a person moves from operating a microenterprise in the informal economy to operating a legally recognized microfranchise in the formal economy, the asset gains legitimate protection and can be maintained indefinitely under the rule of law.

Increased self-esteem Perhaps the greatest personal benefit that comes to people engaged as microfranchisees is that of increased self-esteem that comes from microfranchisees' growing ability to provide adequately for their families. Nothing can bring more hope into people's lives than this simple ability to see oneself as a respectable and contributing member of society, as a participant in a business community, and as a leader of and provider for one's family.

Benefits to NGOs

Due to the fact that microfranchising appears to be the next logical step in development work, NGOs who act as franchisors can also reap significant benefits as they become involved in microfranchising efforts:

Increased ability to bring self-reliance to clients
When NGOs create a network of microfranchises, they are rewarded by establishing an innovative and long-lasting financial opportunity for the people they are seeking to help. NGOs can help some people become microfranchisors and others become microfranchisees. In either case, the clients will be doing better business than they ever could as necessity entrepreneurs. They will be keeping better records, making more profit, and providing employment opportunities for their neighbors, friends, and family members. All of these outcomes indicate that microfranchising is a way for NGOs to establish long-lasting economic improvement for the clients they serve.

Improved self-sustainability of the NGO's program
The establishment of microfranchising networks clearly results in long-term economic improvement for an NGO's clients, but it also results in NGO-sponsored projects that can eventually sustain themselves. Many NGOs rely on donors for a large portion of their operating funds. Meaningful donor involvement is important to the long-term survival of every NGO, but too much reliance on donors can result in donor fatigue – a condition in which donors tire of donating over and over to a cause.

One of the best remedies for this fatigue is the development of self-sustaining programs that can eventually fund themselves. When NGOs act as franchisors, they establish a potential revenue source that can assist in the daily operating costs of the NGO. The NGO benefits financially from franchise and royalty fees, from mark-ups on products they supply to the microfranchisees, and from other microfranchising-related income. If these fees and revenues are carefully planned, they can generate self-sustaining profits for the NGO.

This self-sustaining involvement eventually brings an additional benefit to NGOs. Once their microfranchising networks are self-sustaining, NGOs are able to free up resources to do other mission-driven activities. This can further eliminate donor fatigue as well as NGO staff fatigue.

Benefits to MNCs

MNCs benefit from participation in microfranchising in many of the same ways in which NGOs benefit. First and foremost, microfranchising adds a whole new dimension to a corporation's product-distribution channel. MNCs are generally unable to deliver services and supplies to people who are in extreme poverty or in rural communities in developing nations. Microfranchising enables these corporations to gain access to new levels of clients that the MNC cannot reach on its own. It essentially establishes another distribution channel so more products can be moved down the pipeline to these needy consumers.[41]

Profitable involvement in sustainable development
Sustainable development is not only the next step in solving one of the world's most pressing problems (poverty); it is also the next step in business development. As MNCs participate more fully and centrally in development work, they will gain tremendous benefits. In *Capitalism at the Crossroads* (2005), Professor Stuart L. Hart states that "over the next decade or so, sustainable development will constitute one of the biggest opportunities in the history of commerce. And innovation will be the name of the game."[42] MNCs that can create innovative ways of meeting the needs of the poor and of involving themselves in providing products and services to new markets will ultimately generate more profits and create future business opportunities for themselves and their microfranchisees. The result will be true, sustainable development.

Product creation driven by local need
As MNCs move into new markets, the microfranchisees they work with can help guide the overall product-development and product-distribution efforts of the MNCs. The operators on the ground are intimately acquainted with the local people, with local needs, and with local customs and cultures that might affect the success of various products or services. They can help the MNC tailor its offerings in a way that can bring economic development to the new markets and bring profits to the corporation.

Benefits to US-based Foundations

Although US-based foundations are not yet fully engaged in microfranchising efforts, many of them are beginning to discover the possible benefits of involvement. Microfranchising has the potential to involve US-based foundations in development efforts in a revolutionary way. Hundreds of private and corporate foundations are already moving toward a new type of investment (program-related investments, or PRIs) that enables foundations to pursue their social missions while also fulfilling IRS-mandated giving requirements (all private and corporate foundations are required to distribute 5 percent of their assets annually).

Previously, foundations have satisfied this requirement by giving grants to qualified NGOs and other charitable organizations whose missions align roughly with the mission of the foundation. However, the only return that foundations have received from this involvement is the knowledge of the good their funds accomplish at the hands of the charitable organizations. PRIs provide additional benefits to foundations because they are bona fide investments; they are designed not only to advance the foundation's social mission (just like a grant) but also return to the foundation at least a portion of the principal investment (and in many cases, the foundation also receives interest on loans or capital gains from equity investments). They represent a way for foundations to leverage their assets to help many more organizations and are becoming an increasingly popular alternative (or supplement) to grants as a way that foundations can achieve their mission. PRIs could significantly increase the amount of capital available for charity.

The current trend in PRIs involves foundations investing in microcredit entities.[43] Consulting firms like Princeton Social Capital in Princeton, New Jersey,[44] are educating philanthropists and foundations nationally about this type of investing and are even facilitating it for them. Even major banks are getting involved. Citibank has made PRIs in microfinance and Bank of America recently announced a $10 million PRI to spur small business and microenterprise development in Charlotte, NC. This followed an earlier PRI of $1.1 million to expand loans for microenterprises.

Just as development work progressed from being concentrated on microcredit to being more focused on microfranchising, PRIs may also take this vital step. Microfranchising has proven its ability to provide investors with significant financial and social returns, so many foundations that have previously made grants to help alleviate poverty are recognizing that they can devote more capital to their cause if they make PRIs instead. HealthStore, a microfranchise in Kenya, is already benefiting from a PRI; it has used PRI funds to expand from a handful of small pharmacies to more than 75 rural microfranchises throughout rural Kenya that treated almost 450 000 rural patients in 2005. With increased involvement via PRI funds from other foundations (perhaps from pharmaceutical companies with associated charitable foundations), Health Stores could easily establish pharmacies and wellness clinics throughout rural areas of dozens of countries.

Although PRIs are certainly a new concept in microfranchise funding, they are already doing much good in the developing world. Using this type of investing, US-based foundations can not only fulfill their social agendas but can also help establish tens of thousands of microfranchises throughout the world.

CONCLUSION

Microfranchising, like any new idea, will not immediately revolutionize the development world. Certainly, more time will pass before development organizations and practitioners recognize its full potential. However, many organizations – both NGOs and MNCs – have already begun to recognize that microfranchising is an idea whose time has come. It combines one of the best business ideas to come out of the Western world (franchising) with the passion of major social institutions that wish to permanently change the suffering of the poor through sustainable development. Perhaps microfranchising will prove to be the missing link that combines profit making with poverty alleviation and, at the same time, be the tool that takes additional products and services to the poor. Microfranchising truly provides the next step up on the development ladder.

NOTES

1. Madarang, Imelda (2006) *Negosyo*: *Official Magazine of the Philippine Center for Entrepreneurship*. Note: by any formal or sophisticated definition of entrepreneurship, these "necessity entrepreneurs" aren't really entrepreneurs at all: they don't develop innovative business models or concepts, they don't do much planning, and they don't build teams or gather outside funding. Yet, for our purposes, we will call them entrepreneurs because of their own initiative and determination to survive.
2. Bornstein, David (2004), *How to Change the World: Social Entrepreneurs and the Power of New Ideas*, New York: Oxford University Press.
3. Madarang, Imelda (2006), *Negosyo*: Official Magazine of the Philippine Center for Entrepreneurship, p. 8.
4. Gibson, Stephen W. (2003), *Where There Are No Jobs*: *The MicroEnterprise Handbook*, vol. 3, foreword.
5. Prahalad, C.K. (2004), *The Fortune at the Bottom of the Pyramid: Eradicating Poverty Through Profits*, New Jersey: Wharton School Publishing, p. 11.
6. In *Les Misérables*, Victor Hugo beautifully suggests that people generally have deep-seated but misguided opinions about the plight of the poor. The terms associated with the world's poor (e.g., poverty, disadvantages, downtrodden) "point, alas, rather to the

fault of those who rule than to the sins of those who suffer, to the misdeeds of privilege rather than to those of the disinherited" (Hugo, Victor (1862), *Les Misérables*. Translated into English by Norman Denny, 1982, Penguin Classics, p. 987).

7. Landes, David (2000), Lawrence E. Harrison, and Samuel P. Huntington (eds), in *Culture Matters: How Values Shape Human Progress*, New York: Basic Books, p. 12.

8. In our rush to do good, we must always remember the mantra expressed by William Easterly, author of *The White Man's Burden* (Penguin Press, 2006, p. 7): "First, do no harm." Helping people help themselves always requires more work and more time than giving a handout does, but it brings about more lasting change than giving people things they didn't earn.

9. Landes, David (2000), Lawrence E. Harrison, and Samuel P. Huntington (eds), in *Culture Matters: How Values Shape Human Progress*, New York: Basic Books, p. 12.

10. The State of the Microcredit Summit Campaign Report (2005), The Microcredit Summit Campaign.

11. Felder-Kuzu, Naoko (2005), *Making Sense: Microfinance and Microfinance Investments*, Hamburg, Germany: Mermann Verlag GmbH, p. 29.

12. Counts, Alex (1996), *Give Us Credit*, New York: Times Books, p. xiv.

13. Manwaring, Todd (2001), internship report "Targeting the LDS Third-world poor with microcredit".

14. Sachs, Jeffrey D. (2005), *The End of Poverty: Economic Possibilities for Our Time*, New York: Penguin Group, p. 18.

15. Ibid., p. 20.

16. Felder-Kuzu, Naoko (2005), *Making Sense: Microfinance and Microfinance Investments*, Hamburg, Germany: Mermann Verlag GmbH, pp. 23 and 58.

17. Ibid., p. 73.

18. Hatch, John (11 March, 2005), Panel discussion at the Economic Self-reliance Conference, Brigham Young University, Provo, Utah.

19. Yunus, Muhammad (2003), *Banker to the Poor: Micro-lending and the Battle Against World Poverty*, New York: Public Affairs.

20. Ibid., p. 226.

21. Counts, Alex (1996), *Give Us Credit*, New York: Times Books, p. 316.

22. Justis, Robert T. and Richard J. Judd, (2003), *Franchising*, 3rd edn, Ohio: Thomson Custom Publishing.

23. International Franchise Association. accessed at www.franchise.org/content.asp? contentid =560.

24. Justis, Robert T. and William Slater Vincent, (2001), *Achieving Wealth Through Franchising: A Comprehensive Manual to Finding, Starting, and Succeeding in a Franchise Business*, Maryland: Streetwise, p. 4.

25. http://franchiseusa.net/why.htm.

26. Gerber, Michael E. (2001), *The E-myth Revisited: Why Most Businesses Don't Work and What To Do About It*, New York: HarperCollins Publishers.

27. http://franchiseusa.net/why.htm.

28. This assertion is the subject of widespread discussion. While some researchers and organizations indicate that franchises are much more successful than independent business, others suggest that the failure rate of franchises can reach roughly 35 percent.

29. www.franchise.org.

30. http://franchiseusa.net/why.htm.

31. Spinelli, Stephen Jr., Robert M. Rosenberg, and Sue Birley, (2004), *Franchising: Pathway to Wealth Creation*, New Jersey: Prentice Hall Publishing, p. 98.

32. Hipolito, Helen, personal interview (22 February, 2006), National Pharmaceutical Foundation, Executive Director.

33. Gerber, Michael E. (2001), *The E-myth Revisited: Why Most Businesses Don't Work and What To Do About It*. New York: HarperCollins Publishers.

34. Prahalad, C.K. (2004), *The Fortune at the Bottom of the Pyramid: Eradicating Poverty Through Profits*, New Jersey: Wharton School Publishing, p. 76.

35. At the Economic Self-reliance Conference held at Brigham Young University (Provo, Utah) on 9 March, 2006, Scojo leadership announced that it is now partnering with BRAC (another NGO) to expand the microfranchises into India.
36. Generic templates of some of these tools are contained in the MicroFranchise Toolkit published by the Center for Economic Self-reliance at Brigham Young University.
37. Samie Lim, Vice Chairman for Asia under the World Franchise Council, says that the Philippines government, for example, will make loans to franchisors and microfranchisees, but it won't loan to independent business start-ups. Personal interview, 2005.
38. Magleby, Kirk (2006), *Microfranchises as a Solution to Global Poverty*, Utah: MicroFranchises.org, p. 44.
39. Gibson, Stephen W. and Tina J. Huntsman, (2006), *Where There Are No Jobs*: *The MicroEnterprise Handbook* vol. 1.
40. De Soto, Hernando (2000), *The Mystery of Capital*: *Why Capitalism Triumphs in the West and Fails Everywhere Else*, New York: Basic Books, p. 6.
41. Prahalad, C.K. (2004), *The Fortune at the Bottom of the Pyramid*: *Eradicating Poverty Through Profits*, New Jersey: Wharton School Publishing.
42. Hart, Stuart L. (2005), *Capitalism at the Crossroads*: *The Unlimited Business Opportunities in Solving the World's Most Difficult Problems*, New Jersey: Wharton School Publishing, p. 32.
43. Chapter 12 by Naoko Felder-Kuzu will address some of the 74 funds making distributions to MFIs worldwide. Some funds have more than $50 million under management.
44. www.princetonsc.com.

FURTHER READING

Gibson, Stephen W. and Jason Fairbourne, (2005), *Where There Are No Jobs*: *The MicroFranchise Handbook*, vol. 4.
Gibson, Stephen W. and Tina J. Huntsman (2006), *Where There Are No Jobs*: *The MicroFranchise Handbook*, vol. 1.

3. The informal economy and microfranchising*

Michael Henriques and Matthias Herr

THE INFORMAL ECONOMY: A KEY DEVELOPMENT CHALLENGE

There is little doubt that the informal economy is one of the biggest development challenges currently facing the developing world. The informal economy is where large numbers of poor people work. In addition to low incomes, informal work is most often characterized by poor working conditions, a lack of formal employment contracts, and very limited or no social protection. Particularly women are affected, since they form the majority of workers in this part of the economy.

While there is no accepted single definition of the informal economy (see Box 3.1), it is a phenomena that is clearly visible to even a casual observer. The informal economy reflects a huge diversity of business transactions. The streets of cities, towns, and villages in most developing countries—and in many developed countries—are lined by barbers, cobblers, garbage col-

---

BOX 3.1   DEFINING THE INFORMAL ECONOMY

Economic and financial planners call it the unobserved economy. Labor advocates call it the unorganized sector. Social security officials label it as the unprotected sector. Statistical authorities call them uncounted. Others say they are simply the poor and marginalized who are forced to create their own employment. There is a huge debate on what the informal economy is. There is however one common denominator in all these interpretations—all of them refer to some type of exclusion: exclusion from social security, exclusion from statistical coverage, exclusion from traditional trade unionism, exclusion from GDP estimates, exclusion from productive resources typically available to larger enterprises. (*Informal Economy*, August 2005, 2)

---

lectors, waste recyclers, and vendors of vegetables, fruit, meat, fish, snack-foods, and a myriad of non-perishable items ranging from locks and keys to soaps and detergents, to clothing.[1]

Employment in the informal economy has grown rapidly in recent years in the developing world and in countries in transition. According to International Labor Organization (ILO) estimates from 2002, self-employment, which is generally accepted as an indicator of the informal economy, represents nearly half of total non-agricultural employment in all regions of the developing world. It ranges from 32 percent in Asia to 48 percent in Africa, and 44 percent in Latin America.[2]

As Figure 3.1 also shows, the informal economy has grown substantially in all developing regions of the world.

In nearly all developing countries, women constitute the majority of informal economy workers (see Table 3.1). This is particularly the case in Africa, where self-employed women make up more than half of total non-agricultural self-employment.[3]

In addition to being where large number of people are working, the informal economy also makes a substantial contribution to the economic output. The average share of the informal sector in non-agricultural GDP varies from a low of 27 percent in Northern Africa to a high of 41 percent in Sub-Saharan Africa. The contribution of the informal sector to GDP is 29 percent for Latin America and 41 percent for Asia.[4]

In recent years there has been a growing recognition of the vast entrepreneurial energy and purchasing power represented by enterprises and

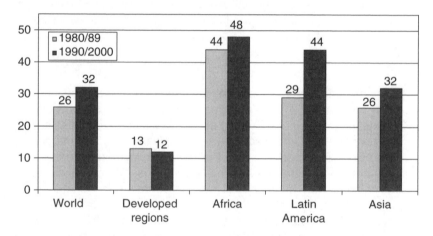

Source: ILO (2002, p. 22).

Figure 3.1 Non-agricultural self-employment, 1980/89 and 1990/2000 (percentage of total non-agricultural employment)

Table 3.1   Self-employment as percentage of non-agricultural employment

Region	1990/2000		
	Total	Women	Men
WORLD	32	34	27
Developed regions	12	10	14
Africa	48	53	37
Latin America	44	54	35
Asia	32	32	30

Source: ILO (2002, p. 22).

individuals in the informal economy. ILO discussions on strategies for upgrading the informal economy to join the mainstream economy[5] recognized the potential for development and poverty reduction that can be unleashed if effective ways are found to help micro and informal enterprises upgrade to become more productive and competitive, and thus able to provide better conditions of work. "It is through job quality, improved health and safety at work and access to basic social services – through adopting 'high-road strategies' – that businesses can enhance productivity and gain access to new markets, and thereby move into the formal economy. This means, of course, that the workers in these enterprises also directly benefit in terms of protected, formal and decent work."[6]

An emerging market with significant potential for informal economy enterprises and for starting the process of linking them with the mainstream economy is the growing trend towards private delivery of public services. In developing countries, many public authorities, faced with increasing populations and shrinking public budgets, look for partnership with the private sector to deliver a growing range of essential public services such as water supply, sanitation and solid waste collection, and recycling. When delivered through a public–private partnership, the public authorities would define certain standards for the services concerned, ensure access to tenders for micro and small enterprises, and rely on the resources and efficiency of the small-scale private sector for actual delivery. But such relationships are unlikely to be successful without well-designed systems to support the partnership and to upgrade and link the small businesses involved.

Below, we will explore the different ways in which microfranchising can be a powerful tool for upgrading micro and informal enterprises. We will start by looking at some of the major constraints faced by enterprises in the informal economy generally, including the factors that mitigate against equitable and mutually beneficial linkages with other enterprises, particularly against linkages with the formal economy.

CONSTRAINTS FACING INFORMAL ECONOMY ENTERPRISES

A starting point for developing sound strategies for upgrading informal economy enterprises requires an understanding of why, at present, these microenterprises generate incomes that are often below the poverty line, and why they generally do not grow over time.

The micro and small enterprises in the informal economy are generally constrained by the following factors:[7]

- *Lack of access to credit, working capital, and investment capital.* While access to credit and financial services is a challenge for many medium and small enterprises, the situation is particularly severe for informal economy enterprises, which suffer from inadequate levels of property rights and, hence, collateral. Credit has to be obtained from informal sources such as friends or relatives or non-banking financial agencies with unfavorable terms; insufficient funds do not allow for further investments. Also, low incomes or lack of regular income as household consumption competes for the use of business earnings often means that inadequate funds get reinvested in the business.
- *Weak networks.* There is much research to show that successful businesses are able to link with other businesses through value chains and "eco-systems," which allow participants to gain advantages in terms of mutually beneficial business transactions and exchange of information and learning. Informal units are much less able to link with other enterprises, particularly with larger enterprises in the formal economy.
- *Low productivity.* Enterprises typically use labor-intensive production methods. Equipment and organization of production are basic, and awareness of improvements in production technology and methodology is low. Because of their small size, they cannot achieve the economies of scale that are often needed to be competitive.
- *Poor working conditions.* Working conditions are often poor. Inadequate lighting, insufficient ventilation, and low standards of occupational safety and health contribute to low levels of productivity and product quality. Child labor is more common in informal economy units.[8]
- *Supply and marketing.* They have limited access to resources and technology as well as to opportunities for bulk purchase of inputs and effective marketing of outputs. Lack of information on prices, viability of products, etc. Also, there are fewer market opportunities due, for instance, to non-compliance to international standards.

- *Education and skills.* Low level of technology and technical and managerial skills compound problems of low productivity, insufficient innovation and upgrading, and low levels of product quality. There is no access to formal education and vocational training.
- *Infrastructure issues.* Poor infrastructure such as transport, storage facilities, water, electricity, lack of working premises, poorly developed physical facilities.
- *Legal aspects—formalization procedure and requirements.* Overly restrictive or cumbersome procedures and regulations for registration and expansion of businesses pose large burdens for informal enterprises contemplating formal registration. Lack of coverage in terms of intellectual property rights and trademarks may discourage the establishment of franchise systems.
- *Harassment.* Informal sector enterprises are often subject to sustained, high levels of harassment and bureaucratic hurdles.

It is clear that the business environment in the informal economy is both difficult and challenging, but also that the most successful informal economy entrepreneurs show much creativity in coping with risk and uncertainty, including engaging in multiple activities, selling a wide variety of products, and ensuring that they have business locations that attract the most customers (which sometimes requires using connections or paying bribes).[9] And there are examples of effective linkages between formal enterprises at local and even global levels and informal enterprises. For example, small-scale producers of footballs in Sialkot, Pakistan, supply global brands with their products, and numerous small, informal vendors sell soap, toothpaste, medicine, newspapers, and home electronics produced by large enterprises.

Nevertheless, for most informal enterprises the realities are marginal, low-productivity activities where linkages with formal sector enterprises tend to be on terms unfavorable for the informal unit. As pointed out by the ILO, "to be able to survive in increasingly competitive markets and make the transition to the formal economy, micro-enterprises need to be innovative, adapt to clients' changing needs and increase their productivity, and they often require support to be able to do these things effectively and efficiently. Business support services that can make a significant difference in establishing and operating a micro-enterprise are credit, training, market information and marketing support, technology, business incubators, promotion of inter-firm and intersectoral linkages, including subcontracting, consultancy services, etc."[10] We will be showing that microfranchising provides a proven strategy to provide many of these services to micro and informal enterprises and, therefore, to promote upgrading and formalization of this part of the economy on an effective and sustainable basis.

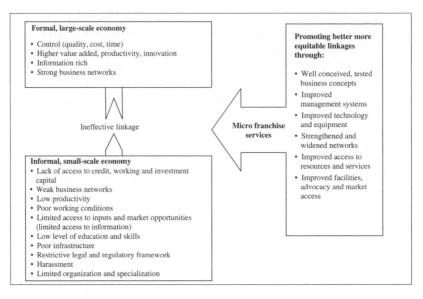

Source: Adapted from Hitchens et al., (2005, p. 12).

*Figure 3.2   Improving linkages between formal and informal economy
            enterprises*

Figure 3.2 highlights some of the reasons why linkages between formal
and informal units are often not as productive, effective, and equitable as
they could be, and also points toward some of the ways in which these
issues may be overcome.

As summarized in Figure 3.2, informal economy enterprise upgrading
might be promoted through a range of services including:

● mechanisms and systems that can help the informal unit become more
   productive and competitive by allowing it to link more effectively with
   other businesses, achieve economies of scale, and develop more professional systems for business management and control;
● partnerships aimed at overcoming some of the external constraints
   facing informal operators including lack of official recognition and
   registration, poor infrastructure and facilities, harassment, and lack
   of access to markets including certain types of public tenders.

The following sections will give concrete indications and examples of
how core concepts and strategies from franchising can be and have been
adapted to provide solutions to some of the particular challenges facing
enterprises in the informal economy.

FRANCHISING AS A MECHANISM FOR INFORMAL ENTERPRISE UPGRADING

The franchise approach effectively combines many of the most successful features of traditional entrepreneurship development programs, such as an emphasis on small business expansion rather than start-ups from scratch, mutually beneficial large–small enterprise linkages, highly focused and sustained training and extension support to the entrepreneur, improved access to capital, and collective purchasing and marketing arrangements. At the same time, franchising can be considered as an innovation that combines the advantages of a large business (economies of scale in purchasing, production, advertising and product development, experience and track record, and specialized in-house expertise) with the strengths of the small-scale entrepreneur (a high level of commitment and motivation, and knowledge of the local area). It is this unique blend of features that allows the franchise-based approach to reduce dramatically the risk in small business creation.[11]

Through franchising, a successful business can be replicated in other locations. If the franchise concept is not used, each new business is created according to what the entrepreneur believes is best for that individual business. Many of the decisions will be made on a trial and error basis. If 15 small businesses were initiated relating to domestic cleaning services for example, there would be 15 different types of businesses, even though the services they provide were similar. Although some of these businesses might be expected to be successful, it might be expected that 80 percent of these independently owned businesses would fail within the first eight years of existence.

By using the franchising concept, a model business might be developed based on an existing successful domestic cleaning services business. The business concept would be carefully examined, and the operations of the business would be determined in a logical manner. Operating manuals would be prepared, along with step-by-step instructions on starting and operating a domestic services business. There are a growing number of examples to show that the franchise approach leads to substantially higher survival rates for new business start-ups. In the United States, according to statistics from the Commerce Department, less than 5 percent of franchises failed on an annual basis from 1971 to 1987, and the continued rapid growth of the franchise sector is an indication that this impressive record has continued to the present time. (International Franchise Association, no date.)

This promise of the franchise approach is being recognized by government authorities and international development agencies involved in enterprise and private sector development. The example of the Chinese Business Start-up Service Centers (BSSCs) (Box 3.2) shows that public–private partnership can combine the franchise concept with traditional business development services to dramatically increase survival rates of business start-ups and help small and informal enterprises grow and link with the formal economy.

BOX 3.2   MAKING FRANCHISING WORK FOR MICRO AND INFORMAL BUSINESS IN CHINA

Franchising is playing an increasingly significant role in China. According to statistical data from the Ministry of Commerce, in early 2004 there were 82 000 franchisees in 1900 individual franchise systems, covering about 50 different trades. It is estimated that some two million employees work for franchise businesses, and the sector is growing by 50 to 60 percent annually.

Developing and supporting indigenous franchises has been recognized as an effective way to help upgrade the informal economy and create employment for groups such as laid-off workers from state-owned enterprises who lost their jobs in the course of economic reforms. Most of them are middle-aged women and men (so-called "4050" people) that are finding it hard to compete in the labor market but nevertheless possess rich working and life experience, and a strong commitment to running their own businesses.

In 1998 the government introduced national policy guidelines to promote employment for laid-off workers. Local cities were encouraged to develop "informal labor organizations" as a semi-registered legal business entity to support businesses run by "4050" people. The intention behind this new organizational form was to allow start-ups in the informal economy to gradually formalize over a period of time.

In September 2003 the government took a further step and established special microcredit guarantee fund programs across the country. One-stop business services including business ideas banks, start-up training, business ideas assessment, start-up counseling, financial services and other follow-up services were delivered to business starters by local Business Start-up Service Centers (BSSCs). The International Labor Organization (ILO) started working with the Ministry of Labor and Social Security (MOLSS) to introduce its "Start and Improve Your Business" (SIYB) training program to China. After an initial trial period the program was launched on a large scale in June 2004. The program is aimed at enabling urban unemployed to start and run their own businesses and to create quality jobs and has reached some 260 000 business starters to date in China.

At the same time, the municipal BSSCs recognized that franchising was an effective supplementary system to help "4050" people to start up a business. The BSSCs started collecting franchise business ideas from franchisors, including them in an "ideas bank," which was made available to the "4050" people alongside the basic entrepreneurship and management skills that were already being provided under the SIYB programs.

The BSSCs now actively encourage trainees to select a franchise business. Once the trainees have selected a franchise idea, the BSSC helps them access commercial loans from banks through a special credit guarantee fund program. The BSSCs thus play an important role in putting franchisors in touch with potential franchisees. The informal labor organization model also makes it possible for the franchising system to be applied to microentrepreneurs in the informal economy.

The results to date have been impressive: 37 SIYB trainees have joined five franchise businesses (garment-making and retail, digital goods retailing, purified water production and retail, domestic service, and traditional handicrafts-making and selling). Eighty-three percent of them successfully run their franchise businesses now. This compares very favorably with 45 percent of other SIYB trainees that have successfully started a "conventional" business.

Source: Baoshan Deng, ILO colleague (2006, unpublished ILO report).

While many features of the traditional franchise model can help address several of the challenges facing informal economy enterprises, experience shows that a number of adaptations may be called for. First, we have found that it is useful to distinguish between two different versions of the franchising model:

- *Top-down franchising*, where the owner of a proven business system (the franchisor) grants the right by contract to an entrepreneur (the franchisee) to establish a similar business. In exchange for franchise fees and the obligation to adhere to quality standards, the franchisee acquires the right to use the franchisor's trademark and receives marketing support, detailed manuals on how to operate the business, start-up assistance, staff training, equipment, raw material procurement, and regular visits by a representative of the franchisor.[12] This is the model embodied in the business format franchising strategies of, for example, McDonald's. A developing country example is the Shuilong Ying Purified Water Outlets in China (see Appendix to this chapter).

- *Bottom-up franchising*, where small enterprises in the same sector (members) decide to join forces under a cooperative (shared service cooperative) or similar structure to enhance their performance and competitiveness by developing a number of "shared services." Shared services often include exchange of information on market trends, joint lobbying of public authorities to ensure a more favorable environment, knowledge sharing and business upgrading, services to achieve economies of scale in such areas as purchasing of equipment and raw materials in bulk, joint marketing and distribution, and shared services in accounting, legal services, and insurance. This model is used extensively in developed countries as, for example, in the German bakery sector where some 17 500 bakers have joined in 362 local cooperatives belonging to 16 regional cooperatives, all integrated in a single central cooperative.[13] A developing-country example is the REDTURS network of community-based ecotourism operators in Central America (see Appendix).

Under both of these franchising models, the central idea is to develop a system that links a group of enterprises into an effective system, which enables the participating enterprises to gain competitive advantages that they are unable to access as individual, stand-alone enterprises. Below in Table 3.2 we identify a number of core services, some or all of which form part of the franchising model.

Even the most advanced franchise systems rarely involve all the different services listed in Table 3.2. And in systems involving microenterprises, particularly those in the informal economy, only just a few of these services may be involved. In the real world, each franchise system like every business enterprise is a unique response to the particular entrepreneurial opportunity it seeks to fill and to the particular environment in which it operates. However, even when just a few of the services form part of the microfranchise system, the involved enterprises can gain very substantial advantages, which allow them to move towards higher levels of productivity and competitiveness, and ultimately formalization.

Because the various service elements are not always achieved through a franchisor, we find it useful to talk about a "systems integrator" function, which performs some or all of these services. While the system integration functions can be carried out by a single actor, such as a franchisor or a shared service cooperative, it can also be performed by several actors working together. For example, in Dar es Salaam, Tanzania, a group of small enterprises engaged in solid waste collection and recycling receive support from a non-governmental organization (supported by ILO) that provides training based on a manual called *Starting Your Waste Collection*

Table 3.2   Overview of possible core franchise functions or services

Franchise Services or Functions	Example: Tianjin Jialijie Domestic Service in China (a top-down franchise)

• *Business concept and management systems*
  – Operation manuals and systems specifications
  – Definition and adherence to quality standards
  – Initial training
  – Right to use trademark
	• *Business concept and management systems*
	The franchisee receives manual covering location selection, staff hiring and training, unit operations, control systems, and marketing, advertising and promotion
	The franchisor has defined clear quality standards including standardized steps for cleaning an apartment The franchisee receives two weeks of training in which s/he learns how to manage the franchise business and is also introduced to basic domestic services and specific vocational skills
	The franchisee has an agreement with the franchisor in which s/he is to use the trademark, is required to protect the business concept with penalty payments for breaches of the franchisors intellectual property rights

• *Provision of equipment*	• *Provision of equipment* The franchisor provides the franchisee with all materials needed to operate the business, e.g., buckets, bicycle, medicament holders, floor washing machine, dust collector, etc.
• *Access to start-up funds*	• *Access to start-up funds* To help laid-off workers with very little capital resources, the franchisor has set up four business franchise formats requiring different amounts of start-up capital (between 25 000 and 60 000 RMB) The cooperation with the public BSSC enables the franchisor to facilitate access to microcredits for potential franchisees

• *Ongoing support*
  – Bulk purchasing
  – Joint marketing
  – Training and consultancy
  – Joint accounting, legal, insurance, and other services
	• *Ongoing support*
	The franchisor purchases equipment and inputs in bulk, and is therefore able to offer these products (e.g., cleaning liquids) at a favorable price to the franchisees
	The franchisor offers training and consultancy on marketing and advertising.

Table 3.2   (continued)

Franchise Services or Functions	Example Tianjin Jialijie Domestic Service in China (a top-down franchise)

– Product development	The franchisor has videos and brochures to promote the franchise concept to potential franchisees, and for them to promote their services to clients
	    The franchisor offers refresher trainings after the first six months and also organizes national qualification and authentication
	    New domestic service products are made available to the franchisees on an ongoing basis.

● *Lobbying toward local and national authorities*
   – Recognition
   – Facilities
   – Market access (incl. public tenders)
	● *Lobbying toward local and national authorities*
	The franchisor has a close cooperation with the local BSSC, which includes the franchise in its business ideas bank, thus helping to promote the business. The BSSC also offers training and access to financial resources to potential franchisees

Source: Adapted from Henriques and Nelson (1997).

Business. The manual offers detailed guidance on operating the business. This organization works closely with the local municipality, which sets standards for services and fees, manages bidding for tenders, and ensures that enterprises operate according to contract requirements. Table 3.3 below gives an indication of the various actors that can be involved in systems integration and of their respective roles.

It is possible for the "integrator(s)" and the individual enterprises to have varying degrees of formality. Thus it is not uncommon for the integrator to be a formally registered organization while the individual enterprises are fully or partially informal, perhaps moving towards higher levels of formality over time. The Chinese Business Start-up Service Centers (Box 3.2) that target laid-off workers illustrate this case very well. Another example is Jialijie Domestic Service in Tianjin, China (see also Table 3.2 and Table A3.1 in Appendix).

Jialijie was founded in 1999 as an "informal labor organization" by Ms Cui Hong, a laid-off worker, who delivered various services (e.g., babysitting) to domestic households. After participating in an ILO "Start Your Business" training program, Ms Cui developed a franchise model of her

Table 3.3   System integrators and their roles

System Integrator	Role	Example
Business format franchisor	• Fairly full range of integrator functions (Table 3.2). • Mainly used as marketing and distribution instrument • Top-down approach (franchisor driven, offers complete system, hierarchical structure) • Advocacy toward public agencies tends to be less emphasized	McDonald's Kentucky Fried Chicken South Africa: Butterfield Bakery Scojo Foundation (reading glasses) Bangladesh: Grameen Village Phones China: Tianjin Jialijie Domestic Service, Shuilong Ying Purified Water Outlet (see also Appendix)
Shared service cooperatives[14]	• Can provide full range of integrator functions (Table 3.2) • Bottom-up approach (member-driven, systems often evolve over time, democratic structure and decision-making); primarily aimed at achieving economies of scale for established enterprises • Tend to have a stronger advocacy function toward local and national authorities (e.g., addressing issues such as harassment of informal units)	Europe: Cooperative Optic 2000, German Bakery Cooperatives USA: VHA Health Care Cooperative India: Anjuman Textiles Handloom Weavers Cooperative Society Ltd. Kenya: Akamba Handicraft Industry Cooperative Society Ltd. Senegal: Construction Workers Cooperative Uganda: Shoe Shiners Industrial Cooperative Society Ltd. (see Appendix)
Sectoral associations and representative organizations	• Advocacy toward local, national and international level often key function • Provide information and business services • Bottom-up approach (member-driven) • Collective marketing and branding (e.g., tourism industry) • Setting of industry standards	Latin America: REDTURS network for Community-based Tourism operators (see Appendix)

Table 3.3   (continued)

System Integrator	Role	Example
Public agencies at local and national levels	• Determine guidelines for standards and access to public tendering systems • Taking the initiative to "organize" informal and microenterprises to promote upgrading and formalization • Facilitate access to credit and other key inputs • Promote physical facilities and rights including property rights	Dar es Salaam and Bangalore: Solid Waste Collection (see Appendix)
Development agencies, franchise associations and other NGOs	• Help franchisors develop system and services through awareness and training • Link franchisors to franchisees • Create synergies with other small enterprise development promotion efforts • Raise awareness of franchising concepts and advantages • Advocate for an enabling franchise environment (intellectual property rights, trademarks, etc.)	Business Service Start-up Centers in China (see Box 3.2)

business as a way to expand her business and meet the strong demand for domestic services in Tianjin. In 2003, the enterprise was registered as a limited company under the "Jialijie" trademark. To support laid-off workers Jialijie has developed four different franchise formats with different levels of start-up capital. This system allows laid-off workers with limited capital resources to join the business as franchisees and to grow over time, reaching increasing levels of formality.

Examples can also be found for bottom-up franchises: the Uganda Shoe Shiners Industrial Cooperative Society Ltd. (see Table A3.1 in Appendix) was founded by five shoe shiners in 1975. It remained an informal unit until 1989, at which time it became a fully registered cooperative society. However, its members often remain informal business operators. The cooperative thus functions as a system integrator, linking its informal membership to the formal economy, and providing them with services (such as training, loans, advocacy, bulk purchase of inputs, etc.) that members would otherwise not be able to access. These shared services allow the participating units to become more competitive and profitable, and open opportunities for the operators to move towards higher levels of formalization.

The matrix in Table A3.1 in the Appendix provides a number of practical examples of how franchising methodologies are being applied in practice, and how they fit into the various frameworks presented here. The examples have been chosen to illustrate the many different ways in which franchise concepts can be applied to a range of different entrepreneurial opportunities and the environment in which the system operates. Below we will discuss some of the key features and lessons that can be drawn from the matrix.

LESSONS FROM INFORMAL ENTERPRISE UPGRADING THROUGH FRANCHISING

Comparing the top-down franchising model to bottom-up franchising systems in the matrix (see Appendix, Table A3.1) reveals differences as well as similarities. These need to be taken into account when discussing upgrading strategies for micro- and informal economy enterprises. Whether a top-down or bottom-up franchising model is most appropriate depends both on the business at hand and on the local and situational particularities. The following summary identifies some key points:

The Top-down Franchising Model

- *Complete and sophisticated operation system.* The franchisor specifies in fairly great detail how the franchisee has to operate the business. This usually includes a detailed manual on most aspects of the business.[15] This makes the top-down model particularly suitable for franchisee target groups with limited entrepreneurial skills and experience, such as young people and laid-off workers from public enterprises. An example includes the Jialijie Domestic Service franchise, where the franchisor has developed a complete system of services and requirements for the franchisees (see Appendix).
- *Market orientation.* Product development and marketing strategies are strongly emphasized in nearly all cases. Top-down franchising can be seen as a potentially powerful tool to market goods and services to the "bottom of the pyramid," assuring affordability, access, and availability of goods and services.[16] Grameen Village Phones in Bangladesh and the Butterfield Bakery in South Africa highlight this point well. Both are aimed at making products and services available to local and difficult-to-access markets (see Appendix).

- *Management skills.* Top-down franchise systems are particularly dependent on good management skills by the franchisor, who must identify and develop the initial business concept and operation system, refine and optimize it further, be responsible for the services delivered to the franchisee, and control the adherence to quality standards. Inadequate franchisor skills are a common cause of failure of franchise systems. The importance of good management skills of the franchisor becomes apparent when considering the often complex systems of the top-down franchises, as illustrated in the Appendix. Developing and maintaining these systems requires a dynamic and skilled entrepreneur. Therefore, franchisor or more general management training programs (such as the ILO's SIYB programs) can be a significant element of effective schemes to support the development of microfranchising.
- *Intellectual property rights.* The protection of trademark and business concept can be an important issue in the overall franchise concept to protect the system from copycats. Many sophisticated systems such as McDonald's, Burger King, and KFC rely heavily on intellectual property protection to defend a distinct and heavily advertised brand. Among the simpler systems included in the Appendix, the Butterfield Bakery in South Africa in the matrix in Table A3.1 is an example where a trademark also plays a significant role. While the limited enforcement of intellectual property rights in the informal economy can pose constraints in incorporating informal economy units into franchise systems, the examples given in this chapter also show that it can over time provide an incentive towards formalization, thereby in effect helping to "pull" microenterprises out of the informal economy, where they can benefit from higher levels of law and order.
- *Good work place practice promotion.* Particularly important in terms of promoting decent work in microenterprises, franchise-based programs can, and often do, incorporate environmental issues as well as occupational safety and health concerns by building appropriate measures into the structure, organization, and training systems of the business that is being franchised. The ILO has worked closely together with local partner organizations and municipalities to improve the working conditions of the franchised units involved in solid waste collection in Tanzania. This has been achieved by incorporating modules on health and security into the franchise concept in which the municipality (the franchisor) delivers public services (waste collection) through informal units (the franchisees) to the community (see Appendix). This module gives the waste collectors advice on how to protect themselves against injuries or how to handle dangerous waste. It also specifies the processes required for environmentally friendly recycling.

- *Advocacy functions.* Individual top-down franchises rarely engage in extensive advocacy towards local and national policy-makers, whereas such functions are often a prominent part of bottom-up franchises (see below). However, some cooperate with public authorities and development agencies in areas such as microfinance and business start-up training, and franchise associations can represent franchise enterprises toward political decision-makers. The cooperation between franchisors and the Chinese Business Start-up Service Centers (BSSCs) (see Box 3.2) is an example of mutually beneficial public–private partnership. On the one hand, the franchise businesses benefit from the services provided by the BSSCs, which in effect become advocates for the franchise approach. On the other hand, the franchise businesses help upgrade the training programs and expend the options available to the Centers' clients.
- *Constraints and disadvantages.* The top-down model also entails a number of constraints to the franchisee:
  - There is usually strict adherence to quality standards.
  - Initial financial inputs may be substantial.
  - The track record of the franchisor may be difficult to assess.
  - Detailed contractual arrangements may restrict creativity of franchisee.
  - Sale or transfer of franchise may be highly restricted.
  - Dependency on franchisor and franchise name.
  - Franchise may have limited product line.
  - Franchisor may lack initiative and flexibility in reacting to local market changes.
  - Franchisee position is weak relative to franchisor.
  - Where local government authorities participate in the systems integration function (such as in outsourcing of social and other public services), strategies are needed to overcome bureaucratic culture and non-businesslike working styles.

The Bottom-up Franchising Model

- *Evolution over time.* Bottom-up systems are a suitable model for upgrading groups of already established enterprises. Such systems therefore start from what already exists and then evolve over a period of time. The integration functions performed by the system, at least initially, tend to be less complete and sophisticated. Experience also shows such systems often need one or more visionaries or lead entrepreneurs who can persuade others to join forces to upgrade their competitive advantage and exploit potential economies of scale.

Often the starting point for a bottom-up system is the identification of at least one key area where substantive economies of scale can be achieved (bulk purchasing for instance) and build the initial collaboration around this function. The Uganda Shoe Shiners Cooperative and the Rwanda Public Transport Operators Cooperative (see Table A3.1 in Appendix) are good examples of such evolutionary bottom-up franchises. The Shoe Shiners Cooperative started with five shoe shiners (the "visionaries") in 1975 with the initial target to provide jobs to young people and to lobby for their recognition and interests towards local authorities. Over time, the cooperative added additional services, such as access to savings and loan services. Plans are currently under way to offer cheap equipment to members through bulk purchasing.

- *Member-driven.* The fact that this model is a joint venture of already established enterprises means that the individual enterprises often enjoy more autonomy than their counterparts in top-down franchises, where a much higher level of control typically prevails. This is another reason why these systems tend to evolve and develop over time. The bottom-up approach is therefore suitable for target groups with well-developed entrepreneurial skills and experience and a desire for considerable autonomy. Again, both the Uganda Shoe Shiners Cooperative and the Rwanda Public Transport Operators Cooperative are good examples of member-driven franchises. Also, the REDTURS network of small-scale eco-tourism operators (see Table A3.1 in Appendix) is an example of where small communities have joined forces to establish national associations and even international cooperation (with the support of the ILO).

- *Marketing.* The model may, initially at least, be less focused on marketing and brand support, but instead offer market access in other ways. This may include access to public tendering systems supported through advocacy towards local government and other actors, as the example of informal waste collectors in Tanzania shows (see Appendix). Here, the local municipality (e.g., of Dar es Salaam) has opened its tendering system to small and informal business operators to deliver public services to hard-to-access urban areas. The REDTURS network in Central America is another example: one of the main objectives of this network is to help small community-based eco-tourism operators gain access to European markets.

- *Intellectual property rights.* There is often less emphasis on the protection of trademark and business concept as individual enterprises enjoy more autonomy. However, the REDTURS example of small eco-tourism operators in Central America shows that a trademark may evolve over time, including objectively defined and enforced standards that apply to all members.

- *Additional group-based services.* Many bottom-up franchises that have a membership base consisting of informal business operators include financial services, such as a savings and credit schemes, to their service portfolio. Other similar group-based schemes in such areas as risk insurance and even employment insurance can help upgrade working conditions and promote decent work in the participating enterprises. The Rwanda Public Transport Operators Cooperative, for example, has created a savings and credit scheme that is based on a tontine system, by which several operators form a savings group, and they take turns using the savings for investments.
- *Advocacy function.* Many bottom-up franchises have a strong advocacy function toward local and national authorities and even international institutions and agencies. The purpose is often to improve the business environment (i.e., the legal and regulatory framework) in which members operate. In the case of REDTURS, advocacy was carried out both at the national and international levels to gain government support in marketing community-based tourism to international markets. The Uganda Shoe Shiners Cooperative also includes a strong advocacy function by actively lobbying for the recognition of informal shoe shining operations as businesses, thus helping to improve the working conditions and environment of its members (e.g., stopping harassments through authorities).
- *Formality.* Bottom-up franchise systems are a potentially powerful instrument to integrate small and informal enterprises into (global) value chains at improved terms. While the members can remain informal, the overall system is represented through the formalized systems integrator, resulting in enhanced bargaining power towards other members of the chain. Most of the bottom-up franchises in the Appendix illustrate this point well. For example, the shoe shiners and transport operators remain informal, while their respective cooperatives are formalized entities that bargain effectively on their behalf.
- *Constraints and disadvantages.* The bottom-up model may also entail a number of constraints to the participating members:
  - Level of ambition of participating enterprises may vary, thus limiting the range of shared services available to members. This may result in frustration and decreasing support of members due to slow progress in some cases.
  - Democratic decision-making may lead to slow and cumbersome decisions on key issues, particularly those involving significant investments.

   – Protecting the brand integrity and reputation of the system may
   be difficult due to inhomogeneous membership. An efficient
   quality control system often requires formalization of standards
   and procedures. This has been evident in the cases of the shoe
   shiners cooperative where a committee on quality control has been
   established, and the REDTURS network, which is currently in the
   process of establishing a trademark based on well-defined quality
   standards and enforcement systems.

Despite these differences, both top-down and bottom-up franchising
models have a number of *similarities* including:

- *Risk reduction.* Both franchise models have shown to reduce substantially the risks of entrepreneurship, thus leading to higher start-
  up and survival rates. The services and operation systems that
  franchisors or systems integrators provide to participating enterprises in terms of start-up support and ongoing guidance are based
  on a proven concept that enhances opportunities for successful start-
  up, upgrading, and expansion.
- *Economies of scale.* A key reason for participating in a franchise
  system is to achieve economies of scale, for example, through bulk
  purchasing. The larger the business network gets, the more bargaining power exists toward suppliers or buyers.
- *Public–private partnership.* Applying the franchise model to the
  informal economy often requires cooperation between private
  sector enterprises, public authorities, representative and sectoral
  associations, and international development agencies. Combining
  the franchise model with traditional business development services,
  as in the case of the Chinese Business Start-up Service Centers
  (see Box 3.2), has proven to be an effective instrument in linking
  informal enterprises to the formal economy. Public actors often
  facilitate access to resources (e.g., microcredit), the provision of
  business training, or the improvement of the legal and regulatory
  framework.

RECOMMENDATIONS FOR TAPPING THE MICROFRANCHISING POTENTIAL FURTHER

There are two basically different approaches to franchising as it is applied
to micro and small enterprises: bottom-up and top-down. Both can deliver
many of the same services and advantages to participating enterprises.

Each has its own strengths and weaknesses, and is particularly suitable in certain situations:

1. In top-down systems, the franchisor generally plays the central role. The franchisor must have strong management skills because the franchisor will introduce the business concept and operation system and develop them further, be responsible for services delivered to the franchisee, and control the adherence to quality standards. Top-down franchising as an enterprise development strategy can be promoted through franchise associations, and governments can set up franchise resource centers, which can assist would-be franchisors. Public entrepreneurship development programs can help link franchisors with potential franchisees as has been shown in the case of China. Since such schemes operate in many countries, a systematic effort to raise awareness of the potential of franchise systems could have an important, positive impact on start-up and survival rates. Special training programs for would-be franchisors should be developed and promoted to complement existing business start-up and expansion programs.

2. The bottom-up approach often requires one or more strong leaders and visionaries among the group of small enterprises that decide to join forces to upgrade their competitiveness through a shared service cooperative or similar structure. Sometimes this initial animating role can be carried out by sectoral associations, the government, or other concerned actors. The process can be promoted through awareness-raising campaigns highlighting potential benefits. The ILO has successfully worked with trade unions to "organize" self-employed workers in a particular sector to allow them to gain increased competitiveness and economies of scale in their microenterprises and to raise their bargaining power with public authorities around such issues as physical facilities and harassment. It is the intention, based on these experiences, to initiate a larger global program to organize microenterprise operators in the informal economy in cooperatives and bottom-up franchise-type structures, and, over time, to move these enterprises toward the mainstream economy.

The general principles behind microfranchising can be promoted through dissemination of good practice examples, perhaps through online databases and rosters and teams of experts drawn from successful programs in different parts of the world. Other activities that can help tap the advantages of franchise-based approaches include:

*   raising awareness among government policy-makers about the advantages of franchising as a strategy for upgrading micro and

small enterprises and the need to create an enabling environment for franchising, including upholding copy and trademark protection and facilitating access to credit for such ventures;

- assisting private and public institutions dedicated to micro and small enterprise development by building their knowledge of and expertise in franchising concepts, strategies, and skills;
- encouraging development agencies, franchise associations, and other NGOs to support franchise systems among small and micro enterprises by making training and consultancy expertise available to potential franchisors for development of operation systems and facilitating start-up.

Public–private partnership can be an important mechanism for delivering integrator functions, including for enterprises delivering social and other services linked to public tenders. The local government, maybe working with other partners, would act as franchisor or "integrator" by specifying an operation system that guarantees an adequate level of quality of public services delivered through private sector enterprises (e.g., solid waste collection). This would often require the establishment of special units in government authorities to overcome the lack of a business orientation in the public sector. An important issue is often to improve access to the public tendering system for micro and small enterprises.

NOTES

*   The authors would like to give special thanks to the following ILO colleagues: Baoshan Deng, Jürgen Schwettmann, Husejin Polat, Angela Mwaikambo, Robertus Zegers, Asha D'Souza, Kees van der Ree, Roel Hakemukter and Carlos Maldonado for helping to write up and collect many of the case examples presented in this chapter.
1.   ILO (2002, p. 9).
2.   ILO (2002, p. 17).
3.   ILO (2002, p. 23).
4.   ILO (2002, p. 24).
5.   ILO (2002).
6.   ILO (2002) and ILC (2002).
7.   BECKER (2004, p. 22); ILC (2002).
8.   ILC (2002, pp. 4, 26).
9.   ILC (2002, p. 23).
10.   ILO (2002).
11.   Henriques and Nelson (1997).
12.   Henriques and Nelson (1997).
13.   Schwettmann, ILO colleague.
14.   Couture (2003).
15.   Bangasser (1996, p. 9).
16.   Prahalad (2005).

FURTHER READING

African Development Bank Group (2002), "Enhancing development in Africa", franchising report, Abidjan.

Bangasser, Paul E. (1996), "Franchising as an integrating approach to the informal sector: some preliminary ideas", working paper on promoting productivity and social protection in the urban informal sector, Geneva: International Labor Office, Development Policies Branch.

Becker, Kristina Flodman (2004), "The informal economy", fact finding study, Swedish International Development Cooperation Agency (SIDA).

Bibby, Andrew and Linda Shaw (eds) (2005), *Making a Difference – Co-operative Solutions to Global Poverty*, Co-operative College.

Birchall, Johnston (2003), *Rediscovering the Cooperative Advantage – Poverty Reduction Through Self-help*, Geneva: International Labor Office, Cooperative Branch.

Birchall, Johnston (2004), *Cooperatives and the Millennium Development Goals*, Geneva: International Labor Office, Cooperative Branch and Policy Integration Department.

Couture, Marie-France (2003), *Cooperative Business Associations and their Potential for Developing Countries*, Geneva: International Labor Office, Cooperative Branch and IFP/SEED.

Couture, Marie-France et al. (ed.) (2002), *Transition to Cooperative Entrepreneurship – Case Studies from Armenia, China, Ethiopia, Ghana, Poland, Russia, Uganda, Vietnam*, Geneva: International Labor Office, Cooperative Branch and IFP/SEED.

Fairbourne, Jason and Stephen W. Gibson (2005), *Where There are no Jobs*, vol. 4

Henriques, Michael and Robert E. Nelson (1997), *Using Franchises to Promote Small Enterprise Development*, in Malcolm Harper (Publisher), Bhubaneswar (India): Small Enterprise Development, March 1997 edition.

Hitchens, Rob et al. (2005), *Making Business Service Markets Work for the Rural Poor – a Review of Experiences*, in Malcolm Harper (Publisher), Bhubaneswar (India): Small Enterprise Development, June 2005 edition.

ILC (2002), "Decent work and the informal economy", report VI, Geneva: International Labor Conference, 90th Session.

ILO (2002), *Women and Men in the Informal Economy – a Statistical Picture*, Geneva: International Labor Office, Employment Sector.

ILO (2005), *Start Your Waste Collection Business – A Step-by-step Guide*, Geneva: International Labor Office.

Prahalad, C.K (2005), *The Fortune at the Bottom of the Pyramid – Eradicating Poverty Through Profits*: Wharton School (USA).

Yu, Sandra O. (Publisher) (August 2005), *Informal Economy, Poverty and Employment in Cambodia, Mongolia and Thailand*, Bangkok: International Labor Organization.

Internet Sources
Scojo Foundation: www.scojofoundation.org.
Grameen Village Phones: www.grameenphone.com.
REDTURS: www.redturs.org.
Butterfield Bakery: www.butterfield.co.za.

APPENDIX: CASE EXAMPLES

Butterfield Bakery in South Africa

Butterfield Bakeries are designed and constructed in such a way that the entire process of baking bread takes place in full view of its customers. The business concept capitalizes on the revival of the village concept of buying fresh products baked throughout the day at the local bakery. The consumer base is very diversified due to the vast social and cultural differences that are evident in the South African market, which is why Butterfield offers four different franchise formats. Since 1997 Butterfield has expanded to more than 100 shops throughout the country. The franchise operation system is highly developed and offers a variety of support and services to its franchisees.

Scojo Foundation (reading glasses)

Scojo Foundation has three goals: (1) increase the number of poor people with access to affordable reading glasses; (2) create jobs for local entrepreneurs – especially women – as so-called "vision advisors"; and (3) facilitate access to comprehensive eye care. The foundation operates in El Salvador, India, and Guatemala and plans to expand its activities to Nicaragua, Honduras, Mexico, Bangladesh, and Afghanistan within the next three years. Scojo Vision LLC provides the foundation with reading glasses at a low cost. Scojo Foundation then trains local women to perform basic eye exams and sell reading glasses at an affordable cost. The women are owners of their operation, that is, they buy and own the products they sell. The foundation continues to support them, for example, by having meetings every two weeks at which the business performance and new products and strategies are discussed and trained.

Grameen Village Phones in Bangladesh

The program is implemented by Grameen Telecom in cooperation with the Grameen Bank, a microcredit institution. It equips women borrowers of Grameen Bank with a GSM technology mobile phone and a subscription. These women then operate an owner-operated pay phone (the "village phone") in their villages. It allows the rural poor who cannot afford to become regular phone subscribers to connect to the outside world. The loan that the women receive from the bank pays for the equipment and incidental expenses. The VP operator receives training from GTC about mode of operation, user charges, etc. Since 1997 the VP program has continuously expanded its outreach: there are currently more than 165 000 VP subscribers who facilitate connectivity to more than 60 million people living in the rural areas of Bangladesh.

Tianjin Jialijie Domestic Service in China
Jialijie provides professional domestic services (such as apartment or house cleaning, baby sitters, elder care, patient nursing, building and office cleaning etc.) through a business system with a unified brand, standardized services, and large-scale operation. It markets the business to resident communities under the cooperation with the community labor service stations, because demand for domestic services is particularly high in these areas. To help poor laid-off workers to join the franchisee business, a business start-up financial plan with four franchise formats was designed by the franchisor. Furthermore, Jialijie offers the franchisees a very specific business system for all aspects of the business including location selection, staff hiring and training, unit operations, accounting, advertising, equipment, etc.

Jialijie was founded by Ms Cui Hong, a laid-off worker, in 1999 as an informal labor organization. After participation in an ILO "Start Your Business" training program at the Tianjin Business Start-up Service Center (BSSC), Ms Cui developed her franchising model based on tremendous demand for domestic services. She developed the franchising business system including location selection method, marketing program, technical and service standards, and training program. So far Jialijie has four franchisees that have 700 workers, 3000 individual family clients, and 56 organizational clients, including banks, big companies, hospitals, governmental offices, schools, etc. Each franchisee earns at least 50 000 RMB a year.

Shuilong Ying Purified Water Outlet in resident communities in China
Shuilong Ying was set up by Tianjin Yadean Environment, Science and Technology Limited Company in 2003. Shuilong Ying is a franchise business that produces and sells purified drinking water from computer-controlled water machines with high technology in outlets located in resident communities. Franchisees buy the machine and operation system from the franchisor, and use the machine to produce and sell water to customers. The franchisor provides the franchisee with a package of services to start and run the franchise business. These services include water station layout and decoration, marketing planning, profit planning, business registration, equipment installation and trial operation, and equipment maintenance and repair. The cooperation with the local BSSCs also enabled Shuilong Ying to help its franchisees (in most cases poor, laid-off workers) in securing start-up funds.

Shuilong Ying was selected by the BSSC in Tianjin and listed on the inventory of business ideas bank. The enterprise has cooperated with the BSSC by taking 13 trainees of the ILO "Generate Your Business Idea" and "Start Your Business" programs as franchisees into the purified water business. All of them run their business smoothly. On average the franchisees employed three employees and generated annual income of 87 000 RMB compared with the initial investment from 44 000 RMB to 50 000 RMB.

Public Transport Operators Cooperative in Rwanda
Facing many problems, such as personal injuries, harassment through local authorities, lack of capital and resources, lack of knowledge and skills, etc., public transport drivers in Rwanda decided to form an Association. The Association de l'Espérance des Taxis Motor au Ruanda (ASSETA-MORWA) has since its foundation helped to improve the situation of public transport operators. It has set up a credit and saving scheme that allows the operators to access credits to purchase a motorcycle. It provides the operators with equipment and uniforms; it has established a training center, which teaches basic mechanics and the highway code. It has also created an anti-AIDS club. Members are able to access these services by paying a small monthly fee.

Uganda Shoe Shiners Industrial Cooperative Society Ltd.
The Uganda Shoe Shiners Cooperative began in 1975 as an informal unit, when five shoe shiners in Kampala decided to establish their own cooperative organization. Their primary objective was to create jobs (in particular for young people who were forced into the informal economy after school) and represent their interests against government authorities. In the meantime, it has become a properly registered cooperative society, the Shoe Shiners Industrial Cooperative Society Ltd. Recently, the numbers of members have increased to over 600, and the cooperative has extended its reach outside Kampala to other cities in Uganda.

The cooperative has struck deals with the KIWI shoe polish company, and also operates a brush-making project producing 50 shoe brushes a day. The cooperation with the Uganda Cooperative Alliance and the Cooperative Savings and Credit Union has opened access to training courses and savings and loan services to members. The support that shoe shiners receive from the cooperative helps them to run their small and informal businesses and generate higher incomes.

Solid Waste Collection in Dar Es Salaam
The municipality of Dar es Salaam is using a franchise approach for delivering public services to private households. It allows small and informal operators to collect solid waste in a predetermined area. As franchisor, the municipality sets the operation system, which determines frequency of collection, a minimum fee that households pay to the collectors, a central gathering point to dump the waste, etc. It has established cooperation with the ILO that has developed a training kit for solid waste collectors. This

training kit provides informal collectors with basic knowledge about business operation and management, health and safety standards, access to financial resources, etc. It is provided through local partner organizations. Small and informal operators have proven to be ideal partners in delivering public services to difficult-to-access city areas. However, they lack bargaining power towards the municipality that still prefers to negotiate with larger business units. For this reason, the ILO is currently helping small waste collectors to create associations.

REDTURS Community-based Tourism (CBT) in Latin America

The REDTURS network in Latin America promotes alliances between rural and indigenous communities, private enterprises and public institutions to facilitate access of community-based tourist enterprises to business services and new markets. REDTURS provides technical assistance and institutional support to communities so that they have access to training, information technologies for the promotion and marketing of their products under a collective trademark, and to enter into fair-trade commercial agreements. The REDTURS Internet portal is one means by which CBT is supported in accessing European markets. It supplies tourists, tour operators, public and private institutions with comprehensive and updated information about such community destinations.

REDTURS is an initiative started by communities in Ecuador and the ILO. It has rapidly included further countries in Latin America. As a result of this local and international cooperation, national tourist associations have been set up, to act as intermediaries between local communities, the local and national government authorities and final customer markets. Already today, these associations support the CBT operators in many ways, for example, in accessing financial resources to set up their businesses. It is planned to expand the delivery of services such as training and marketing support through these national associations. It is also planned to establish a collective trademark in the near future, which would set and regulate quality standards for CBT. The ILO has facilitated this process by providing a training manual for CBT operators and also helping them to build associations.

Table A3.1 outlines the business concepts, management systems and ongoing support areas of the above microfranchises.

Table A3.1   Selected top-down and bottom-up franchises

Case	Business Concept and Management Systems				Provision of Equipment	Start-up Funds
	Operations manuals & systems	Adherence to quality standards	Initial training	Right to use trademark		
Top-down franchising						
Butterfield Bakery in South Africa	Manuals on technical and operational management of a bakery, business format franchise	Operational standards, quality control system	Four weeks of theoretical and practical training	Franchisees operate under a trademark; rights and duties are defined in agreement	Baking equipment and shop interior is included in start-up fees	Starting at 800 000 Rand (minimum contribution of franchisee: 20%). Franchisor provides contacts to banks for loan
Scojo Foundation (reading glasses) in El Salvador	Three-tier management system with Scojo Foundation as intermediary	Ten pairs to be sold per month, reference to clinics for complicated cases	Local women trained in marketing, eye health screening, financial management and women's empowerment	Women call themselves "Scojo Vision Advisors"	Initial inventory of 20 glasses with display and carry case, eye charts, uniform, repair kits, ad-sign	US $130 Initial setup either provided for free or on consignment basis
Grameen Village Phones in Bangladesh	Village women receive an operations manual for wireless phone, three-tier franchising system	Standardized user charges, urban/rural price level secured by GP (price protection), selected women must have a good (loan) record	Basic instructions on how to operate business	Franchisee responsible for phone's maintenance, use and local marketing for a per-minute fee charged from customer	GSM mobile handset, subscription	$220 pays for equipment and incidental expenses, monthly subscription charge (min. $3), Grameen Bank lease finance program

Ongoing Support					Success
Marketing	Product development	Training and consultancy	Bulk purchasing	Advocacy	

Top-down franchising

Advertisement is done by franchisor; brand; some local marketing freedoms	New business formats are developed continuously; latest format: Butterfield Espresso	Franchisor has a training facility that provides training on demand	Franchisor conducts negotiations with suppliers (e.g., flour) for more than 100 outlets		Since 1997 growth from 0 to more than 100 stores country wide, further rapid expansion
Sign to put up in front of home, flyers, posters, radio advertisements	Scojo Vision LLC	Bi-weekly training meetings for teaching new strategies and performance analysis, replenishing inventory	Low-cost reading glasses from Scojo Vision LLC (5% of profits are donated)	Strong international recognition; awareness raising for women empowerment and local entrepreneurship	El Salvador: 25 (since 2002); India: 60 (since 2001); Guatemala: in operation since 2004; expansion to other countries planned
Newspaper ads	Internet access, email and fax services can be offered additionally	Connected to services provided by Grameen Bank	Grameen Telecom purchases bulk airtime for discount price and sells it to franchisees at a discounted rate	Strong international recognition; no direct lobbying for village phones, but GB has strong public linkages and support	165 000 VP subscribers since 1997; further rapid expansion; provides connectivity to 60 million rural population

Table A3.1   (continued)

Case	Business Concept and Management Systems				Provision of Equipment	Start-up Funds
	Operations manuals & systems	Adherence to quality standards	Initial training	Right to use trademark		
Top-down franchising						
Tianjin Jialijie Domestic Service in China	Manual includes: location selection, staff hiring and training, unit operations, accounting, advertising etc.	Quality standards defined by franchisor, e.g., standardized cleaning steps for apartments or hygiene rules	Half-month training: business system and management, basic domestic service knowledge, specific vocational training	Franchisee agrees to operate under trademark; penalty payment in case of contract breach	Unified materials: bicycle, medicament holders, floor washing machine, polishing machine, bucket, dust collector, etc.	Four categories form 25 000 to 60 000 RMB; franchisor cooperates with BSSC that facilitates microcredits
Shuilong Ying Purified Water Outlet in resident commun-ities in China	Technical and business operations manuals given to franchisee	Quality and safety standards manual, approval of authorities, 24-hour quality monitoring screen, inspections	Water station layout, marketing planning, profit planning, business registration, installation, maintenance and repair	Direct (five-year agreement) and indirect (three years) use of trademark, commitment to protect the business concept; ongoing royalty fee	Franchisee acquires purification machine and equipment (e.g., water station layout and decoration) with fee	41 500 RMB (for five years) cooperation with local BSSCs that provide access to microcredits
Bottom-up franchising						
Public Transport Operators Cooperative in Rwanda (ASSETAM ORWA)	Managed along cooperative democratic principles; highway code	Limited working hours			Uniforms, motorcycles (on loan)	Member-ship in co-op costs 200 FRW/day (75% operation costs, 25% forced savings),

	Ongoing Support				Success
Marketing	Product development	Training and consultancy	Bulk purchasing	Advocacy	
Top-down franchising					
Franchise sales video and brochures; training and consultancy on marketing strategies	New domestic service products are made available to franchisees	Refresher training after six months; recommendation to participate in national occupational qualification and authentication	Franchisees purchase equipment at lower price than market	Only cooperation with local municipal BSSCs (that are supported by the ILO)	Four franchisees that have together 700 workers, 3000 family clients, 56 organizational clients (since 1999). Each franchisee earns at least 50 000 RMB/year
Marketing program and materials: advertisement on website, newspapers, TV. Flyers, posters and special demonstrations	Continuous upgrading, e.g., new anti-freezing technology to update old machines	Marketing, staff recruitment, business operation and management training and consultancies	Filter, spare parts and water containers/ bottles can be bought at discount price	Only cooperation with local municipal BSSCs (that are supported by the ILO)	Started in 2003; every small franchisee creates three jobs and generates annual income of 87 000 RMB (on average); steadily growing
Bottom-up franchising					
Yellow colored uniforms, co-op helps to improve image	Garage and spare parts depot, health and insurance fund	Training facilities established (teaches highway code and basic mechanics), anti-AIDS club	57 motorcycles have been bought for members (on loan)	Negotiations with traffic police and local authorities	2500 members; bought 57 motorcycles; established a training center, garage, anti-AIDS

Table A3.1   (continued)

Case	Business Concept and Management Systems				Provision of Equipment	Start-up Funds
	Operations manuals & systems	Adherence to quality standards	Initial training	Right to use trademark		
Bottom-up franchising						
						saving and credit initiative
Uganda Shoe Shiners Industrial Cooperative Society Ltd. Remained informal until 1989	Managed along cooperative democratic principles; lack of funds to develop training and manuals	Recommendations on material for brushes, dryness, right color of shoe polish; quality standards committee carries out periodical checks	Peer-education, informal on-the-job training	Full and part-time membership share allows members to use the name of the cooperative, no branding	Arrangements for provision of brushes cupboard, umbrella and aprons polish are under way. Rent of polish kits, KIWI shoe polish, shoe brushes if possible	US$ 200 (covers brushes, chairs, benches, creams, umbrella, uniforms, work permit, etc.); cooperation with Uganda Cooperative Savings and Credit Unions opens access to savings and loan services
Solid Waste Collection in Dar Es Salaam (Tanzania)	Operations manual based on the ILO training kit "Start your Waste Collection Business"	Requirements in frequency of collection, minimum fee, restricted geographical area, protective clothing and equipment, monitoring	Training on waste collection business management provided by local partner institutions and organizations of the ILO	Registration includes right of collection-monopoly in a pre-determined area	Due to lack of resources and funds, provision of equipment had to be given up	

Ongoing Support					Success
Marketing	Product development	Training and consultancy	Bulk purchasing	Advocacy	

Bottom-up franchising

					club and a savings and credit initiative (with 18 tontine groups)
Marketing of shoe polish and brushes, expansion of cooperative all over Uganda	Penetrates new markets: shoe polish marketing, shoe brush production and sale, shining kit renting; plans to import shining kits to be placed in various locations in Uganda	Consultant company engaged to train members in management (with support of the ILO); cooperation with Uganda Cooperative Alliance opens access to training programs and other services to members	Deal with KIWI shoe polish company; plans to extend bulk purchasing services	Represents interests of members towards government;. lobbies for recognition of shoe shiners business; plans to form a regional association for East Africa; awareness raising at local and international level	Started in 1975 with 5 shoe shiners and has grown to more than 600 recently; expanded to other cities in Uganda
Facilitated access to the public tendering system		Business development programs provided by partner organizations of the ILO		The ILO is facilitating the creation of associations that would give small collectors more bargaining power	Mixed success; municipali-ties are reluctant to cooperate with micro informal units

Table A3.1　(continued)

Case	Business Concept and Management Systems				Provision of Equipment	Start-up Funds
	Operations manuals & systems	Adherence to quality standards	Initial training	Right to use trademark		
Bottom-up franchising						
REDTURS Community based Tourism (CBT) in Latin America	Training manual that outlines how to operate a CBT business (written by the ILO); international network system	Planned: code of conduct, peer review system, annual external evaluations	Based on training manual for CBT	Planned: create a collective trademark with quality standards	Depends on services offered; communities are given support in negotiating financial funds	National tourism association provides contacts to donors, finance institutions and the tourism ministry

Ongoing Support					Success
Marketing	Product development	Training and consultancy	Bulk purchasing	Advocacy	

Bottom-up franchising

Internet platform REDTURS; ILO facilitates contacts to European tourist operators	In the case of Ricancie community network in Ecuador: regular regional knowledge sharing meetings; cooperation with universities	Some local networks have developed own capacities; national associations are planned to provide further training and consultancy		National tourism associations represent CBT operators at national and international level	Started in 2001; has since then created 12 national tourism associations, training modules, Internet portal, confer-ences, etc.

4. Current international development tools to combat poverty

Warner Woodworth

The current context of global poverty is wide-ranging and linked to multiple factors. This chapter attempts to ascertain the basic elements of human poverty, especially in the Third World, and to describe briefly some of its features. I next explore traditional solutions for alleviating world poverty – what has worked, as well as what has not – and how microcredit seems to be succeeding as a current innovation. The success and limitations of microcredit are analyzed, and we then turn to microfranchising as a new tool, attempting to elucidate its potential for moving the poor up the economic ladder.

POVERTY AND ITS FEATURES

The plight of the global poor and the causes of their impoverishment have been debated for decades, even centuries. From time to time, experts offered grand solutions and predicted the alleviation of human suffering. New voices continue the cause, even calling for an "end to poverty" (Jones, 2004; Sachs, 2005).

When I speak of poverty, I mean *extreme* poverty, that which resides in the many so-called "developing nations," the Third World, or what the World Bank refers to as "low-income countries." The bank asserts that some 1.1 billion of the poorest attempt to live out an existence on merely a dollar a day. Some 400 studies carried out in 100 countries, mostly by government researchers conducting random samples, substantiate this figure. The sample size consists of over a million households, and the surveys have sought numerous details about the sources of income, amounts spent, the number of individuals dependent on that income and so forth (PovCal Net, 2006).

Unfortunately, the future picture does not suggest an acceptable rate of progress. Clearly, more must be done. But poverty is not a simple economic factor. It includes a number of other facets that help to explain its impacts, or, conversely, to exacerbate human suffering. They include the following: inequality, homelessness, refugee status, international debt, monies spent on military uses, lack of access to clean water, consumption patterns, education, and so on. Below are a few "poverty facts and stats" assembled by Anup Shah (2006). While some specific numbers may be debatable, the overall picture of inequality shows disturbing trends:

- The gross domestic product (GDP) of the world's poorest 48 countries is less than the combined wealth of the three richest individuals on the planet.
- Some 20 percent of industrialized nations consume 86 percent of the world's goods.
- Developing nations spend $13 to repay their foreign debt for every $1 of grant money received.
- Approximately a billion people are unschooled and illiterate.
- Fifty-one percent of the world's 100 major institutions are not nations, but corporations such as Wal-Mart, Exxon, and IBM.

Lack of access to new technology, racism, oppression of women, environmental degradation, and disease such as HIV/AIDS all foster poverty. Natural disasters accelerate the increase in poverty – events such as the 2005 Pakistan earthquake, and the 2004 Asian tsunami that hit 11 countries bordering the Indian Ocean, killed over 260 000, and left four million homeless. There were the terrible El Salvador earthquakes in 2001, and Hurricane Mitch destroyed much of Central America in 1998. When one adds these factors to civil wars in Sudan, Uganda, East Timor, Haiti, Afghanistan and Iraq, one sees how poverty and suffering continues to plague much of the Third World.

HISTORICAL OVERVIEW OF DEVELOPMENT MOVEMENTS TO COMBAT POVERTY

Much conventional public opinion assumes that the improving economies of the industrialized nations is matched by similar success in Third World nations, but such assertions may be erroneous (Herman, 1995; Broad and Landi, 1996; *Economist*, 1996; Kristof, 1997). Over the past 40 years, large-scale strategies of traditional development programs have each been attempted, and at times they led to questionable results. They include the following:

- 1960s Modernization strategies often produced unintended, negative outcomes that contradicted indigenous cultures and values.

- 1970s   The green revolution attempted to superimpose Western agricultural methods (big tractors, chemical fertilizers and toxic pesticides) on the Third World. The outcomes included short-term yields, rising cancer rates, and depleted soil.
- 1980s   Basic needs were the next focus, such as health care, access to clean water, education/literacy, and so on; but such programs were enormously expensive and hard to sustain.
- 1990s   There began to occur a dramatic shift away from huge, macro solutions that were inefficient, costly, and often wasteful, funded by major donors such as the World Bank or the United Nations. Experts from such institutions too often described their projects in high-level abstractions, which seemed ethereal to indigenous groups in the Third World. New approaches in the 1990s started with emphasis on small, concrete projects, which the local community could manage, grow, and improve, thereby impacting the members.
- 2000   In the new millennium, the emerging approach began to accelerate dramatically from the bottom up. Needs and problems were identified at the grassroots level and participants were able to later engage consultants to assist. In this alternative development paradigm, Third World citizens began to operate in partnership with outside experts – each having a voice, each involved in the process of defining problems and generating solutions. Above and beyond traditional strategies that were run by the World Bank and other huge institutions that focused on economic matters primarily, social development began to be addressed – factors such as health and education. Hence the need for different foreign aid and development strategies that would work. We now turn to several of these methods.

MACRO TOOLS FOR DEVELOPMENT

Within these major paradigms of development described above, a number of specific tools began to be utilized to combat poverty. The items below are not a complete list, but they suggest the range of methods for aiding developing nations. My initial emphasis will be on describing and advocating each tool, accepting its use and viability as a means to empower the poor. Such an approach may be referred to as a "generous interpretation" (So, 1990, p. 14), or "appreciative inquiry" (Srivastva and Cooperrider, 1990). The first tools listed are macro in nature, while I later review more micro approaches.

Health Care

Evidence began to be shown in the last couple of decades that economic investment was not the sole answer to the problems of the global poor. Third World development could also be enhanced by strategies for improving people's health, the assumption being that as disease is prevented or reduced, economic improvements will occur. Infections lead to poverty, and vice versa. Continuous ill health is a main explanation as to why the poor stay poor. Hence, over recent decades, many development tools have focused on bettering women's reproductive health, prenatal care, and infant well-being. Others have emphasized childhood disease prevention methods, such as vaccinations against polio, which was eliminated globally but is now again on the rise.

Clearly, without ongoing programs to control and reduce traditional disease, as well as being alerted quickly to fast-spreading new epidemics that may arise, human morbidity and mortality can greatly disrupt economic and social development. The Third World in particular requires a global health system that can rapidly identify and contain public health emergencies in order to prevent the disruption of trade, economic growth and travel.

To understand the uses and treatments for many of the above-mentioned health problems, global organizations have been established to treat, educate, vaccinate or otherwise combat these problems: the UN's World Health Organization (WHO), UNICEF, the Pan American Health Organization (PAHO), the International Labor Office (ILO), and many others, including national and local government agencies. Also, private foundations have been established within countries and regions, along with thousands of NGOs that seek especially to improve the physical well-being of the Third World poor.

Finally, a new phenomenon is unfolding – the rise of global business and corporate partnerships, which channel funds and medicines to fight disease among the poor. They mount awareness campaigns, fund medical research, recruit and train doctors and other medical practitioners in public health. They raise capital, operate vaccination programs, and attempt to scale up prevention and treatment of disease.

Even small NGOs I have worked with in recent years have had positive and significant health impacts. For instance, the Ouelessebougou–Utah Alliance has worked for two decades in a group of 72 villages in Southern Mali where we have established indigenous pharmacies, trained over 100 health care workers, given prenatal education courses and demonstration projects to pregnant women taught by Utah midwives, conducted HIV/AIDS education, provided millions of dollars in donated pharmaceuticals, offered medical surgeries by US physicians to reconstruct cleft palates, and club feet, sent expeditions of dentists who performed needed teeth repairs, and so forth (OUA, 2006). All these small, grassroots health programs have had a significant impact on the economic development of the 36 000 villagers in that region. And OUA is simply one illustration of hundreds of thousands of NGO health care strategies around the globe (Woodworth, 1997).

Literacy

Related to the above, adult illiteracy is largely a function of lacking education for Third World children. The low literacy levels of Sub-Saharan African adults, as well as much of South Asia, are critical barriers to national development in those countries where 40–50 percent of adults cannot read or write. In Latin America and East Asia, the rates are 10–15 percent (UNDP, 2005).

If the young could be schooled, the logic suggests, more adults would read and write. But sadly today, some 800 million school-age children around the globe are not enrolled or attending school. In certain cases this is because there are simply no such facilities in various Third World areas. More likely, the problem is that parents cannot afford the costs of registration, books, or perhaps, the required uniforms. To make matters worse, many peasant families depend on even their young children to work in the fields in order to enjoy greater earning power. Still more seriously, in my mind, the bulk of children who miss out on education tend to be girls. Gender discrimination usually favors boys' schooling.

In recent years, development experts have began to stress the need to improve a nation's social capital through the building of schools for all children – rural or urban, young or old, male or female. Huge amounts of funding for child education are currently offered to poor countries, especially in Africa and South Asia, to reduce illiteracy and enable the young to grow up and obtain employment by having at least a rudimentary education. One only has to see the educational impacts in countries like Botswana, Chile, Singapore, South Korea, Taiwan and China to appreciate how building schools and educating society's youngest can produce important developments in nation-building within just a few decades of effort.

Foreign Direct Investments (FDI)

Monies from the so-called industrial nations have long been a traditional tool for development. Such funds often flow from multilateral agencies such as large transnational corporations (TNCs) and capital sources such as the International Monetary Fund (IMF) or World Bank. Foreign trade is the basic tool here, a method that may include selling and purchasing foreign equipment and technology. The G-7 industrial nations often lead this movement, using such mechanisms as the World Trade Organization (WTO) to set policies and establish cross-national agreements. Funds from such activities are used for capital investments in ventures like factories, highways, mines, ports, and so on. They are used to improve society, creating jobs while generating incomes and tax revenue for the host country. The success of South Africa's development through mining and shipping enterprises illustrates this approach.

Internal Productive Investments

Development tools such as taxation and confiscatory devices, as well as capital generated from government bonds, stock markets and banks can channel money into national coffers and thereby build the economy. The ultimate goal is to modernize the Third World and help it mature until a mass consumption society is attained. Hence, aid takes the form of generating capital, technology and new abilities or expertise. Perhaps an example of this is the tremendous investment of Japan's government and corporations in recent years, a move that rapidly shifted it toward becoming an economic powerhouse.

Political Systems Evolution

This tool consists of differentiating elements of a nation's structure of politics, democratizing them, secularizing them, and enhancing society's political capacity (Coleman, 1968). Key elements include shifting toward a self-orientation rather than that of the collective, personal status rather than that of the group, creating a secular worldview rather than a sacred perspective, specialization instead of generalization, complexity rather than simplicity and such factors as legal norms, administration skills, citizen rights, and equality. The context for political development is often that of Europeanization/Americanization, the assumption being that the Third World can be transformed into a highly industrialized democratic society. The rise of Brazil as a global power from its Third World status a few decades ago to a fully-functioning democracy today is an illustration of political evolution.

Human Capital and Entrepreneurship

This development method implies that macro investments in infrastructure or businesses are not sufficient. Instead, what is needed, according to

McClelland (1964), is the fostering of native or local entrepreneurs. Designing new political systems or sending in foreign-aid and expertise will not transform the Third World character. What is needed is achievement motivation, such that citizens seek to spend their time in economic production, not leisure. According to this perspective, countries with high economic development possess high scores on achievement motivation. Conversely, Third World nations often tend to be characterized by leisure, family ties, and a "laid-back" mentality. In other words, the emphasis is on affiliation, relationships between family and friends, not success. McClelland argues that development can be attained by training individuals, by improving contacts with industrial nations, by changing parental and educational socialization – so that the young grow up seeking to excel, get good jobs, be known and respected for their individual accomplishments, not for being loyal to their families, or a good member of the neighborhood, or clan. Examples might include Hong Kong and South Korea, countries that were transformed over several decades, from being clan-based religious societies into valuing personal success, economic achievement, and post-Confucius/Buddhist belief systems. For industrial nations using this approach, economic development can best occur by building a Third World entrepreneurial culture.

Counter-dependency Tools

In contrast to the above modernization paradigms, another theory is that the Third World is behind because of *underdevelopment* (Frank, 1967). It is seen as a condition fostered by the Northern Hemisphere to keep poor countries of the South down. This view argues that colonial nations have always sought to repress impoverished regions: Europe in Africa and Asia, and the United States in Latin America. It is held that the *core* controls the power and wealth, keeping the Third World out on the *periphery* where it continues to be exploited over decades.

To counter this condition of dependency, some analysts, especially in countries south of the United States, have argued the need to reject foreign intervention in order not to be trapped in the web of control from outside. Attempts to protest against external controls grew into mass movements in Latin America, especially during the 1960s–80s. But these independent movements were often put down by military repression and "junta" regimes. Cases include Argentina, Chile, Peru, Bolivia, and so on. Negative economic results followed, consisting of high inflation, mass unemployment, loss of or unfair trade, and the devaluation of local currencies.

In 2006, Venezuela's oil wealth has enabled Hugo Chavez to build a booming economy within, while thumbing its nose at the United States and other imperialists from the North. Similarly, the new President of Bolivia, Evo Morales, was recently elected as the first *quechua* indigenous president in the country's history. His platform? Reject US power and build a pro-poor society to empower its native people. Lead the peasant struggle to retain oil and mineral wealth for Bolivians, not outsiders. Both leaders have threatened to nationalize foreign investments and expel American corpo-rations and even US embassies if necessary. Those nations stress solidarity with each other and rejection of US intervention. They seek to cancel their national debt to such institutions as the IMF and World Bank, arguing that those financial burdens were foisted on the masses by Latino elites collab-orating with the US and are therefore onerous burdens to be cast off, not repaid. The hope is that genuine development will occur in accordance with Latino values, not "gringo" capitalism, "fair trade," not free trade. The working classes, whom Marx referred to as the "proletariat," must rebel and launch an ongoing revolution in order to build a just and democratic society. Counter-dependency, defined as class struggle, is the path to a better world, according to this tool.

The preceding pages regarding major development tools for the Third World cover the basic paradigms: modernization, dependence, the green revolution, basic needs, education, and health care. With the macro approaches to development summarized above, we next turn to more micro-specific tools.

MICRO LEVEL TOOLS FOR DEVELOPMENT

The tools highlighted below are specific methods used in current develop-ment practice in smaller, more concrete ways. While big business, big gov-ernment, and multi-lateral institutions tend to emphasize the macro approaches described earlier, these next strategies tend to focus on narrowly-built change tactics. They are often operated by an NGO or local government to address concrete problems of underdevelopment, regardless of a national policy or priority. Practitioners work to design and implement these tools, often out in the trenches. Many may be considered as "grass-roots" or "bottom-up" approaches to change, as opposed to massive, top-down solutions for development.

Small-scale Farming

A number of NGOs now engage in development projects to aid the rural poor by helping them to grow cash crops for selling in village or town mar-ketplaces. Instead of large agribusinesses that harvest millions of acres with heavy farm equipment, the "small is beautiful" (Schumacher, 1973) approach stresses family agriculture, low-tech methods and local markets.

Definitions of such a practice vary, but they usually refer to poor, rural families who either own or lease a mere one to three acres upon which they labor. There are generally no hired farm hands, the work being done, instead, by a father, mother and their children. The annual gross income tends to range between several hundred and several thousand dollars, depending on the country. Often, NGOs or government extension services provide technical assistance in order to facilitate small-scale farm success. These provide expertise for establishing the farm's operation—plants and fertilization, managing, harvesting, storing and distributing one's produce.

Development researchers advocate small-scale farming both as a means for economic survival of poor rural families, sometimes referring to it as an "agroecology" model (Altieri, 1989), as well as an alternative path to the growing concentration of the global food supply in the hands of just a few large agribusinesses (Shiva, 2000). The latter worry about giant MNCs like Cargill and Continental Grain, which own an estimated 25 percent each of global soybean trade, grain, and seeds. Such massive institutions undermine and negatively impact small farm families, as well as global consumers. Hence the need to strengthen small-scale agriculture. While some observers bemoan the plight of small family farms in the Third World, others see the growing fair trade movement over coffee and/or the rising organic produce preference by consumers as roads to a re-emergence of small-scale crops (Raynolds, 2000).

The potential benefits of small-scale family farming often include family self-reliance, less crop erosion, new organic food supply chains, preservation of indigenous farming methodologies, increased food security, and the retention of rural life. With the assistance of NGOs or progressive government extension programs, basic needs may be met, local produce markets can survive, ecological resources may be conserved and farmers may become socially organized through group empowerment to increase purchasing power of raw materials, achieve access to markets, and enjoy a better quality of life

Economic Cooperatives

These often consist of a few hundred industrial workers who have taken over their factory, or groups of agricultural field workers in rural areas who join together to survive and grow collectively (Moskin, 2004). These structures have been long-practiced as solutions to Third World poverty. Thus, today millions of worker-owners from the Philippines to Kenya, from Canada to Costa Rica, own their workplace (Ellerman, 2005). They emphasize democratic decision-making, equal ownership of shares, election of members to boards and even, in many cases, to managerial positions. There are a number of long-term, viable cooperative organizations that have generated higher productivity, greater profits, and extremely high rates of worker motivation and longevity. These include the plywood co-ops of Northwestern United States, the Israeli *kibbutzim* that outproduce capitalist firms and have existed for a century, and the 200 Mondragon co-ops that have built a strong Basque economy in Northern Spain (Woodworth, 2002).

Other forms of cooperative economics include housing co-ops, credit unions, retail store co-ops, insurance cooperatives, and additional collective systems in which members band together and leverage their group power to reduce costs, provide quality service, increase buying power and so forth. The International Cooperative Alliance (ICA), founded over a century ago in 1895, represents approximately 760 million members of various co-op organizations around the globe that serve to build economic development, much of it in the Third World (ICA, 1996).

Emerging Development Methodologies

Of course there are numerous other micro interventions, some of which have arisen quite recently, but describing them in depth is beyond the scope of this chapter. A brief listing will have to suffice:

Legalizing the informal economy
Initiated by Peruvian economist, Hernando de Soto, the thrust is on establishing quick and simple processes by which the poor may obtain legal title to their squatter land, register their small businesses, etc. (de Soto, 1989, 2000).

Women's empowerment
Since the "Fourth World Conference on Women" held in Beijing in 1995, the movement to strengthen development efforts on behalf of females has exploded—gender equality, education for girls, political rights, reproductive health, protections from domestic abuse, and laws against human trafficking have all become major initiatives for hundreds of government agencies and thousands of NGOs globally (Eade, 1999; Bennett, 2002; Beneria, 2003; UNIFEM, 2006).

Community organizing and development
Advocacy and conflict resolution have become chief tools for mobilizing communities to fight racism, preserve the local ecological system, maintain

jobs, and build a better quality of life—whether for peasants of an Asian rural village or squatters in an urban *barrio* of Latin America (Schwartz, 1981; Hirschman, 1984; Collier, 1994; Tarrow, 1994; Lean, 1995; Krishna, 2002).

Social entrepreneurship (SE)
An emergent development tool of the last several years, SE reframes traditional businesses entrepreneurialism, risk, vision, new inventions and new services to fight societal problems. Rather than seek business profits, the objective is to build a genuine civil society where the masses can find fulfillment (Leadbeater, 1997; Bornstein, 2004; Bruyn, 2005; Korten, 2006).

Environmentalism
The greening of development has become a major thrust over the past few years. It emphasizes everything from forest preservation and sustainable economics to clean air and socially responsible business practices (Devall and Sessions, 1985; Daly and Cobb, 1989; Adams, 1990; Orr, 1991; Peritore, 1999).

Appropriate technology
This movement began with the visionary insights of Britain's E.F. Schumacher, articulated in the 1970s in his books. Today his theory for Third World development consists of partnering with the poor in building intermediate, simple tools and equipment that are inexpensive, easy to repair, etc. Schumacher's legacy is currently manifest in research institutes and college programs named after him, as well as NGOs and thousands of articles and books that have built off the original concepts and spread across the globe (Schumacher, 1973; McRobie and Schumacher, 1981; Basu et al., 1996; Nardi and O'Day, 1999; Hazeltine and Bull, 2003).

Bottom (or base) of the pyramid (BOP)
Perhaps one of the hottest recent development tools is the idea of alleviating poverty through capitalism-for-the-poor: Providing goods and services to the three to four billion impoverished people on earth who survive on or under $2 per day. If MNCs could view the poor as value-conscious consumers and begin designing and selling cheaper products to them, whole new markets could be created at the base of the global social pyramid. The argument suggests that entrepreneurial creativity, innovative trade, and emerging prosperity may combine to eradicate poverty through low-end capitalism, a feat not yet attained by governments, NGOs and other non-profit sectors (Boyer, 2003; Prahalad, 2004; Hart, 2005).

Having reviewed a number of macro development tools, as well as briefly highlighting several small-scale interventions, including new or emerging ones, we now turn to the topic of microfinance.

MICROFINANCE AS DEVELOPMENT

Perhaps the most innovative development tool to empower millions of poor families in recent years is that of microcredit. It was hardly known until a decade ago, but is becoming widely practiced in the contemporary Third World. It is impressive for several reasons: it defies the traditional assumption that solutions are best invented in industrialized nations and that top-down development is required because national political leaders' support is essential for success. Instead, microfinance essentially turns traditional borrowing and finance upside down.

As microcredit has been recognized for its contribution to poverty alleviation efforts, many government and multilateral organizations (such as USAID, the World Bank, the United Nations, etc.) have become involved, as well as NGOs. Likewise, there are important microcredit industry research and policy organizations helping to further the impact of microcredit for the poor: some of these organizations are the Consultative Group to Help the Poorest (CGAP) and the Small Enterprise Education and Promotion Network (SEEP).

In 1997, microcredit began to accelerate through the establishment of an annual microcredit summit, which brought together several thousand NGO leaders from more than 100 countries. Conceived of by Sam Daley-Harris of Results International, an NGO that focused on hunger, the summit campaign established the goal of extending microcredit to the planet's poorest families, hoping to impact 100 million by 2005. In 2005, it was reported that 3164 MFIs had reached 92 million clients with microloans, benefiting over 333 million individuals in poor families (Harris, 2005). The microcredit campaign has grown 776 percent since its inception in 1997, averaging a bit more than 36 percent annual growth. The summit plans to expand its outreach over the next several years. With the UN declaring 2005 as the "International Year of Microcredit," the movement has continued to grow (UN, 2005).

New Microfinance Developments

A variety of new tools are being rolled out to facilitate the practice of microlending and self-employment. Several of these are identified below:

Government initiatives

National governments are beginning to experiment with new approaches to microcredit. For instance, the government of Bangladesh has established Palli Karma Sahayak Foundation (PKSF), a national wholesale fund that, in turn, channels monies to NGOs for microcredit purposes. So far, it has extended about $262 million to approximately 200 Bangladeshi NGOs, greatly expanding the availability of microcredit to the nation's poorest regions where, before PKSF, there were few such opportunities. Because of this success, other countries such as Pakistan, Nepal, and the Philippines, have likewise created national wholesale funds.

Various loan products

Microcredit services are being offered above and beyond simply obtaining a loan to start a microenterprise. Some NGOs are giving other types of loans. For example, the Aga Khan Development Network operating in Egypt, Syria, and elsewhere, has started providing health microinsurance for poor families at extremely low costs. They also give school loans so impoverished children can get an education. With support from the World Bank, Aga Khan will be able to grow from its available $35 million in micro-credit for small businesses of 25 000 borrowers per year into a larger MFI that offers numerous types of financial loans to the poor. Other NGOs are offering housing loans to improve one's shelter, agriculture-crop loans to insure peasant field work, and so forth.

Microcredit and ecology

Environmentalists have begun to partner with new types of "green" micro-credit NGOs to provide financial services for the poor that are ecologically appropriate and sustainable. They are teaming up with Rotary International to send solar ovens to poor families victimized by the 12/26 Asian tsunami in Sri Lanka Several NGOs and universities are collaborating on research about pro-green policies for microcredit, as well as holding conferences and funding student internships in green microcredit. HELP International, an NGO we established at Brigham Young University in 1999, trains its college-student volunteers to implement Square Foot Garden methods, using compost to double or triple vegetable produce for poor families in Central America. A number of other NGOs are giving loans for environmentally sustainable projects like bio-gas systems, micro-drip irrigation, Lorena Stoves to reduce in-house smoke particles, low-tech water pumps, and so on.

Commercialization

For some, what started as a non-profit NGO providing humanitarian loans to the poor has evolved into a formal, for-profit bank. Depending on the legal environment and social-political structures of the national government, the trend for doing this seems to be growing. The first example of this was ACCION's project in Bolivia to transform itself beginning in 1984. A partner NGO, PRODEM, was organized, and with a native board of business experts and a skilled staff, training and loans began to be provided. But the demand for microcredit was so huge in a country so poor, PRODEM soon realized it could simply not do the job as an NGO. A committee was formed to launch a new formal financial "institution," Banco Solidario (Solidarity Bank). It opened in 1992 and quickly outgrew its need for donors and unpredictable government support. Instead, profits generated operating capital to fuel its growth. Today, Banco Sol is the largest bank in Bolivia, providing a vast array of financial services to the country's poor, while enjoying a high rate of return on its loan portfolio.

MFI acceleration
Critical challenges today are how to expand microcredit from its current important but limited impacts into a major tool for empowering the poor. So far, even though microcredit provides loans to 100 million individuals, this represents a small percentage of the projected global demand for microcredit. UNITUS has led the charge in showing that most microcredit NGOs serve an average of only 2500 poor clients. Only a handful of major NGOs such as FINCA, Grameen, and ACCION, serve well over 100 000 borrowers each.

An MFI I founded and served as board chair, UNITUS, has launched an innovative acceleration model to exponentially expand microcredit around the world. It evaluates high-potential NGOs that have only a few thousand clients and, upon deciding to partner with them, provides capital and consulting services to enable them to expand dramatically. UNITUS typically invests $2–4 million for several new partners annually. So far it has fueled the growth of such MFIs in Kenya, Mexico, India, and Argentina to a total of over 2 million clients. By 2015 its objective in India alone is to have ten million poor families receiving microcredit.

Better banking tools
New tools for financial transactions are being provided through microcredit institutions in some countries. For example, ADOPEM in the Dominican Republic, a partner of Women's World Banking, offers ATM services for its poor female clients. And, in a dozen or so countries, microentrepreneurs can now obtain a VISA or MasterCard to access needed capital for microenterprise expansion.

New technologies

Providers of microcredit services are rapidly embracing the use of new technologies to expand their impact: computers, smart cards, personal digital assistants (PDAs), cell phones and other tools, etc. For instance, the Andhra Pradesh partner of UNITUS, Swayam Krishi Sangam (SKS), began using smart cards for each of its clients spread throughout the hard-to-travel rural areas of India. Before this innovation, paper, pencil, and manual ledgers were used. But the SKS staff now uses PDAs to record borrowers' efforts. The clients' loan and savings transactions are recorded automatically. Instead of paper passbooks and collection sheets, everything is computerized. Elsewhere in Uganda and Bangladesh, cell phones have begun to be used, not only to enhance client communication, but as microenterprises that can sell minutes to the public. Such services are a hot commodity in rural villages where there is no regular phone system. Some "phone ladies" in Uganda today have incomes of $1000 per year, a sharp contrast to annual compensation of $300 when they were only raising goats.

Recent Microfinance Experiments

In Uganda, FINCA discovered that 80 percent of its 30 000 clients were raising at least one AIDS orphan, and that 75 percent of client incomes went to health care providers. So, it started health insurance to treat medical problems, as well as life insurance to mitigate the high burial costs for borrowers and their family members who may die.

In the Philippines, Freedom from Hunger and the World Council of Credit Unions (WOCCU) began to partner so that credit unions could offer microloans to poor clients. WOCCU has seen its Filipino client base mushroom from 2000 to 13 000 microentrepreneurs over the past several years.

Children are becoming microentrepreneurs too. In Bangladesh, street children 11–18 years of age go through training programs on health, AIDS, hygiene, and financial well-being. When graduating, the MFI PMUK gives small loans of $10 or so to those youth who want to start a microenterprise of shining shoes, selling flowers, etc.

In rural Slovakia where people are spread out too widely for an effective MFI operation to be established in a central location, one NGO has begun taking its services to potential clients as a "traveling road show." The Integra Foundation (TIF) moves around the country, recruiting single mothers and abused women, providing training, accepting loan applications, and disbursing loans.

Finally, it should be pointed out that the preceding innovations are but a sample of the numerous creative solutions being experimented with by MFIs and others around the world. Many of them are in the early stages of innovation that hold the promise of future breakthroughs on a large scale. We next articulate several complaints regarding microfinance as a tool for Third World development.

MICROFINANCE CRITICISMS

There are a number of questions about the viability of microfinance services for empowering the poor. Several major conflicts between advocates and critics exist, including those briefly mentioned below.

Microloans Only?

One debate centers around whether a microcredit business loan ought to be the only offering to poor individuals, or if additional services should be provided. Many NGOs claim that they should strictly focus on doing one thing – microcredit – and do it well. Their view is that organizations need to have a single, clear mission, but that many flounder by trying to offer multiple services, none of which is extraordinary.

Conversely, other practitioners hold the opposite view. In their minds, microcredit is a necessary, but not sufficient, resource for the poor. They stress the need for additional programs that, if not provided, will likely lead the poor to slip back into their earlier suffering state. Perhaps the most well-known NGO advocating this view is Freedom from Hunger, a California-based non-profit that pioneered the provision of various services, (Freedom, 2006). Started in 1946 to fight hunger, it shifted in 1988 to integrate microcredit with nutrition and/or education. The result was "Credit with Education," which combines microloans with such things as HIV-AIDS awareness, polio vaccinations, family nutrition, women's health, literacy, and management skills.

Microentrepreneurial Education?

In scanning the horizon of microcredit, there is ongoing debate about whether the NGO practitioner should only provide microloans, or whether small-business training ought to be included. Some MFIs such as Grameen simply provide microloans. They claim that the poor are trustworthy, capable, and merely need extra capital to start or grow their business ideas. Small organizations point out that training is costly and takes time, thereby reducing the growth of poor borrowers, many of whom can't afford the time or travel costs to attend seminars, even if such training events are free. Other NGOs argue the opposite. What good is a loan if a person can't use it effectively? They note the high rate of failure among new firm start-ups in most countries and suggest that training lessens the likelihood that the microenterprise will fail. Enterprise Mentors International (EMI), an MFI I started with Brigham Young University students in 1990, argues the need for extensive training. With a dozen NGO partners today in five countries, EMI continues to emphasize training and management skills first, and credit later.

Questions of Gender

Another matter is whether loans should go to only women, mostly women, or males and females equally? The trend over time has mostly been toward giving loans to female microentrepreneurs. This is because women tend to be better risks, they pay their microloans back at a higher rate, and they use their profits to grow the business and/or help their children. Males often are not so responsible. However, others primarily loan to men. They argue that men can be responsible, too, and that loaning only to women upsets the traditional patriarchal structure in their culture, leading to unintended consequences, such as role loss, marital conflicts, and so forth. As an illustration, the case of BASIX, a new MFI in India emphasizes microcredit for males.

THE NEW TOOL OF MICROFRANCHISING

An innovative addition for fighting Third World poverty, recently being designed and implemented, is the new concept of microfranchising as development. It is viewed by some as an extension of the set of already existing microfinance practices. Essentially it builds off of the traditional microfranchise business model prevalent in industrialized nations. Examples of the traditional system range from fast-food cases like McDonald's, Pizza Hut, and Subway sandwiches to automobile dealers and gas stations.

The basic feature of a microfranchise is that it is replicable. The franchisee is trained and mentored, buys into the business in order to get a license, adheres to the parent organization's established operational systems and marketing practices. The parent firm, or franchisor, finances the microfranchisee who, as the business grows, pays off the debt while making a share of the profits from his/her microenterprise. At the same time he/she enjoys a greater income for one's family.

Other chapters in this volume spell out the details of how microfranchising operates. In addition, several cases of success are described and analyzed in considerable detail. The expectation is that this latest innovation may help to accelerate the broader field of microfinance by providing an additional tool for speedier economic growth.

Potentially, on one hand, microfranchising may obtain deeper impacts because of its capacity to be replicated and to expand since it has a proven product or service. In other words, the microfranchisee is not having to "reinvent the wheel" by launching a new start-up business. Rather, she or he works within an existing structure to scale up the firm that is already operating and successful. The hunch is that by so doing, the individual faces less risk and is able to generate more profits, revenue, and family income by using this method than the traditional microenterprise. In addition, because the franchisor is already incorporated, has a business license and so forth, the franchisee will likely be able to move from the informal or underground economy to the formal economic system more efficiently. Thus, poor families may enjoy greater success in moving up the socioeconomic ladder throughout the Third World.

On the other hand, microfranchising may have a few weaknesses. I do not believe it is appropriate to over-hype this new form of microfinance as the "one big answer" to the problems of poverty in general. What might be some of its limitations? My guess is that it will require more money and time spend on training potential new microfranchisees, getting them up to speed with more sophisticated business processes than, for example, simply buying fruit wholesale and selling it retail as a street vendor on a city sidewalk. Indeed, one can also hypothesize that a microfranchise business will more likely work for individuals who are better educated, have the math and reading skills required to fill out reports and handle larger financial transactions than simple microenterprise efforts.

Another critique is that establishing microfranchises will more likely require larger amounts of capital, better infrastructure such as roads and bridges, in order to receive raw materials or ship products. Such requirements are often difficult to achieve in heavily impoverished regions of the Third World.

A related concern is the viability of franchising under conditions of conflict, violence, war and natural disasters. For instance, just a few months after the Asian tsunami hit, several traditional MFIs such as Grameen Foundation-USA started giving microcredit. The same was true with Katalysis in Central America after Hurricane Mitch. My assumption is that trying to attract microfranchisors into hard-hit disaster areas would be much more difficult because of the business risks involved. In contrast, traditional microcredit NGOs will tend to respond rapidly with humanitarian aid, as well as microenterprise loan capital, because of their commitment to social development, not just business deals.

A final question to be considered is the fear that microfranchising may create a larger spiral of individual debt than traditional microcredit. Franchisees will likely have to borrow more and they may end up with repayment amounts that are clearly over their heads in the ability to pay back such large loans. If conditions worsen, as they often do in the Third World, it may be exceedingly difficult to overcome such crises as regional conflict, genocide, terrorism, drought and/or flooding.

In conclusion, we have examined the stress, strain, and manifestations of poverty in today's Third World. Trends, paradigms, and correlates of global impoverishment were analyzed, as well as macro and micro tools for empowering those who suffer. Microfinance, in several variations, was reported on, along with its challenges and state-of-the-art innovations. Finally, microfranchise was briefly discussed, along with several potential criticisms that were identified and highlighted. However, because it is such a new model for development, I suggest we consider microfranchising's further potential with an open mind.

REFERENCES

Adams, W.M. (1990), *Green Development: Environment and Sustainability in the Third World*, New York: Routledge.
Altieri, Miguel A. (1989), "Agroecology: a new research and development paradigm for world agriculture", *Agriculture, Ecosystems and Environment*, **27**, 37–46.
Basu, Susanto et al. (1996), *Appropriate Technology and Growth*, Cambridge, MA: National Bureau of Economic Research.
Bennett, Lynn (2002), "Using empowerment and social inclusion for pro-poor growth: a theory of social change", working draft of background paper for the social development strategy paper, Washington, DC: World Bank.
Beneria, Lourdes (2003), *Gender, Development and Globalization: Economics as if People Mattered*, New York: Routledge.
Bornstein, David (2004), *How to Change the World: Social Entrepreneurship and the Power of New Ideas*, Oxford: Oxford University Press.
Boyer, Nicole (2003), *The Base of the Pyramid (BOP): Reperceiving Business from the Bottom Up*, San Francisco, CA: Global Business Network.
Broad, Robin and Christina Melhorn Landi (1996), Whither the North–South gap?, *Third World Quarterly*, **17** (1), 7–17.
Bruyn, Severyn T. (2005), *A Civil Republic*, Bloomfield, CT: Kumarian Press.
Coleman, James S. (1968), "Modernization: political aspects", in David L. Sills (ed.), *International Encyclopedia of the Social Sciences*, New York: Macmillan, pp. 395–402.
Collier, George (1994), *Basta! Land and the Zapatista Rebellion in Chiapas*, Oakland, CA: Institute for Food and Development Policy.
Daly, Herman and J. Cobb (1989), *For the Common Good*, Boston: Beacon Press.
de Soto, Hernando (1989), *The Other Path: The Invisible Revolution in the Third World*, New York: Basic Books.

de Soto, Hernando (2000), *The Mystery of Capital: Why Capitalism Triumphs in the West and Fails Everywhere Else*, New York: Basic Books.

Devall, Bill and George Sessions (1985), *Deep Ecology*, Salt Lake City, UT: G.M. Smith.

Eade, Deborah (ed.) (1999), *Development with Women*, Bloomfield, CT: Kumarian Press.

Economist, The (1996), "Reforms lagging, hopes dying", 30 November.

Ellerman, David (2005), *Helping People Help Themselves: From the World Bank to an Alternative Philosophy of Development Assistance*, Ann Arbor, MI: University of Michigan Press.

Frank, Andre Gunder (1967), *Capitalism and Underdevelopment of Latin America*, New York: Monthly Review Press.

Freedom (2006), accessed 25 April at www.freedomfromhunger.org.

Harris, Sam Daley (2005), *State of the Microcredit Summit Campaign Report 2005*, Washington, DC: The Microsummit Summit Campaign, accessed 3 June, 2006 at www.microcreditsummit.org/pubs/reports/socr/2005/SOCROS.pdf.

Hart, Stuart L. (2005), *Capitalism at the Crossroads: The Unlimited Business Opportunities in Solving the World's Most Difficult Problems*, Upper Saddle River, NJ: Pearson Education.

Hazeltine, Barrett and Christopher Bull (2003), *Field Guide to Appropriate Technology*, Boston: Academic Press.

Herman, Edward S. (1995), "Immiserating growth (2): the Third World", *Z Magazine*, 22–27 March.

Hirschman, Albert (1984), *Getting Ahead Collectively: Grassroots Experiences in Latin America*, Elmsford, NY: Pergamon Press.

Human Development Office (UNDP) (2005), *Human Development Indicators*, New York: UN.

ICA (2006), International Co-operative Alliance's cooperative sectors, accessed 3 June at www.coop.org/coop/sectors.html.

Jones, Gareth Stedman (2004), *An End to Poverty? A Historical Debate*, London: Profile Books.

Korten, David C. (2006), *The Great Turning: From Empire to Earth Community*, San Francisco, CA: Berrett-Koehler.

Krishna, Anirudh (2002), *Active Social Capital: Tracing the Roots of Development and Democracy*, New York: Columbia University Press.

Kristof, Nicolas D. (1997), "Why Africa can thrive like Asia", *The New York Times*, 25 May.

Leadbeater, Charles (1997), *The Rise of the Social Entrepreneur*, London, UK: Demos.

Lean, Mary (1995), *Bread, Buicks, and Belief: Communities in Charge of their Future*, Bloomfield, CT: Kumarian Press.

McClelland, David (1964), "Business drive and national achievement", in Amitai Etzioni and Eva Etzioni (eds), *Social Change*, New York: Basic Books, pp. 165–78.

McRobie, George and E.F. Schumacher (1981), *Small is Possible*, New York: Harper and Row.

Moskin, Julia (2004), "Helping Third World one banana at a time", *The New York Times*, 5 May.

Nardi, Bonnie A. and Vicki O'Day (1999), *Information Ecologies: Using Technology with Heart*, Cambridge, MA: MIT Press.

Orr, David W. (1991), *Ecological Literacy*, Albany, NY: SUNY Press.

Ouelessebougou-Utah Alliance (OUA) (2006), accessed 30 May at www.sistercom-munity.org.

Peritore, N. Patrick (1999), *Third World Environmentalism: Case Studies from the Global South*, Gainesville, FL: University Press of Florida.

PovCal Net (2006), "Introduction", accessed 28 May at www.iresearch.worldbank.org/PovcalNet/introduction.html.

Prahalad, C.K. (2004), *The Fortune at the Bottom of the Pyramid: Eradicating Poverty Through Profits*, Upper Saddle River, NJ: Pearson Education.

Raynolds, Laura T. (2000), "Re-embedding global agriculture: the international organic and fair trade movement", *Agriculture and Human Values*, **17** (3), September, 297–309.

Sachs, Jeffrey (2005), *The End of Poverty: Economic Possibilities for Our Time*, New York: Penguin.

Schumacher, E.F. (1973), *Small is Beautiful: Study of Economics as if People Mattered*, New York: Vintage.

Schwartz, Norman B. (1981), "Anthropological views of community and community development", *Human Organization*, **40** (4), 313–21.

Shah, Anup (2006), "Poverty facts and stats", cases of poverty updated 3 April and accessed 1 June at www.globalissues.org/TradeRelated/Facts.asp.

Shiva, Vandana (2000), *Stolen Harvest: The Hijacking of the Global Food Supply*, Cambridge, MA: South End Press.

So, Alvin Y. (1990), *Social Change and Development: Modernization, Dependency and World-system Theories*, Newbury Park, CA: Sage.

Srivastva, Suresh and David L. Cooperrider and Associates (1990) (eds), *Appreciative Management and Leadership: The Power of Positive Thought and Action*, San Francisco, CA: Jossey-Bass.

Tarrow, Sidney (1994), *Power in Movement: Social Movements, Collective Action and Politics*, Cambridge, UK: Cambridge University Press.

United Nations (2005), International Year of Microcredit, New York: UN, accessed 7 June, 2006 at www.yearofmicrocredit.org.

UN (2006), "Millennium Development Goals", accessed 29 May at www.un.org/millenniumgoals.

United Nations Development Fund for Women (UNIFEM) (2006), accessed 23 May at www.unifem.org.

Woodworth, Warner (ed.) (1997), *Small Really is Beautiful: Micro Approaches to Third World Development – Microentrepreneurship, Microenterprise, and Microfinance*, Ann Arbor, MI: Third World Thinktank.

Woodworth, Warner (ed.) (2002), *Economic Democracy: Essays and Research on Workers' Empowerment*, Pittsburgh, PA: Sledgehammer Press.

5. Opportunities for partnership: how microfinance and microfranchising complement each other

John Hatch

INTRODUCTION

These words are written as I'm about to complete my first year of exposure to one of the newest poverty-alleviation concepts—micro*franchising*. The concept of has intrigued me from the first moment I heard about it at a two-hour workshop at Brigham Young University (BYU) in March 2005. Perhaps it was because the concept surfaced among colleagues who I've known and admired for years. Or maybe it was the déjà vu memory they awakened in me of my early village banking days. In any event, since the BYU event I've done some serious reading on the subject, starting with Stephen W. Gibson and Jason Fairbourne's sourcebook *Where There Are No Jobs (2005)*, followed by Kirk Magleby's *Microfranchises as a Solution to Global Poverty (2006)*. In late 2005 I began working with four graduate students from George Washington University who wanted to research the feasibility of launching one or more microfranchise pilot projects among FINCA[1] affiliates in Africa. In January 2006 these students and several FINCA staff attended a "microfinance learning lab" held in Washington DC, hosted by the Millennium Challenge Corporation. Following the MCC event, Kirk Magleby and my GWU interns pitched microfranchising to FINCA senior management. Fundraising by FINCA for an African microfranchise pilot is now underway.

The fact is I'm absolutely *not* attracted to microfranchise by itself, and certainly not as an alternative to microfinance.[2] Rather, what *does* attract me are the potential synergies between the two concepts. Both have strengths and deficiencies, but the strengths of the one balance the deficiencies of the other. Only microfinance has the proven service outreach capacity to reach *all* of the world's low-income households, but the self-employment businesses it finances generally have modest growth potential and create few additional jobs. In contrast, microfranchise seeks more exceptional, more entrepreneurial clients – perhaps one in 20 of those families attracted to microfinance – but it has the capacity to develop businesses strong enough to generate continuous growth in sales, jobs, and profits. Microfinance provides its clients with working capital loans that are usually disconnected from business skill training or technical assistance. Microfranchise normally does not provide loans to its clients, but it does offer proven business models, technical training, supervision, quality control, and marketing expertise. Microfinance already rules at the bottom of the world's income pyramid, but with few linkages to global capitalism. Microfranchise is well-connected to global capitalism, but lacks the distribution networks and marketing skills needed to penetrate the millions of neighborhoods and villages where the poor live. In summary, what should fascinate not just me but the practitioners of both camps is the possibility of *integrating* their respective tools into a single coordinated strategy.

Hence, the purpose of this chapter is to explore how microfinance and microfranchise complement each other. To make this discussion less tedious – and with apologies to Milton Friedman – I propose to substitute the acronym "M1" for the word microfinance, and "M2" in place of microfranchise. I like this convention because it suggests two separate components of the same poverty-alleviation vision. Or to use a family analogy, you can also think of M1 as the older sister and M2 the younger sister of the same "micro" household. My conviction is that a well-crafted partnership between M1 and M2 could make a big difference in the global war against poverty. In making my case I intend to document some of the under-recognized strengths and weaknesses of both M1 and M2, employing whenever possible the facts, figures, and findings of survey research on 23 FINCA country programs and based on interviews with over 6000 microfinance clients.[3]

STRENGTHS AND WEAKNESSES OF MICROFINANCE

The World's Largest Infrastructure for Reaching the Poor

During the last quarter-century, over 100 million low-income families worldwide have gained access to microfinance services.[4] *I* submit that no social movement or foreign aid program in human history has impacted more of the world's most disadvantaged citizens, nor done so more quickly and less inexpensively, than microfinance. And given its current infrastructure – estimated at 10 000 programs worldwide and possibly serving as many as five million neighborhoods and villages – microfinance has the location and momentum, I believe, to reach another 100 to 150 million low-income families by the year 2025. Thus, if you want to help the world's poor, the global infrastructure of microfinance appears to be the best venue available. Microfinance is like a highway system that can accommodate many different vehicles. And regardless of the service or product you have to deliver – be it related to food security, health, housing, education, or the endless other needs of the poor – there is room for an almost infinite volume of traffic.

Survivors

Promoters of microfranchise commonly assert that M1 businesses are mostly "copycat" ventures, with little growth potential, serving miniscule and insecure niche markets, highly vulnerable to seasonal market fluctuations, poorly capitalized, managed without written records, and closer to subsistence activities than to formal businesses. All these criticisms are valid in certain contexts but by no means in all or even most. For every example of deficiency you can find its exact opposite – business multiplicity, rapid initial growth, low start-up capital requirements, flexibility of product offerings from one season to the next, memory-based accounting, and above all, *survival*. The truth is, the self-employment activities supported by microfinance routinely generate – on average – an extra US$3 of profit per day (see next section), which is the equivalent of two to three minimum-wage jobs in the poorest developing countries. *That* is a huge return for an average loan investment of $140 per microfinance client. In my experience, microfinance has the highest business survival rate in the world. Why? Because if nothing else, the world's poor are survivors. Self-employment is how they survive. Failure is not an option. Failure means they starve.

Client Income Gains From Microfinance

Providing the world's poor and poorest families with access to self-employment loans, a safe place to accumulate savings, and other financial services can truly have a major impact on the lives of the poor. As mentioned above, FINCA research since 1996 shows that the typical village banking client – with an average microloan of $140 – can generate about US$3 per day in net profits from his or her self-employment business. At first glance this gain appears quite trivial. But for a family living on a daily per-capita income of US$2 or less – which describes at least one of every four families on our planet – an income gain of US$3/day is an achievement that is likely to transform these families' lives (see next section).

Improving Living Standards

FINCA research also shows that an extra US$3 per day is indeed enough to achieve major gains in family well-being. Our data show that 93 percent of all school-age children of FINCA clients are currently in school or have completed primary school, while 53 percent have begun or completed secondary school. Since starting a FINCA-financed business, one of every two clients has installed electricity in his or her home, one in three has made a sanitation improvement, and one in three has a cell phone. Client-reported gains in household health care and food security – after one year in the program – are in the 12–15 percent range. Such gains suggest that if the client is severely poor when he or she joins the program, his or her extra $3/day is enough to lift his or her family to a level of moderate poverty. If he/she joins at a level of moderate poverty, his/her daily $3/day will lift his/her family to just above the poverty line. Considering that the average FINCA loan is $140, with 97 percent on-time repayment and without subsidy, these results suggest that the poverty-alleviation results of investments in microfinance are measurable, significant, and arguably the most efficient form of foreign assistance currently available.

Gains Among Non-clients

FINCA research also reports that the typical client, with an average loan of US$140 dollars, purchases supplies for his or her self-employment business several times per month, spending a total of about US$300 per month or US$3600 per year. This is income that benefits the *suppliers or wholesalers* of microfinance clients. In turn, these supplier-wholesalers – unlike their much smaller clients – are likely to be more experienced business people, better capitalized, and far more likely to create new jobs.

. . . But Arrested Business and Job Growth

Unfortunately, the income gains (and possible job creation) mentioned above disguise a more troublesome reality that M2's supporters have rightly identified. FINCA research reports that for nine of every ten FINCA clients, their self-employment businesses *stop growing* after three to four consecutive loans.

Upon closer inspection we see that the typical M1 client's (say, a woman) business size tends to level off when its owner-operator arrives at her maximum daily sales potential – that is, the total amount of product she is able to sell by herself in a six- to eight-hour period – without hiring an additional laborer who might help her further grow her sales. Why is this? If we consult the data on client demographics we will discover the average age of FINCA clients is around 39–41 years. This is old enough for the typical client to have one or more children who have already reached employment age (15–24 years). Thus, not only is this mother nearing the end of her productive life, but her (usually better-educated) children are old enough to support themselves, and possibly assist their parents as well. Under such circumstances, it would appear that most M1 clients simply do not have sufficient incentives or capacity's incentive to further grow her business and/or assume the additional responsibility of employing non-family workers?

. . . With High Youth Unemployment

But there is still another challenge that microfinance is not effectively addressing. The ILO reports[5] that unemployment worldwide is now estimated at almost 200 million, and of this amount a disproportionate 47 percent represents young adults (ages 15–24). Moreover, this share has more than doubled from only a decade ago, suggesting a rapidly-growing global crisis. In the words of ILO Director General, Juan Somavia, "We are wasting an important part of the energy and talent of the most educated youth generation the world has ever had . . . Enlarging the chances of young people to find and keep decent work is absolutely critical to achieving the UN Millennium Development Goals."

In 2004 FINCA conducted survey research on 1500 of its clients in Mexico, Guatemala, Honduras, El Salvador, and Haiti. What we found was quite shocking. Only one in six of our clients' children with partial or complete secondary education were successful in finding a job in the formal sector (defined as a salary of at least $8/day). The rest were either unemployed (including young mothers with babies or pregnant) or employed at an informal sector rate of less than the $3/day earned by their mothers (and usually much less). So the strategy of FINCA clients educating their children so they can qualify for formal sector employment – even for entry-level jobs such as secretaries, teachers, bank clerks, drivers, security guards, fast-food restaurant workers, and sales people – is not succeeding for the majority of our clients.

I believe this crisis presents an important opportunity for both M1 and M2. It should be obvious that most current M1 clients – many of whom are now the mothers of unemployed youth – will never fully succeed in lifting their families out of poverty in a sustainable way as long as their own businesses stop growing (after creating only one self-employment job) and while their employment-age children can't find decent jobs. By mostly restricting M1 services to only mothers, we also undercut the family's capacity to create additional sources of income for itself. However, by developing "second-generation loan products" – including the finance of M2 businesses – MFIs will enable their clients to (1) generate additional self-employment activities that will lift them safely above the poverty line, and (2) help jump-start the growth of currently stabilized family microbusinesses.[6] Furthermore, today's young adults are more energetic and better-educated than their parents, making them more suitable candidates for (1) business training, and (2) creating businesses that can keep growing and can generate more jobs. These young adults would also constitute the kind of talent pool for not only supporting the creation of M2 businesses but also for supplying those M2 businesses with better-qualified laborers (many of whom might themselves become future franchisees and sub-franchisees). To my mind, this need (decent jobs for young adults) and this cure (second-generation loan products) constitutes the most powerful rationale for M1-M2 partnership.

The Ladder of Financial Services

For many years I have been describing the role of microfinance in relation to a nation's "ladder of financial services." For the typical developing country, 25 years ago its financial services ladder consisted of only two to three rungs located at the top of the structure and designed to serve that nation's economic elites – wealthy families, large businesses, and (in the best of cases) the upper echelons of an emerging middle class – but excluding access to the majority of its citizens (80 percent or more), who were defined as too poor to be bankable. What the microfinance movement did was to start building rungs near the bottom of this ladder so that the very poor, moderately poor, and non-poor could get on to the ladder.

In justifying the need for microfranchise, I have noticed a tendency for M2 advocates to equate microfinance with only a single rung (the one closest to the ground); while associating microfranchise with rungs two, three and higher. This view not only greatly misrepresents the spectrum of M1 services currently available but unnecessarily limits opportunities for building M1-M2 partnerships. To correct this misperception it might be helpful to view the lowest ladder rungs in terms of average loan amounts. I consider the lowest rung – designed for very poor clients – as offering loans in the range of $50 to $300. The second rung – for less-poor clients – offers loans in the range of $300 to $600. The third rung – from $600 to $10 000 or more – offers loans for the non-poor (including clients who began very poor or less-poor). In over two decades of experience in microfinance, I have *never* met an MFI that restricts its maximum loan amount to $300 or less. To the contrary, all MFIs seek to "grow with their clients", to help them climb as high as they want to climb. In fact, one of the biggest debates in microfinance today involves the fact that the majority of MFIs say they serve the poor, but in practice most of their new clients are *above* the poverty line when they join the program.[7] In view of the fact that many M2 programs do not provide credit at all, and that most M2 business prototypes require start-up capitalization of $300 to $5000, it seems to me that existing M1 programs offer the single best source of loan capital for M2 businesses. M1 programs also mature their borrowers so they are better prepared (either themselves or their children) to grow the business to levels where it can begin to generate additional jobs within the community.

Leveling Business Growth But Not the Loan Request

FINCA research confirms that when an M1 client takes out their first loan, it is not uncommon for them to invest 75–100 percent of that first loan in their business. But after three to four loan cycles (12–16 months) this typical M1 client (at least in the poorer nations of Africa and Latin America), after leveling off the growth of their microbusiness, now only invests 25–50 percent of their FINCA loan in that business.[8] Many clients partially compensate for the increased burden of larger loans by recycling their reduced business capital more rapidly – for example, re-supplying their business twice as frequently (every three to seven days instead of their original seven to 14 days). This behavior nets them increased profits because every re-supply presents a new mark-up opportunity. But still, what do these clients do with the rest of their loans? The truth is we still don't know. Is it spent on subsistence needs of the household – food, health, housing? Are these funds what keep their school-age children in school? Are these funds sponsoring *multiple* family business start-ups?[9] If so, who runs them – their children? Perhaps an indigenous version of microfranchise is already underway and we don't even know it?

WEAKNESSES AND STRENGTHS OF MICROFRANCHISE

Targeting a Minority

As M2 advocates are quick to point out, "microfranchise is not for everyone." Among the poor and poorest there are leaders and followers, entrepreneurs and the risk-averse, good managers and bad managers, the disciplined and the easily distracted. M2 advocates suggest that perhaps only one out of every ten or 20 low-income adults will have the personality or skill to succeed in a microfranchise business.

To lay claim as a strong poverty-alleviation role, M2 would have to show how the business development activities of the relatively few franchisees generate sustainable jobs for the many who lack the personality and skills to be franchisees themselves. But as of this moment, I have not yet seen an information system – among either M1 or M2 practitioners – that tracks how many new jobs these franchises are creating, for whom (family versus non-family labor), and how much they pay. The last question is the most critical. If microfranchisees pay the equivalent of their country's legal minimum wage, that does not constitute a poverty solution because it is not a "living wage." Furthermore, because most M1 clients – at an average of $3/day profit – earn two and three times their country's legal minimum wage, an M1 solution may still be preferable to attempting an M2 business.

Business Training But Not Business Loans

The strength of M2 is that it provides a business development training and support package—a proven product, management guidance, quality control, technical supervision, marketing support, and brand identity. It also provides a building-block strategy for market expansion, sub-franchising, and (potentially) endless job creation. All this is critical to success, but for the franchisee *to get started* he or she needs to provide a share of the start-up capital required by the franchisor. Where will this all-important start-up capital come from? I would argue that, throughout the developing world, the necessary capital—nine times in ten, or 18 times in 20—will come *not* from a franchisor (on consignment, or as supplier credit) but from an existing microfinance program serving the neighborhood or the village where the would-be microfranchisee lives.

Meeting Start-up Capital Needs

In their sourcebook *Where There Are No Jobs*, authors Gibson and Fairbourne (2005) provide some 50 examples of microfranchises, of which nearly all can be launched with less (and often much less) than US$5000. Given a solid microfranchise candidate, there is hardly an MFI anywhere in the world who would not want to finance such a business, especially when linked to a technical support package and an existing market virtually guaranteed by an international corporation. And who would be a "solid" microfranchisee candidate? Well obviously, the well-educated but unemployed, 20–24-year-old son or daughter of a *current* microfinance client, who has an established credit history of perfect repayment and who, moreover, is willing to co-sign or personally guarantee the loan made to capitalize his or her child as a franchisee.

I'm not speculating here. In FINCA's research on youth unemployment in Central America, we asked hundreds of respondents (mothers) if they would be willing to co-sign for a second-generation loan benefiting their son or daughter aged 15–24 years of age – thus placing at risk their own positive credit history and automatic loan access. With virtual unanimity these mothers replied with an enthusiastic "yes" for any son or daughter aged 20–24, whom they defined as sufficiently mature and reliable to justify their loan guarantee. In contrast, for younger sons or daughters (ages 15–19) their mothers' responses were an equally resounding "no," precisely because these young adults were considered still too immature to take on such an obligation. So not only would M1 clients be willing to guarantee loans for capitalizing M2 businesses for which their children might be eligible, but these mothers would carefully screen out which of their children has the *least* potential to be a franchisee.

Microfranchise as a Tool for Addressing Diverse Social Needs of the Poor

In the last analysis neither M1 nor M2 are ends in themselves. Rather, they are both tools for addressing the multiple needs of the poor and fit hand in glove. In reality these needs are virtually endless. Not only do they include better food security, health care, housing, and education but also such services as telecommunications, insurance, retirement pensions, employment searches, market information, entertainment, and many others. Most of these social goods are supposed to be provided by the government, not the private sector. But when governments are too poor, too corrupt, or too distracted to provide needed social services, it becomes necessary for that nation's citizens to fill the gap with private sector initiatives. Gibson and Fairbourne's sourcebook, cited previously, provides a marvelous assortment of M2 businesses that address basic needs. A short list of examples—with their start-up capitalization requirements – include Scojo Foundation's low-cost eye glasses (US$130), SHEF's drug shops (US$1200), rural Internet kiosks (US$1200), HP village photographer (US$1300), Vodacom rural phone kiosks (franchisee cost: US$3400), ApproTEC brick-making (US$375) and hand-operated (US$75) water pumps, Grameen-style cell phone service (US$220), n-Logue Internet kiosks ($1200), door-to-door courier ($2300), and Honey Care Africa beekeeping (US$160). One must conclude that given a little ingenuity and capital, virtually *any* human need can be addressed by means of an M2 business. One can also conclude that virtually any community-level M2 business can be readily financed by an M1 program. The rationale for partnership between M1 and M2 appears to be obvious and overwhelming.

CONCLUSION: TOWARD A FAMILY VISION FOR POVERTY ALLEVIATION

Meet Your Family

When at the outset of this chapter I introduced the acronyms "M1" and "M2" I was merely seeking a simpler syntax for discussing the respective strengths and weaknesses of two different "micro" movements. But as I bring this chapter to a close it has finally dawned on me (I've been a slow learner my entire life) that my accidental family reference contains a very powerful, unifying truth. First, what unites us is that all of us are children of the same God, members of the same human family, and – if we go back millions of years – all of our ancestors were very close relatives. Second, what unites many of us is that we all belong to the "micro" family. In the context of M1 and M2, "micro" has a very important and specific meaning. *Micro means trying to serve the world's most disadvantaged citizens, be they the poorest, the moderately poor, and/or the vulnerable non-poor.* By logical extension of this concept, the world's poor have many needs. Yes, they need access to business loans and business development skills. But they also need greater food security, improved housing, better health care, enhanced educational opportunities, and a more abundant offering of jobs for young adults. So, in a not so distant future, could we not expect the creation of an expanded family of micros? – for example, M3 (microinsurance), M4 (micropensions), M5 (microhealth care), M6 (microhousing), M7 (microfarming and gardening), M8 (microemployment services), M9 (microtelecomunications), M10 (microengineering), etc. As was suggested earlier, each of these service categories could be provided – at the local neighborhood and village level – as an M2 business. Each of these M2 businesses could benefit from an M1 loan, and each, in turn, could generate an increasing number of jobs for unemployed young adults – for the sons and daughters of poverty.

I wish to end this article by alluding once again to the ladder. This time substitute the "ladder of the financial system" for the "ladder of economic development," an image often referred to by Dr Jeffrey Sachs in his celebrated book *The End of Poverty* (2005). Sachs describes extreme poverty or "poverty that kills" as those individuals and families who are unable to gain a footing on the lowest rung of the ladder of economic development. Once they make the first rung, he argues, they are no longer extremely poor, and what they now need is the opportunity to keep climbing. I see M1 as primarily targeting the first two to three rungs of this development ladder. I see M2 as targeting the next three rungs. And I see the conventional commercial banking system serving the final three to six rungs on the ladder.

The higher the rung, the fewer the climbers, but without an abundance of rungs the climbers will ultimately have nowhere to grow, and development stagnates. This is why, ultimately, development can never succeed if it gets hijacked by only a few institutions, a few models, a few services, and focuses on only a few rungs. The M1/M2 partnership faces an exciting opportunity to serve and accelerate more climbers than ever before in the history of humankind.

NOTES

1. FINCA stands for the Foundation for International Community Assistance and its microfinance network (FI) with programs in 23 countries of Africa, Latin America, Eastern Europe, Central Asia, and the Middle East. In 2005 the FINCA network provided nearly 400 000 clients – organized in some 28 000 "village banks" – with loans totaling $323 million, with an on-time loan repayment rate of 97 percent.
2. In this chapter I make no distinction between "microfinance" and "microcredit." The current debate between these two terms, in my opinion, is a question of semantics. In practice, both describe the provision of *mainly* financial services to the world's most disadvantaged citizens – be they the poorest, the moderately poor, or the still vulnerable non-poor.
3. Using graduate student interns, since 1986 FINCA has been conducting survey research interviews on a representative sample of its clients. All of FINCA's current country programs are surveyed at least once every two years, and our largest programs every single year. Each intern uses a palm pilot-based (PDA) interview tool known as FCAT (FINCA client assessment tool) to conduct ten-minute interviews with a minimum of 300 clients per summer. Thanks to a grant from the John Templeton Foundation, FINCA is currently organizing all of its client data in a Global Data Warehouse accessed by an online portal, so that FINCA senior management, investors, and others can formulate queries and obtain the findings that most interest them for decision-making purposes.
4. The Microcredit Summit Campaign, with only 3164 institutions reporting, estimates that as of December 2004 the number of *current clients* exceeds 92 million, of whom 73 percent were among the poorest when they took their first loan. See Sam Harris (2005). This figure excludes tens of millions of ex-clients who have already graduated to their own savings. Thus, total clients served since 1980 could already exceed 150 million.
5. See ILO (2004).
6. By "second-generation loan products" I refer to such products as (1) loans to complete secondary education, (2) loans to complete vocational training, (3) loans for self-employment, and (4) loans for microfranchises.
7. Indeed, a growing number of MFI practitioners allege that the very poor are inherently unable to use microfinance loans effectively (not even at the lowest rung) and thus need other kinds of assistance – like subsidized food, health, housing, and education services, or "savings-led" rather than "business-led" interventions. Another aspect of this debate involves "poverty outreach versus program sustainability." It is correctly perceived that the very poorest clients are the most expensive to serve, and their tiny loans do not generate enough interest income to cover the costs of servicing them. Thus, the business models of most MFIs – at least until they reach their break-even point – is to make the objective of poverty outreach subservient to, or at least compatible with, the achievement of program sustainability. In achieving the latter it is commonplace for them to seek out non-poor clients whose larger loans generate more interest and thus accelerate the MFI's achievement of sustainability. Many MFIs would argue that loans to the non-poor enable them to *subsidize* the costs of serving the poor and poorest.

8. In Eastern Europe and Central Asia, being former Soviet bloc republics, virtually all FINCA clients have 12 or more years of schooling (a major Soviet priority). And despite their socialist experience (where being a self-employed capitalist was illegal), many FINCA clients have become smart and aggressive entrepreneurs, managing two to three additional storefronts and kiosks, borrowing much larger loans, rotating all of their FINCA loan capital every two to three days, and earning profits of US$9–12/day, three and four times the FINCA global average.
9. FINCA research shows that at least a third of FINCA clients have multiple businesses.

REFERENCES

Fairbourne, J. and S.W. Gibson (2005), *Where There Are No Jobs*, vol. 4.
ILO (2004), *Global Employment Trends for Youth*.
Harris, S. (2005), *State of the Microcredit Summit Campaign Report*.
Magleby, K. (2006), *Microfranchises as a Solution to Global Poverty*, Utah: MicroFranchises.org.
Sachs, J. (2005), *The End of Poverty: Economic Possibilities for Our Time*, USA: Pearson.

6. Microfranchising and the base of the pyramid

Molly Hoyt and Eliot Jamison

From the earliest days of commerce and trade – from Marco Polo to the Dutch East India Company – enterprising individuals and companies have searched for new sources of goods, and new markets for those goods, in faraway lands. In that era, knowledge of the existence of markets, and ability to access them were key differentiators, which set those entrepreneurs apart. In our era, information about global markets is prevalent, though knowledge of the best way to access them remains hotly debated in the management and economics realms. Like the enterprising pioneers of a former era, the multi-national corporation of today is interested in finding lower-cost sources of goods and labor, and new growth markets to which they can sell. However, unlike many organizations from the past, today's global companies operate in an environment of substantial NGO and government scrutiny and have become aware of the importance of ensuring that their activities are beneficial to all the countries and communities where they operate. As we will see, this is having a major impact on how companies pursue the expansion opportunities that are open to them.

OVERVIEW

Our approach in this chapter is to take the perspective of a company interested in initiating or expanding its emerging markets operations; what role can and should microfranchising play in such a company's strategy? A starting point for answering this question can be found by considering the major challenges that companies face in emerging markets, especially companies that are doing business with the lower-income segments of those markets and committed to doing so in a mutually beneficial way (what is being called "base of the pyramid business"). The challenges faced by companies include their:

- need for local partners and intelligence;
- need for distribution channels with broader reach;

- need to re-engineer cost structures;
- need to give communities a stake in the success of the business.

Each of these challenges has the potential, in certain circumstances, to be addressed through the use of a franchising strategy.

After covering in more detail the nature and extent of corporate interest in emerging markets we turn to the concept of base of the pyramid business specifically and explain its rationale and implications. Then we explain the potential role of microfranchising and provide examples of how it could play a role. We have divided the uses of microfranchising in BOP business into two broad categories. The first is the use of microfranchises as part of a distribution channel. Local entrepreneur franchisees will know their markets intimately and often can tap into pre-existing distribution channels that might not be available to a larger company, especially one based outside the country. The second is the use of microfranchises as part of a supply base. Local entrepreneurs operate without the overhead of many larger businesses and can be an important part of bringing costs down. In addition, local franchises will be able to provide services to larger companies that are appropriate for the local operating environment. And finally, by providing the opportunity to build local wealth, a franchise system can increase the receptiveness of communities to the presence of multi-national companies – this benefit applies if the franchise is a supplier, a distributor, or is playing some other role entirely.

CORPORATE INTEREST IN EMERGING MARKETS

Corporate focus on emerging markets is driven first and foremost by strong growth. Since the early 1990s, developing countries have been the fastest-growing market in the world for most products and services (Khanna, Palepu and Sinha, 2005). GDP growth in recent years is more than double in emerging markets as compared with advanced economies (IMF, 2006).

Doing business in emerging markets is not without risk, however. Foreign currency fluctuations, political instability, unfamiliar business practices, and a lack of knowledge of partners and market behaviors mean that the risk of failure is high. However, there are many factors that continue to drive corporate interest in emerging markets.

The Opportunity: Higher Growth, Lower Costs

The financial opportunity for doing business in emerging markets falls primarily into two categories: the opportunity to find new sources of revenue and the opportunity to reduce costs by sourcing products or labor in lower-cost countries.

At a macroeconomic level, there are a number of trends that are further enabling these opportunities. These include:

1. Higher growth rates. While the pattern is not uniform, economic growth rates on average continue to be substantially higher in emerging markets than in more developed markets. For the period from 2004 to 2006, economic growth is expected to average 7.2 percent in developing countries versus 3 percent in high-income countries, according to the International Monetary Fund (see Figure 6.1).

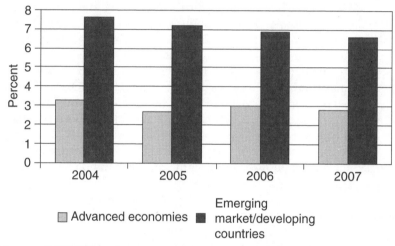

Source: IMF (2006).

Figure 6.1   Comparison of GDP growth

In specific industries, the growth differential can be even more dramatic. In the wireless industry, for example, mobile cellular subscriber growth in low-income countries grew 88.7 percent from 1999–2004, compared with 16.3 percent in high-income countries over the same period. Compare growth rates over that period for some specific countries (ITU, 2004):

Nigeria   225.6 percent
Kenya   154.7 percent
India   90.5 percent
Italy   15.7 percent
Sweden   12.5 percent

2. Technological change. Lower transportation, computing, and commu-
    nication costs make cross-border economic transactions more feasible
    and open up opportunities that were unthinkable even a short time ago.
    For example, the opportunity for geographically dispersed production
    allows companies to optimize each activity in their value chain by
    moving it to the location with a comparative advantage in that activity.
    The most direct benefit of optimizing production in this manner is to
    lower costs but it can also be a source of product innovation and new
    revenue opportunities.
3. Improvements to the enabling environment. Countries around the
    world are making progress on strengthening their governance and legal
    and regulatory environment. Restrictions on trade and capital flows
    are decreasing. While not all countries are moving in the right direc-
    tion, and corruption in some countries remains rife, both the World
    Bank and Political Risk Services (an independent advisory firm)
    confirm that the overall trend is significantly positive.[1]
4. More receptive partners. Government development agencies, charit-
    able foundations, non-governmental organizations (NGOs), and other
    potential partners have begun to recognize the essential role that busi-
    ness and private enterprise play in poverty alleviation. As a result, they
    are more receptive to partnerships with the private sector. There has
    also been increased interest from private sector companies in exploring
    emerging market business opportunities in collaboration or "clusters"
    with each other.

How Companies are Reacting

In addition to new product sales in emerging markets, there is an opportunity for companies to involve local entrepreneurs and workers in
their supply and distribution chains. This is not simply outsourcing or
moving production to lower-cost regions (although it may include both
of these) but using the knowledge and capabilities of people and communities in emerging markets to develop new and better products and
business practices. In fact, moving production into emerging market
countries can be closely linked to finding new revenue opportunities in
those markets:

> Multinational companies have invested abroad for two main reasons: to
> expand their customer base by entering new markets . . . and to reduce costs
> by locating production in countries with lower factor costs . . . we see the
> two motives as increasingly complementary, as companies are forced to
> reduce costs in order to be able to expand their markets. (McKinsey Global
> Institute, 2003)

The compelling nature of these opportunities is reflected in the substantial increases in private capital flows into emerging market countries. Net private capital flows reached a record level of $490.5 billion in 2005. This included $237.5 billion of foreign direct investment (FDI), a level that is up substantially from the range of $160–180 billion that was typical in the late 1990s and early 2000s (World Bank, 2006).

WHAT IS BASE OF THE PYRAMID BUSINESS?

Business activity in emerging markets faces some unique challenges and opportunities, which are causing many companies to consider non-traditional approaches. As described in the prior section, companies that are successful in emerging markets are learning to see low-income individuals and communities as sources of opportunity rather than as reasons to stay away. Their approach to business consciously brings lower-income people into the market as consumers and producers and focuses on creating value for everyone involved, including the company and the community. A number of prior writers and practitioners have described approaches to business that have these characteristics, but the descriptor that has received most attention in the business press is "base of the pyramid business."[2] Others have used the terms "sustainable livelihoods business" (WBCSD, 2004) or "sustainable enterprise" (Wheeler et al., 2005).

While some of the methods advocated by these authors have been practiced for many years, often by local entrepreneurs, the systematic approach to, and definition of, this type of business is relatively new. As with many new markets and new ideas, definitions are being debated and usage is not yet consistent. As a result, it will be useful to start with a brief history and review of some of the major definitions. From there we will turn to a more detailed analysis of best practices and lessons learned.

C.K. Prahalad and Co-authors

C.K. Prahalad, along with other authors including Kenneth Lieberthal, Stuart Hart, and Al Hammond, wrote a series of articles in the late 1990s and early 2000s that developed his thesis around the opportunity, primarily for multi-national companies (MNCs), to expand and innovate by serving the vast numbers of untapped customers in emerging markets.[3] Prahalad conceptualized the world population as a pyramid with the top being a small number of high-income consumers, mostly in developed markets, and successive tiers having lower income but being larger in absolute numbers. His contention was that the bottom of the pyramid (BOP) was a source of substantial overlooked opportunities. He pointed out that the aggregate market is large even if each individual has a very modest income. Furthermore, many of these consumers were not well served by existing market mechanisms; they often paid a substantial "poverty tax" in the form of higher prices and/or lower quality.

At a microeconomic level, emerging markets are often the site of the most extreme market inefficiencies—lacking sufficient competition, and/or sufficient scale to make basic goods and services affordable and available. As a result, the world's poorest often pay *more* than the rich for their basic needs. For example, people in a poor neighborhood near Mumbai, India pay up to 37 times more for clean water and up to ten times more for diarrhea medication than their wealthier counterparts in the same area (Prahalad, 2004). A related characteristic of these markets is the high ratio of informal (unregistered and untaxed) economic activity to formal sector activity; it is estimated that up to half of economic activity in some low-income countries is in the informal sector. Similarly, households in these markets are in possession of an estimated $9 trillion in unregistered assets (De Soto, 2000). Addressing the "poverty tax" and moving more activity into the formal sector can be a source of new growth opportunities for companies.

The World Business Council for Sustainable Development

The World Business Council for Sustainable Development (WBCSD) has been another leader in developing both the theory and practice of emerging markets business designed to benefit low-income communities. The WBCSD is a membership organization of over 180 multi-national companies; it undertook a project in 2002 to better understand and advocate for what it calls "sustainable livelihoods" business. It defines this as "doing business with the poor in ways that benefit the poor and benefit the company" (WBCSD, 2004). In a series of publications during 2004 and 2005, the WBCSD presented a variety of case studies from its members as well as guidelines and resources for companies interested in expanding their sustainable livelihoods activities.[4] One of the important additions that the WBCSD makes is to consider more fully the roles that low-income individuals can play as producers, distributors, and marketers of products and services. Where Prahalad focused largely (although not exclusively) on the idea of selling products to a new class of consumers, the WBCSD work pays equal attention to "buying from" low-income individuals and communities and to the complementarity between these approaches.

This addition is important because it is through "buying from" low-income individuals and communities that some of the most important benefits – namely, local integration – accrue to both the company and the community. This local integration serves several purposes. First and foremost, it builds sustainability into the business model through the alignment of interests. By buying from local vendors and hiring local people, new incomes are created that raise the community's standard of living. Depending on the scale of this activity, these effects can extend across a country or region, and can be significant and long-lasting. This benefits the company as well, as the higher incomes and job creation mean greater economic stability, and new potential consumers for the company's products (see Figure 6.2).

Second, local integration helps counter the negative reception that companies often face in emerging markets. Large companies are often perceived by local interests as threatening, whether they be government, civil society groups, or the private sector. Job growth, through use of local suppliers and hiring local people, is almost universally welcomed by governments and the communities being affected. Similarly, greater local ownership and its attendant opportunities for wealth creation will be viewed positively.

New business models

Businesses buy from and sell to low-income communities, making profits while creating jobs and fulfilling basic needs

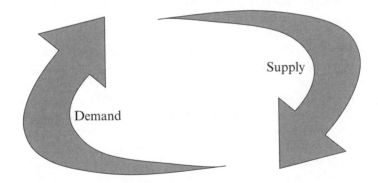

Increased purchasing power

The activites of pro-poor businesses increase local income and ability to meet basic needs

Figure 6.2   The virtuous cycle of business in development

Other Research

At much the same time, researchers, including David Wheeler and Kevin McKague, have been writing about the role of business in international development and have paid particular attention to the role of smaller, local enterprises. They conceive of business in low-income markets as most appropriately being fostered through what they refer to as sustainable local enterprise networks (Wheeler et al., 2005). Such networks have a profit-making business as their anchor but also can include participants from the development sector, community groups, governments, corporations, and outside investors.

Throughout this chapter we will use the terms "base of the pyramid" or BOP since these have become the most commonly used and accepted. However, we use them in their broadest sense, referring to business strategies that engage low-income people and communities as producers, consumers, and business partners.

COMPANY EXPERIENCE WITH BOP BUSINESS

Through our review of the literature on BOP business and direct experience with enterprises operating in emerging markets, we have distilled some of the common lessons learned and pitfalls to avoid. In our experience working with companies that are entering or expanding their activities in emerging markets, we have found two common reasons for lack of success:

- *Business as usual.* Some companies have approached emerging markets with the same products and operating practices as in their traditional markets. This ignores the fundamentally different economic environment that exists in these countries, in particular the existence of widespread poverty and underdeveloped infrastructure. This approach typically leads to political or business problems, and often to both.
- *Not business at all.* Other companies (or other divisions of the same companies) have had the opposite problem. Often this occurs among companies with a strong commitment to philanthropy and corporate social responsibility. They may see emerging markets as an area where they can "do good" and therefore enter these markets with economic development or philanthropic outcomes as their goals. This typically leads to unprofitable and non-scaleable businesses that become "orphans" within the company.

The trick is to navigate between these two extremes. We have found that companies that follow four simple guidelines are most likely to manage this difficult balance in a successful way:

1. Maintain business focus. Companies entering emerging markets, even more than otherwise, should focus on their core competencies and build on the things they do best. They need to ensure that operations in emerging markets align with broader corporate strategy and are not one-off or ad hoc efforts. A strong business focus will keep the whole team on track to achieve the desired results.
2. Integrate local knowledge. Companies should build relationships with the people who live and work in the region they want to enter in order to learn about the local culture, beliefs, and lifestyle. Even better, local residents should be encouraged to become an integrated part of the company's business model so they have an incentive to help it succeed.
3. Be open to unusual partnerships. New forms of collaboration can accelerate emerging-market success. Joining a "cluster," a group of private businesses focused on achieving common emerging-market goals, is one approach that has shown promise. Similarly, partnering with NGOs can provide on-the-ground expertise and access to social purpose capital.
4. Define and articulate a clear story. It is critical to make sure that all stakeholders – employees, partners, customers, and investors – know what the company is doing and why it is doing it. This common understanding can provide meaning, build team spirit, and inspire commitment.

Cutting across these four guidelines is the idea of a systems-based approach to business. It is critical that companies approach BOP business opportunities from a whole systems perspective and not just focus on their own role and assets. While focusing their activities around their competencies, companies should fill in the missing pieces of a systems solution through carefully planned partnerships and by taking advantage of existing local resources whenever possible.

MICROFRANCHISING AS A DISTRIBUTION STRATEGY

Large companies, both foreign and domestic, that operate in emerging markets have typically focused their marketing efforts on the middle- and upper-income population segments, often in urban areas. These people tend to have the most disposable income and can be reached through

---

BOX 6.1   CEMEX: COMMUNITY FINANCED HOME IMPROVEMENTS IN MEXICO

Cemex, the third largest cement company in the world, has demonstrated an exceptional ability to innovate for low-income consumers. Their program, "Patrimonio Hoy," incorporates numerous cultural insights into the marketing and sales of powdered cement to low-income Mexicans. As a result of the program, participating consumers have increased their cement consumption 300 percent, and 18 percent more families in areas where Patrimonio Hoy is active have begun building new rooms onto their homes. Patrimonio Hoy utilizes a common community financing mechanism wherein groups of families pool money to pay for additions to their houses. In addition to organizing community financing and providing cement, however, Cemex delivers the expert advice, blueprints, and the other building materials necessary for building new additions to one's home. This unique combination of supplies and services profoundly simplifies the process of adding to one's home.

---

relatively familiar marketing and distribution channels. This business mode can work to an extent but will not maximize long-term growth prospects. Companies are increasingly seeing the value of approaching base of the pyramid market segments as a strategy for increasing growth and innovation. To reach these markets, distribution strategies that reach further into urban slums and out to rural villages are needed. In addition, distributors and retailers that come from, and are intimately familiar with, the needs of lower-income customers will be most effective. The WBCSD's report (2004) *Doing Business with the Poor: A Field Guide*, makes this point well in its discussion of the need to look for what it calls "naturally occurring distribution systems": "You may need to develop different, more informal distribution systems. These may not be able to cover their costs based on one product alone, so cooperation and leveraging of existing resources become even more important than usual." It should be clear that microfranchising has a role to play here – it is a way to tap into local knowledge and resources while maintaining quality and brand control.

Selected Corporate Experiences

Before exploring the role of microfranchising in detail, it will be useful to review a couple of examples of how multi-national companies are currently approaching distribution challenges in emerging markets. These examples, which illustrate varying degrees of success, are not necessarily about microfranchising directly but they highlight features of the distribution challenge that could be addressed through franchising.

The classic example of a company with wide distribution in emerging markets is the Coca-Cola Company. Coke, in addition to being one of the most recognizable brands, is one of the most widely available products in the world. For example, the Coca-Cola system is the largest private employer in Africa. It has a presence in every country in Africa, it has 170 bottling and canning plants and it works with 900 000 retail partners (Coca-Cola, 2006). Despite this impressive presence and reach, Coca-Cola has seen the need to continually innovate in the methods that it uses to sell its product, especially in underserved and rural markets. One example of this is its entrepreneur development program in South Africa. In 1999, Coca-Cola decided that in order to expand beyond its strongholds in the most developed areas of South Africa, it needed to take an approach that leveraged the talents and knowledge of local entrepreneurs. However, these entrepreneurs needed training in business skills, access to equipment, and monitoring over time. As a result, Coca-Cola developed a comprehensive program that trains local entrepreneurs and sets them up with a variety of sales options from small containers of sodas (known as "mamas buckets") to larger sales depots (WBCSD, 2003). While not an explicit franchise arrangement, this program illustrates a number of the characteristics of a franchise distribution model including risk sharing, training and monitoring.

A very different experience from that of Coca-Cola can be found in Merck's long-standing work to treat river blindness. Merck's experience with the treatment of river blindness (onchocerciasis) is a good example of how lack of distribution can be a limiting factor. In this case, Merck had already made the decision (in 1987) to give away its drug Mectizan for free to anyone who needed it. Despite this commitment, and the clear efficacy of the drug for treating a painful and debilitating disease, getting the pills to people in need was such a challenge that for many years only a small fraction of the people who could benefit from Mectizan were able to get it. Merck learned early that traditional distribution channels did not exist to the remote villages that they needed to reach; as a result they worked with a wide range of public and non-profit sector partners to distribute Mectizan. Eventually the program achieved significant success but would have done so much sooner if there had been a better way to reach local villages (Weiss and Hanson, 1991).

Distribution of Energy and Water Products: The Role of Local Entrepreneurs

One sector that provides good examples of both the challenges and opportunities inherent in bringing new products to low-income consumers is rural electrification, in particular the use of solar panels to bring electricity to non grid-connected areas. Solar has long been appealing for such markets because it can be implemented on a small scale, does not rely on central infrastructure, is non-polluting and recently has become more cost competitive. However, many of the early schemes that involved subsidized installation of solar panels were failures. The reasons varied but included insufficient customer education about the benefits and uses of the panels and, more importantly, a lack of ongoing maintenance and support. Many of these schemes failed to create any ongoing, local commercial interest in the wider adoption of solar electrification technologies and in the upkeep of these systems. In one extreme case, a return trip to a project site found recipients of the subsidized panels using them to cover holes in their roofs rather than to generate electricity!

Recently, both Shell and Electricité de France (EDF) have developed more successful models for selling and installing solar energy systems in emerging markets. Common elements of their successes include the creation of a selling and distribution force that is dispersed throughout the targeted communities and an ongoing commitment to service and support. Both companies have also used partnerships to bring in carefully tailored grant funding and/or small loans to cover up-front capital costs, which otherwise would be a significant barrier (see Box 6.2 for more detail on the EDF program in Morocco). The need for an ongoing presence and relationship to handle issues that come up post-installation suggests that in this market it may be more advantageous to have local business partners who have a formal structure and presence rather than just sales agents. As a result, this is another instance in which the franchise model could be attractive.

In addition to these examples from the electricity sector, a franchise approach is being contemplated as part of an effort to provide clean water in Madagascar, according to the UNDP. Bush Proof, in a partnership with local and international NGOs, has developed and will soon be selling innovative household drinking water solutions to low-income families. These tools could increase access to clean water, reduce water-borne disease and most importantly, allow the people themselves to be in control of these things. Bush Proof's business plan contemplates a variety of distribution channels including microfranchising. Because much of the market for these products is rural and lower income, distribution challenges are significant and franchising has already been identified as a potential solution.

BOX 6.2 EDF: BUILDING BUSINESSES AROUND RURAL ELECTRIFICATION

This solar electricity project in rural Morocco is a joint venture between Morocco's National Electric Office (ONE), Electricité de France (EDF), Total, and Tenesol. Together, they created Temasol. Temasol based its activities on EDF's Access Program, which uses a strategy of creating small, locally run companies to provide services to rural customers. These companies are intended to stimulate local economic activity as well as to provide basic services including both electricity and water.

Temasol's program involves the sale of a solar panel, a battery, and a controller to individual rural households. ONE provides a grant for each installation in order for all Moroccans to have equal access to the service. Temasol actually installs the system, and provides most services after that, including providing maintenance on existing systems. They do this out of stands that they run in the local *souks* (markets). This presence gives Temasol employees a chance to interact with clients and potential clients, keep an ear to the ground, and truly understand their markets.

Another aspect of this program that accounts for its success is its pricing. Before the program started, local household budgets and electricity expenditures were studied. The company was able to devise a plan, including assistance from the government and donors, to provide an affordable product with costs similar to what people paid for other sources of energy such as batteries, candles, and gas.

Source: WBCSD (2005).

An Example From the NGO Sector

While EDF and other companies have begun to see the benefits from approaches that have much in common with microfranchising, there is more that can be learned from the NGO/non-profit sector – some of these organizations have developed approaches that have applicability to the distribution challenges of larger companies. CARE Canada, an international relief organization, has done pioneering work with enterprise-based strategies for alleviating poverty. One of the key obstacles that it has identified is the lack of linkages between microentrepreneurs and the formal economy; in order to address this it is helping to spur the creation of "gateway agencies" that serve as intermediaries. In one specific example – Village Women Entre-preneurs in Bangladesh – they have created a multi-tiered distribution system for companies interested in selling affordable and quality products to women in rural villages. The central organization, local coordination units and vendor groups each earn a commission from end user sales. This system has allowed Bata (a shoe company) to reach markets that it was previously unable to reach because the women's local knowledge allows them to find and access markets that are not obvious to people outside of the village. This has helped the women to build livelihoods for themselves while delivering a product to their fellow villagers at an affordable price (CARE Canada, 2006).

Microfranchising Compared with Alternative Distribution Systems

The examples described so far illustrate the challenges of distribution into remote and low-income communities and also the potential of franchising and other mechanisms that tap local entrepreneurship. Microfranchising is certainly not the answer in all cases but the specific characteristics of the distribution challenges in emerging markets suggest that it will often have attractive characteristics and should be seriously considered as part of an overall strategy for approaching these markets.

Compared with a distribution model that relies on established whole-salers and retailers, microfranchising more effectively taps into entrepre-neurial incentives and allows for local wealth creation through ownership of the franchise units. Also, because the franchises can be smaller than most existing retailers (at least those in the formal sector) and because they can be quickly started wherever demand exists, the franchise strategy can tap into local market knowledge at the village or sub-village level.

Compared with using individual commissioned salespeople, franchising provides greater opportunities for quality control, brand consistency, and building a deeper relationship with customers. A franchise business, even if it is very small-scale, will have more permanence than an individual sales-person and the franchise relationship allows the franchisor to exercise some control over business practices. Furthermore, the long-term relationship inherent in a franchise provides incentives for both sides to invest. This investment includes both physical capital and investment in human capital through training in business skills and practices.

MICROFRANCHISES AS A SUPPLY BASE

Procurement is one of the most important functions a business under-takes. Companies can wield tremendous power through their sourcing or procurement decisions as large amounts of money are often at stake. Using this power responsibly and intelligently is important for any business, especially one entering the base of the pyramid.

Sourcing locally at the BOP can be an important way to build local integration into the business. As described earlier in this chapter, these benefits of "local integration" extend to both the community and the company, and can be significant and long-lasting. For the community, economic development is fostered through job creation and income growth. For the company, new potential consumers are created, while the company gains greater receptivity into the community.

In addition to the benefits of local integration, when a company sources locally *from a microfranchise*, additional benefits are often accrued in the form of lowered costs and decreased risks of doing business. We will discuss these benefits below.

The Low-cost Imperative

One of the first places companies often look as they seek to re-engineer their cost structures for the BOP is the sourcing of product and labor inputs for their business. Just as it has for its distribution strategy, a multi-national has a variety of options when it comes to its sourcing, or procurement, strategy. It can buy resources locally from the market in which it is providing goods and services, it can buy them directly from the parent or head-quarter operations, or it can buy them from the international suppliers used by its other global operations.

Historically, the traditional view was that the ability to source from the international market was a key differentiator for a multi-national. It allowed the multi-national the option to access goods at a lower cost elsewhere within its network of global operations and suppliers. However, some recent studies have indicated that there are additional costs, not readily apparent, in the global sourcing process. These studies suggest that when using global sourcing, multi-nationals incur monitoring, coordination, and transportation costs that they would not have incurred had they sourced locally (Chen and Cannice, 2006). Logistical difficulties due to weak or inadequate infrastructure, high energy and transportation costs, potentially high import tariffs, and other factors can have disastrous impacts on a business in the form of high costs, delayed deliveries, and damaged goods. Sourcing locally, when done in the right way, can be an effective means to circumvent these potential problems, and reduce costs.

Among the alternatives for sourcing locally, a microfranchise offers unique benefits, which may translate into even lower costs for the companies buying from it. Whether it is a franchised courier service, temporary staffing agency, or parts manufacturer, there are some common characteristics that make microfranchises attractive to corporate purchasers.

The core business processes of most franchises are streamlined, standardized, and very likely, documented. Not only does this generate operational efficiencies, which can be converted into cost savings, but, as any entrepreneur can attest, the early days, months, and even years of one's business are often spent trying and discarding numerous strategies and tactics that ultimately failed. Providing a proven, documented business model directly to the franchisee translates into significant time and cost savings for him or her, especially in comparison to its non-franchised competitors in the market.

There may be other cost savings through shared operational "infrastructure" among the franchisees, such as back office support, branding, and marketing. The franchisees may share certain capital infrastructure as well, such as a delivery vehicle or a warehouse. Any investment that is leveraged across multiple franchisees will offer cost savings to each of them.

Finally, the scale that microfranchises can attain, relative to other options in the local market, means that additional efficiencies can be attained. For example, a franchisee typically poses a lower risk to creditors than a stand-alone business, because it is part of a larger network or family of businesses. It can therefore receive more favorable terms for obtaining credit. Franchisees can also aggregate their purchasing power when buying products or services from their vendors. For these and other reasons, microfranchises have several cost advantages relative to other suppliers in the local market. By extension, these savings can be passed on to its customers as well.

Risk Management

Despite the clear benefits to a company for sourcing locally, many companies still do not do so. Even when operating in emerging markets, where costs are traditionally assumed to be low, there are many reasons why a multi-national may still wish to source its inputs internationally, or internally. It may have a subsidiary in another country from which it can purchase components, thereby keeping business within the company. The supplier relationships, even if not company-owned, may have been established over a long period of time, providing a high degree of trust and familiarity. The capabilities of the vendor and the quality of the output may be known to the company, valuable for mitigating risk.

In essence, then, it is usually a question of risk mitigation and familiarity that prevents companies from sourcing locally. The issues of quality, reliability, and scale are too critical to the core of the business to take chances with. These vendor qualities may be present in the emerging market, but are often too hard to find, or require taking significant risks in the process of sorting the good from the bad.

An example of this can be found in the experience of McDonald's Corporation in Russia in the early 1990s. McDonald's Corporation, with roughly 27 000 outlets around the world, makes a point of sourcing its products from locally approved suppliers. As Jack Greenberg, Chairman and CEO of McDonald's Corporation, stated at the World Economic Forum in Davos in 2000, "Our global supply infrastructure is the most critical part of our success today and I think it is unique."

However, when McDonald's moved into Russia in 1990 shortly after the fall of the Berlin Wall, it was unable to find local suppliers. It offered contracts to several of its European vendors, without success. McDonald's eventually built up the supply infrastructure itself. It imported cattle from Holland and russet potatoes from America, and identified some Russian farmers and bakers it could train and finance in order to work with. It built a 100 000-square-foot McComplex in Moscow to produce beef, bakery, potato, and dairy products. It also set up a trucking fleet to move supplies to restaurants. In short, McDonald's built a vertically integrated operation in order to compensate for the lack of scaleable, reliable vendors at the outset (Khanna et al., 2005).

This lack of adequate vendors is often exacerbated by a further lack of "specialized intermediaries" in emerging markets. From market research firms, to credit bureaus, to legal and regulatory systems and more, these institutional voids can make it even more difficult for a foreign firm to navigate business in emerging markets. All aspects of a business are affected, though they are especially apparent when a company wishes to source product and labor from the local market.

Generally speaking, microfranchises represent a lower risk alternative for doing business with the local market. For one, microfranchises operate within the formal economy, unlike many other small businesses at the BOP. As a registered entity operating within the bounds of the law, the microfranchise is a more reliable partner and vendor. Furthermore, there is a greater chance for recourse should problems arise in the business dealings.

Second, microfranchises offer transparency, and standardization of processes. They can confidently offer a high degree of reliability and consistency in their products and services. Their own, as well as their fellow franchisees' reputations are at risk. This sense of shared responsibility works to the advantage of all parties.

Finally, there are a multitude of other microfranchise characteristics, which, either directly or indirectly, decrease the microfranchise's risk as a potential supplier to a company operating at the BOP. These reasons can include:

- scale, or ability to scale, to the desired need;
- uniform systems and training;
- strict controls on quality;
- internal auditing and inspection of operations;
- local knowledge and networks;
- ability to work with, or through, the institutional voids that may exist.

BOX 6.3   MONDI RECYCLING

South Africa's Mondi Recycling provides a good example of how local integration can reduce a company's costs and risks, while providing benefits to the community. Mondi, which holds a dominant position in the South African paper recycling industry, decided in 2001 to create a new community-centric business model. One of the major aspects of this new model was the introduction of owner-drivers – essentially individual franchisees. Mondi sold these former employees pick-up vehicles at a reduced rate and contracted business out to them. This system allowed the owner-drivers to earn more money, as they were paid according to the amount of paper they picked up, and to own a stake in their own small businesses. These economic benefits to the community are expected to serve Mondi well in the long run.

In this example, Mondi was able to help the community, by creating a sustainable livelihood for its people, and the owner-drivers were able to help Mondi by increasing the amount of paper picked up, lowering operational costs, and improving the company's standing within the community and with the government.

Source: WBCSD (2005).

With a lack of specialized intermediaries, and a lack of known entities for quality, scale, and reliability, the BOP presents significant challenges to the company wishing to source its goods and services locally. Fortunately, a successful microfranchise operation is one that has implemented the controls and practices necessary for a scaleable business. Working with these companies as vendors can offer a multi-national not only access to reliable, low-cost products and services, but also a way to develop networks and ties into the local community. In the long run, it is these investments in products and people that will help the communities raise their incomes and standards of living, and will increase the multi-national's chance of success at the BOP.

NOTES

1. Over the period 1993 to 2003 Political Risk Services (http://www.prsgroup.com/index.html) reports that its average risk score in lower- and middle-income countries improved from 59 to 64 and almost three times as many countries saw an improving risk climate as a deteriorating one. The World Bank (2006) reports that 99 countries from its sample made their regulatory climate more conducive to doing business while only 20 made it more difficult to do business (see: http://www.doingbusiness.org/).
2. C.K. Prahalad and Stuart Hart (2002) brought the term into the literature; some have suggested that "base of the pyramid" may be more appropriate than "bottom of the pyramid," the two terms have the same meaning.
3. See, among others, Hart (1997), Prahalad and Lieberthal (1998), Prahalad and Hammond (2002), Prahalad and Hart (2002), Hammond and Paul (2005).
4. See references for list of publications. Origo Inc., the firm where the authors of this chapter work, was closely involved in the research of the WBCSD's Sustainable Livelihoods project and the writing of its 2004 publications.

REFERENCES

CARE Canada (2006), website accessed at www.care.ca/CEP/CEPportfolio_e.shtm.

Chen, R. and M. Cannice (2006), "Global integration and the performance of multinationals' subsidiaries in emerging markets", *Ivey Business Journal*, 1–2.

Coca-Cola (2006), "The Coca-Cola Company in Africa: key facts and figures", Coca-Cola Africa website, accessed 6 June, at www.africa.coca-cola. com.

De Soto, Hernando (2000), *The Mystery of Capital: Why Capitalism Triumphs in the West and Fails Everywhere Else*, Basic Books.

Hammond, Allen and John Paul (2005), "Technology innovations at the edge", World Resources Institute Development Through Enterprise report, accessed at www.nextbillion.net/innovations-at-the-edge.

Hart, Stuart, L. (1997), "Beyond greening: strategies for a sustainable world", *Harvard Business Review*, (January-February), 66–76.

International Monetary Fund (IMF) (2006), "World economic outlook: globalization and inflation", *Economic Prospects and Policy Issues*, April, 1–3.

International Telecommunications Union (ITU) (2004), *Mobile Cellular Subscribers Factsheet*.

Khanna, T., K. Palepu and J. Sinha (2005), "Strategies that fit emerging markets", *Harvard Business Review*, (2),12.

McKinsey Global Institute (2003), "Impact on global industry restructuring", *New Horizons: Multinational Company Investment in Developing Economies*, 1.

Prahalad, C.K. (2004) *The Fortune at the Bottom of the Pyramid: Eradicating Poverty Through Profits*, Wharton School Publishing.

Prahalad, C.K. and A. Hammond (2002), "Serving the world's poor, profitably", *Harvard Business Review*, (September), 48–57.

Prahalad, C.K. and S. Hart, (2002) "The fortune at the bottom of the pyramid", *Strategy and Business*, **26** (first quarter), 2–14.

Prahalad, C.K. and Kenneth Lieberthal (1998), "The end of corporate imperialism", *Harvard Business Review*, (July-August), 69–79.

Weiss, S. and K. Hanson (1991), "Merck & Co., Inc.: addressing Third World needs (A, B, C, D)", Harvard Business School Press, case study.

Wheeler, David et al. (2005), "Creating sustainable local enterprise networks", *MIT Sloan Management Review*, **47** (1) (Fall), 33–40.

Wheeler, David and Kevin McKague (2002), *The Role of Business in Development*, Washington, DC: World Bank, also accessed at http://iris.yorku.ca/projweb/SustainableLivelihoods/Publications/file_Role_of_Business_in_Development.pdf.

World Bank (2006), Global Development Finance, Washington, DC: World Bank.

World Bank (2006), Doing Business 2006.

World Business Council For Sustainable Development (WBCSD) (2003), "Coca-Cola: the entrepreneur development program in South Africa", WBCSD case study, accessed 8 June, 2006, at www.wbcsd.org.

World Business Council for Sustainable Development (WBCSD) (2004), *Doing Business with the Poor: A Field Guide*.

World Business Council For Sustainable Development (WBCSD) (2005), "Empowering supply chains: Anglo American's Mondi Recycling", WBCSD case study accessed 8 June, 2006 at www.wbcsd.org.

World Business Council For Sustainable Development (WBCSD) (2005), "Electricité de France, Tenesol, Total: electrifying rural Moroccan households", WBCSD case study accessed 8 June, 2006 at www.wbcsd.org.

PART II

Microfranchising in practice

7. Microfranchise business models

Kirk Magleby

MICROFRANCHISES AS DEVELOPMENT VEHICLES

In the struggle to alleviate world poverty, institutions matter. The US Agency for International Development (USAID) recently observed that institutions are more important than resources.[1] Exploitative, predatory institutions like mafias, corrupt bureaucracies, and commercial monopolies cause poverty. That is why historically, intractable global poverty is called *structural* or *institutional* poverty. Benevolent, uplifting institutions such as microfinance institutions (MFIs), self-help groups and some non-governmental organizations (NGOs) help people lift themselves out of poverty. Lasting change throughout a community or a nation requires locally-owned egalitarian institutions with deep roots such as good schools, reliable employers, and fair markets. Profitable businesses matter because all wealth comes from successful enterprise. Large numbers of locally-owned, networked businesses called microfranchises may be pivotal institutions to help many people escape poverty.[2]

In drought-prone Ethiopia where a culinary water system blesses many lives, World Vision (WV), one of the world's great NGOs,[3] invested millions of dollars drilling, capping, and equipping bore holes. Most of those wells, so celebrated when they first began supplying clean water to villagers a few years ago, are no longer functional. They filled with silt, or the pump broke, or the bore hole technician moved to Addis Ababa and beyond searching for economic opportunity.[4] WV bore hole caps dot the countryside, dusty little concrete reminders that you can pour resources into a community but unless indigenous institutions arise from the grassroots, little sustainable economic development occurs.[5]

NGO Magitek also drills, caps, and equips bore holes in Tanzania and neighboring countries. But, rather than training technicians and moving on, Magitek sets up tiny water companies as microfranchises.[6] These locally-owned small businesses are networked among themselves with Magitek supplying ongoing training, replacement parts, repair and reclamation services, etc. Because Magitek employs a superior form of business organization, their microfranchisees are building sustainable local institutions that should be supplying clean water for generations. Other clean water microfranchise organizations include Play Pumps in South Africa and UV Water in the Philippines.

Structural poverty can be alleviated[7] by deploying appropriate technology and effective business models. One of the most successful business models on earth is franchising. Microfranchising employs proven franchise concepts and techniques among marginalized entrepreneurs with small-scale businesses at the base of the income pyramid (BOP).[8] This chapter will explore various microfranchise business models that show great promise as institutional vehicles to alleviate global poverty.

TOWARD A MICROFRANCHISE HEURISTIC

For many people, the word "franchise" conjures up a mental image of a McDonald's fast-food restaurant, and for good reason. With more than 31 000 locations in 117 countries, McDonald's is so ubiquitous that economists have devised the "Big Mac index" as a convenient way to compare relative purchasing power in disparate economies around the globe. Subway has 23 000 locations in 77 countries, Burger King 11 000 locations in 61 countries, and dozens of other franchised restaurant brands operate transnationally.

The franchise business model, though, extends well beyond the food service industry. Isaac Singer created modern franchising to distribute his famous sewing machines in the nineteenth century. Henry Ford launched the automobile dealer concept as a means of spreading his enormous inventory carrying cost among hundreds and then thousands of local capitalists. Oil companies adopted the franchise model in their petroleum retailing operations. The Marriotts and other hoteliers quickly discovered that it is more profitable for them to operate a lodging property under a franchised management contract than it is to own all of that real estate outright. Coca-Cola bottlers, State Farm insurance agents, and NFL football teams all operate under franchise agreements. Tyson chickens are produced on franchised poultry ranches. Students hone their math skills in franchised Sylvan Learning Centers. As the most successful network business model on earth, the diverse forms of franchising (the "franchise economy") account for 15–25 percent of gross domestic product (GDP) in most developed countries, and that percentage is steadily increasing as industries from construction to health care and financial services to transportation embrace the win/win productivity inherent in the franchise model.

Franchising also works well in the developing world. Goldman Sachs recently coined the acronym "BRIC" meaning Brazil, Russia, India and China.[9] These four transitional countries are the world's current economic development superstars. All four have well-established and fast-growing franchise sectors. In Brazil, for instance, 25 percent of all small and medium-sized enterprises (SMEs) are now franchises. In a 2006 paper submitted to the World Bank[10] I demonstrate a direct relationship between the degree of penetration the franchise business model has achieved in a given country and that nation's per capita GDP. A key reason why franchising fosters economic development is that the franchise economy in most countries is growing much faster than the overall economy. India, for example, has experienced annual economic growth of 6–10 percent in recent years. India's franchise economy has grown by 20–30 percent per year during that same time period.

The franchise business model is viable around the world in practically every industry. Dozens of microfranchise networks demonstrate that the model also works with very small businesses owned by entrepreneurs of modest, even negligible means. Many organizations are now seeking the holy grail of microfranchising: replicable business formats that are inexpensive enough for low-income entrepreneurs to afford, yet profitable enough for the owner/operator to support a family with some degree of dignity. NGOs, MFIs, multi-national companies (MNCs), domestic companies (DCs) and indigenous franchisors (IFs) are all building microfranchise networks. We are witnessing the birth of a new social movement that can positively change the economic development paradigm in millions of low-income neighborhoods.[11]

The definition of microfranchising is not yet entirely settled. If business start-up costs in Mexico are $10 000, is that small enough to be considered a *micro*franchise? In Malawi? Many networked businesses exhibit various degrees of franchise-like characteristics. It is generally agreed that franchises are of two basic types: product franchises and business format franchises. Each type has many variations. All exhibit certain key franchise traits:

- local owner(s) in a symbiotic relationship with an enabling institution;
- a brand or other significant intellectual property;
- mentoring;
- shared know-how codified in an operating system;
- potential for replication; and
- an overt social mission to alleviate poverty through enterprise.

A Chevrolet dealer is a common example of a product franchise. Dealers typically publicize their own names prominently on signage and even on decals or insignia permanently affixed to their cars. Dealer A may build a sleek glass and steel showroom and advertise on TV. Dealer B may sell cars from a circus tent and advertise with a giant inflatable gorilla.

A Jackson Hewitt income tax service typifies a much more standardized business format franchise. The franchisor controls myriad details of the operation including human resource management, price schedules, and computer systems. Some business format franchisors even go so far as to control operating hours, interior decor and key vendor relationships. In general, product franchises focus on "what" while business format franchises are more concerned with "how." Product franchises offer autonomy and measure sales results. Business format franchises control processes in an effort to produce predictable sales results.

Most extant and conceivable microfranchise networks fit into this product-based or business format taxonomy. In an effort to facilitate the global microfranchise movement, I have identified 14 discrete microfranchise business models and categorized them as either a product or a business format franchise. Within each category, the models are organized in ascending order by complexity. Examples are from both the developing and the industrialized worlds since many good business models work in both emerging and mature markets.

PRODUCT FRANCHISES

Hunter Gatherer

One summer I was in Eastern Kentucky and got to know a fellow who worked three months out of every year in Indiana, which gave him enough money to almost survive the rest of the year in a tiny shack at the head of a mountain "holler." "What do you do when you run out of money?" I asked him. "Oh, I just tramp the mountains and gather ginseng," he replied. As my friend explained, an experienced person in Appalachia can collect a burlap sack full of ginseng root in a day and make themselves $100. Ginseng is prized as an aphrodisiac in a number of Asian countries.

Fores Trade offers about 500 Indonesian villagers a similar part-time business opportunity. They can earn extra cash collecting certain plants that have value in the spice trade from the Indonesian forest. Fores Trade does not deal in endangered species and they train their affiliates in sustainable harvesting techniques. They limit the number of affiliates in each region to preserve the forest's regeneration capacity. Fores Trade products command premium prices in niche markets because the forest mystique enhances their global brand image.

This microfranchise-like model is extremely simple with very low start-up costs for the local entrepreneur. Ongoing mentoring is minimal. Replication potential is limited to the carrying capacity of the underlying ecosystem and world market demand. The brand is largely incidental to the local harvester, who benefits primarily from a guaranteed market at a firm and favorable price.

Agricultural Producer

The certainty of a future commodity sale at a contracted price, the fundamental value proposition behind the Chicago Board of Trade, underpins much of the North American agricultural economy. Farmers and ranchers are able to focus on efficient production rather than worry about the vagaries of regional, national, or global commodity markets. Brokers and processors, on the other hand, are assured a steady supply of agricultural products with dependable prices and delivery dates.

Unilever, a most enlightened MNC, manufactures soy sauce at a plant in Indonesia. Rather than purchase soy beans on the spot market for the cheapest possible price, Unilever has entered into a long-term contractual agreement with dozens of local soy farmers. Unilever supplies some inputs and facilitates best practices knowledge-sharing among the farmers in its network. The farmers have a guaranteed buyer who pays a fair price and Unilever has a reliable source of quality raw materials. This egregious win/win is typical of successful microfranchise projects. Other agricultural production projects with some microfranchise characteristics include the Grameen Motsho fish farms in Bangladesh and ES Coffee in Ecuador and Central America. Each of these networks has an enabling institution providing services to local farmers, a brand, some degree of training, and a sense of social mission to alleviate poverty.

Contrary examples are tragically typical in the developing world. Pyrethrum is a plant with natural insecticidal properties that grows in Kenya's Great Rift Valley. SC Johnson's Raid insecticide uses pyrethrum. Pyrethrum-impregnated bed nets protect many sleeping Africans from malaria mosquitoes. Unfortunately, the parastatal Pyrethrum Board of Kenya (PBK) controls the national market. Kenyan farmers can only sell their pyrethrum to the PBK, largely comprised of political hacks and cronies who treat the organization's coffers as a slush fund.[12] Kenyan pyrethrum farmers sometimes wait over a year to get paid. PBK board members have lucrative factoring businesses, offering farmers 60 cents on the dollar to accept immediate payment rather than wait for the oft-delayed PBK check. With corrupt intermediaries siphoning off most of their profits, most Kenyan farmers have simply stopped growing pyrethrum. Dwindling natural supplies led to the development of synthetic pyrethrum. MNC chemical giants now dominate an industry that could potentially benefit thousands of small Kenyan farmers.

Agriculturalists are marginalized in many societies. Some form agricultural cooperatives, but co-ops have a problematic history in the developing world. In a typical pattern, as soon as a co-op grows large enough to be truly effective, a "strongman" emerges who gains control of the organization and then misappropriates assets or absconds with funds.[13] Agricultural cooperatives have been frequent victims of fraud because the farmers are often unsophisticated in their administrative and managerial skills. Networks of agricultural producers organized with microfranchise principles and techniques could empower tens of millions of small farmers and ranchers. Amul in India is a good example. Eight million small dairy farmers, many of whom own a single cow, are organized in 10 000 local milk processing co-ops. The co-ops are then networked to form the powerful Amul brand of milk, cheese, yogurt, whey and ice cream products—the largest dairy enterprise on earth. India's recent "white revolution" has benefited the country almost as profoundly as the vaunted "green revolution" that preceded it. Improved nutrition from widely-available milk products is only part of the story. Many Indian dairy farmers now enjoy increased earning power because they are networked in a win/win relationship with a superior business organization.

Small-scale agriculture exists in virtually every inhabited part of the planet. What are often missing are the intermediate storage and processing facilities to take advantage of this production and the market mechanisms to distribute it fairly. Microfranchise models could be key organizational vehicles to help scattered producers organize effectively. In parts of Africa, foreign transportation firms make handsome profits distributing US and European food aid from seaports to the NGOs inland (themselves contractors to the Washington DC and Brussels foreign aid industry), which in turn distribute this food to malnourished Africans. Ironically, as it is being transported, much of this foreign food aid passes locally-produced food that is rotting or rat-infested because the indigenous infrastructure to store, process, and distribute the food is simply non-existent. The market-poisoning effect of free US and European food dumped into the domestic economy practically guarantees that this crucial local infrastructure will never develop. What is wrong with this picture? Does Africa need more aid? Or do African farmers need better business models?

Sales Agent

A dizzying variety of franchise relationships expect the franchisee to sell a product or service. Avon ladies go door to door, taking orders from catalogs. New York Life agents in the United States must be licensed by the state before they can work from home or an office downtown. Snap-on tool dealers drive step vans to shops that employ mechanics and give impromptu demos. Manufacturers' reps supply specialty construction materials and help contractors prepare bids. Various degrees of product knowledge or after-market support may be required, but ultimately sales agents get paid a commission based on their sales volumes.

Some of the best known microfranchises in the developing world, such as the Grameen village phone ladies in Bangladesh, Uganda, and Tanzania and the Hindustan Lever Shakti Amma ladies operating kiosks in India, employ direct sales agents. Scojo Foundation, operating in India, Bangladesh, Guatemala, and El Salvador, has evolved an innovative consignment model that allows a vision entrepreneur to begin selling reading glasses from a portable kit with little or no up-front capital investment.

The sales agent microfranchise model has tremendous potential worldwide. Traditional wholesale to retail supply chains don't work very well in low-income communities and direct marketing creates large numbers of jobs, which are sorely needed in the developing world. Unilever Vietnam, for example, employs nearly 100 000 microfranchised sales agents to distribute its products in that country, while Avon Brazil has about 800 000 local dealers. Sales agents can work part-time or full-time, and many can be home-based, rather than storefront-based. Women can be very successful sales agents. Detailed product knowledge is not usually a prerequisite, so training can be expeditious. Young people who achieve some success in a direct sales business can springboard to more advanced careers.

Specialized Equipment Operator

For decades, any American who owned a backhoe was assured of practically lifetime employment as an excavation contractor. Since the developing world is acutely resource-constrained, many products could utilize this business model. Cement mixers, chain saws, computers, entertainment systems, and sewing machines come readily to mind. One principal asset acquisition can provide a virtual "business-in-a-box" for the owner/operator.

Kick Start, headquartered in San Francisco, implements this model with simple technology aimed at small farmers and entrepreneurs in the developing world. Their best-known product is a human-powered treadle water pump that tens of thousands of Kenyan and Tanzanian farmers use to irrigate their crops. Kick Start also supplies manually-operated brick presses and oilseed presses. Kick Start tools enhance productivity through appropriate, affordable technology. Kick Start is a social enterprise, not a franchisor. Franchise networks can be built, though, based on these kinds of tools. For example, MFI Yehu Bank is building a coconut oil microfranchise in Kenya based on a hand-operated coconut oil press.

Kit Assembly

Many computer servers are not delivered directly from a factory. A technician assembles a customized server from dozens of components. Products as diverse as volleyball nets and backyard sheds typically require assembly. Ikea has built a global furniture empire based on a do-it-yourself kit assembly model.

Beginning in 1995, Arvind Mills, the largest textile manufacturer in India, developed a very successful piecework microfranchise that made 4500 local tailors important links in the supply chain for denim jeans. Arvind Mills sold its franchisees a $6 "jeans kit" that included denim fabric along with a zipper, rivets, and ready-made pockets. Customers got a well-fitting pair of jeans and Arvind Mills got 4500 points of sale all across India. Ruff 'n Tuffs quickly became the top-selling Indian jeans brand.

With success, Arvind Mills repositioned its brand. Ruff 'n Tuffs are now sewn in factories and sold at Big Bazaar retail stores, but rural Indian tailors continue to sew denim jeans from kits. Kit models could build significant microfranchise networks assembling furniture, shelving, appliances, bicycles, garments, small structures, etc.

Field Service Technician

Globus Relief operates a large humanitarian warehouse in Salt Lake City. Hospitals donate used medical equipment, which Globus ships to NGOs around the world. Hospitals get a tax write-off and NGOs acquire life-saving equipment for cents on the dollar. The problem is that once it gets installed at medical facilities in the developing world, much of this equipment does not stay in service very long. Bulbs burn out and hoses break. A culture of equipment maintenance hardly exists in many developing countries. Many hospital storage rooms throughout Peru, for instance, are practically overflowing with valuable donated equipment needing minor repairs.[14]

Microfranchising could end this Peruvian tragedy as an example from North Africa illustrates. Temasol is a leading supplier of roof-mounted solar electric systems in rural Morocco. Photovoltaic installations require occasional maintenance, so Temasol has trained a group of electricians who work on Temasol equipment. These microfranchised trades people own their own tools and cover specific territories. They perform routine preventive maintenance as well as restorative and repair work. The cost of much of this ongoing service is built into the price of the Temasol equipment itself.

Product Franchise

Traditional product franchises tend to be capital-intensive with considerable local autonomy. Automobile dealers, soft drink bottlers, and professional sports teams are examples. The defining characteristic of these businesses is exclusive access to a highly merchantable product within a defined geography.

Unilever has developed sophisticated technology to micro-encapsulate iodine in ordinary table salt. This enables the salt to remain iodized, even after withstanding the rigors of sometimes brutal ethnic cooking customs. In India, Hindustan Lever markets this advanced salt successfully under the brand name Annapurna. When Unilever introduced Annapurna salt in Ghana, they avoided centralized sourcing or traditional wholesale retail supply chains. Rather, Unilever licensed its technology to a number of existing Ghanaian salt producers who are the exclusive Annapurna franchisees in their market territories. This allowed Unilever's brand to capture significant Ghanaian market share quickly. It also allows a number of locally-owned businesses in Ghana to flourish through a win/win franchise relationship with one of the world's great MNCs. Each Ghanaian Annapurna plant in turn supplies products to an army of direct sellers, making this a bi-level franchise. New York-based Our Community Works LLC plans to use this model with its Options mini-plants, manufacturing cleaning products that will be distributed by legions of sales agents.

Product franchising can be expensive. A manufacturing facility with proprietary technology is often involved. Developing countries desperately need this kind of import substitution activity, which is a fundamental building block of economic development. The product franchise business model is an appropriate way for large companies to engage people at the BOP as customers, employees, business partners, and sales agents.

BUSINESS FORMAT FRANCHISES

Agricultural Enterprise

NGO Honey Care Africa offers a unique value proposition to smallhold farmers in Kenya, Uganda, and Tanzania. Honey Care supplies high-quality beekeeping equipment and training. More importantly, Honey Care contracts to purchase 100 percent of a beekeeper's honey production at a fair price. Honey Care packages the honey and distributes it through traditional retail channels in East Africa and abroad. The system works well enough that 7800 beekeepers supplement their income with a reliable cash crop and Honey Care is emerging as a strong regional brand.

This model is brilliant in its simplicity. Prospective microfranchisees are not required to own the land they work. The franchisor provides equipment, tools, training, agricultural inputs, bulk commodity transportation, intermediate processing, packaging, and marketing services. Dozens of specialty products such as mushrooms, nuts, berries, etc. could use this model in most countries on earth. This model is somewhat more sophisticated than the Agricultural Producer model described in the Product Franchises section because Honey Care supplies a complete package, an agricultural "business-in-a-box."

Informal Business Format

The Tropical Sno company of Draper, Utah has helped several thousand entrepreneurs in dozens of countries open a shaved ice business. Tropical Sno sells the prospective business person an electric ice shaver, uniforms, signage, carts or kiosks, cups, and packages of various flavorings. In other words, Tropical Sno supplies a business-in-a-box plus ongoing branded supplies. Tropical Sno does *not* control site selection, pricing, sales territories, hours of operation, or any of the other myriad details that a more standardized business format franchisor may care about. Tropical Sno is an informally managed brand. As long as franchisees purchase their raw material inputs from the network, Tropical Sno enterprisers have wide operating latitude.

Mexico is home to a similar organization, the remarkably successful Paleterias La Michoacana. A "paleta" is a frozen confection on a stick. An American might call it a "popsicle," while in the United Kingdom they say "ice lolly." Nearly 16 000 Mexican outlets are La Michoacana microfranchisees. Thousands of copycats and knock-offs piggy back on the popularity of the brand. Some La Michoacana outlets are stand-alone storefronts. Others occupy a corner of another retail business establishment. And some La Michoacana microfranchisees push wheeled carts and sell their frozen treats on the street from an insulated cooler. Entrepreneurs share a brand and purchase their concentrated base, molds, and sticks from the network. Each outlet decides which flavors to stock, and freezes its own paletas. The Mexican diaspora has brought La Michoacana with them to the United States and the brand is growing rapidly north of the border. Lijjat snacks from India are another instance of an informal business format microfranchise.

The informal business format model allows a franchisor to grow large without the overhead investment and compliance mechanisms that more tightly controlled networks require. The ongoing supply of proprietary ingredients in customized formulations keeps the franchisees coming back to the source for their raw material inputs. Counterfeit competitors are the natural downside of so much informality. In many developing world environments where intellectual property protections are tough to enforce, this informality may be a pragmatic adaptation of the franchise business model to the reality on the ground. This model would lend itself to a wide variety of products where an intermediate processing step is required before final production or assembly. Oven-ready bakery products are one example.

Independent Operator/Sub-franchisee

When I get my hair cut at the local Fantastic Sam's salon, there is a two-level franchise at work. The Fantastic Sam's franchise is owned by a lady in a neighboring town. But the stylist who cuts my hair is an independent operator with her own clientele who temporarily controls one of the ten chairs in the facility. When I pay the stylist $12 for a haircut, she earns $7.20 and $4.80 goes to the salon which eventually remits about $0.30 to the franchisor's headquarters in Beverly, Massachusetts.

This same model is at work in more than 200 microfranchised Reyes Barber Shops in the Philippines. Barbers with their own loyal customers attend to new walk-ins on an as-available basis. Each barber splits the day's receipts with the shop owner, in essence "renting" their chair. The shop owner in turn pays royalties to the Reyes organization, which controls the brand, organizes group buying, coordinates group marketing campaigns, etc.

The independent operator microfranchise model works in a public market where individual shop owners rent a space or stall. It is appropriate for personal services, professional services, and retail businesses.

Local Promoter

Cemex, the world's third largest cement producer, has created a successful system that is helping 120 000 Mexican, Nicaraguan, and Colombian families build high-quality houses efficiently and cost-effectively. The Cemex program is called "Patrimonio Hoy" or "Equity Now." It is based around a microfranchised local promoter wearing a Cemex shirt who organizes homeowners into small self-help groups, advised by a local architect or construction specialist. In most Latin American countries, mortgages are rare and building codes irrelevant. Families gather building materials on a catch-as-catch-can basis and build their houses one room at a time. It is not unusual to see piles of sand or bricks washing away in the rain or being pilfered by neighbors while a patient homeowner is trying to get enough money together to finish the next room in their house. A typical room can take up to five years to complete. In the structured Patrimonio Hoy system, each family in the self-help group pays about $13 per week into a fund. After the second week, Cemex supplies the equivalent of $130 worth of building materials. After the twelfth week, Cemex supplies the second $130 and so on through a 70-week cycle. After 70 weeks, each family in the self-help group has a new room built to high architectural standards. The microfranchisee local promoter, meanwhile, is off organizing other self-help groups and collecting a small royalty on the accumulated building materials sales they have facilitated.

The model of a microfranchised local promoter organizing and mentoring self-help groups is pregnant with possibilities. The developing world generally suffers from an acute lack of public trust and cooperation. Self-help groups empowered by an enabling franchisor institution could help overcome these deep-seated sociological barriers to development. MFIs have shown that positive peer pressure from organized self-help groups can transform social capital into a powerful change agent.

Owner Operator

For many years, American trucking companies operated primarily with company-owned vehicles and regular employee drivers. There is now a growing trend toward owner operators. In the owner operator model, a driver owns his or her own truck and leases it to a trucking company. This results in a consummate win/win. The trucking company has far less capital tied up in rolling stock, and overall fleet maintenance costs decline because owners tend to take better care of their own equipment than employees do of a company vehicle. Safety records often improve for the same reason. As a result, the trucking company can grow more quickly than it could if it were the sole financier and paymaster for the entire fleet. The owner operator, on the other hand, can build up equity in a major asset over time, which eventually results in higher income than a regular employee could expect. Many owner operators acquire a second and even a third truck. Successful trucking companies offer a variety of benefits to their owner operators such as group insurance, group purchasing plans, etc. to keep these valued drivers loyal to the network.

This owner operator microfranchise model is very much in evidence throughout the developing world. Taxi companies, microbus public transportation lines, moto-taxi, pedi-cab, and delivery services all employ a combination of company-owned and driver-owned vehicles. What is often lacking in low-income communities is the egregious win/win orientation that makes well-managed transportation companies so productive and successful in the developed world.

Refinements to the owner operator microfranchise model could yield significant productivity benefits to hundreds of thousands of transportation companies throughout the developing world. One taxi driver in Lima, Peru owns two vehicles: one that he drives himself for 12 hours per day and another that he leases out to two independent contractor drivers, each of whom drives a nine-hour shift. The owner of the two vehicles complains that he makes a reasonable living from his own taxi, but he profits very little on the second vehicle because maintenance and repair costs are so high. In his mind, the second vehicle represents a lose/win scenario. The two drivers of the second vehicle, on the other hand, see it as a win/lose. They think the owner of the taxi gouges them, taking more than his fair share of the daily proceeds. They respond to this perceived injustice by abusing the vehicle. This creates a lose/lose situation and productivity predictably suffers. The developing world does not need increased external resource flows nearly as much as it needs mutually beneficial business models that result in win/win scenarios for both the franchisor and the franchisee. Valet Taxi in Lima is one fast-growing company taking this win/win approach.

Finance Franchise

One of the most successful franchise organizations on earth is Western Union, with over 100 000 locations in almost every country on the planet. One doesn't walk into a Western Union store—they don't exist. Rather, Western Union offers an auxiliary financial product that an existing retail storefront business can offer as an extra service to its clientele, at the same time generating an additional revenue stream for the store. Western Union franchises tend to proliferate anywhere there are retail businesses with high liquidity serving unbanked or low-income populations displaced through economic migration.

A number of exciting finance microfranchise models are now in operation around the world. The Uganda Microfinance Union (UMU), an Acción affiliate, offers savings and credit services to clients in low-income communities. UMU does not employ the traditional rural branch network that has kept costs so high for many MFIs. Rather, UMU works with existing local retailers such as pharmacies who already have cash in the till, cash handling expertise, and some accounting controls in place. UMU microfranchisees assess credit risks, disburse loan proceeds, collect loan payments and accept savings deposits. Under the aegis of market leaders such as ICICI Bank in India,[15] the franchise business model is quietly infiltrating and revolutionizing microfinance service delivery. ·

Another example deserves mention. Smartcom, the largest wireless telephone carrier in the Philippines, pioneered a transaction processing platform triggered by SMS text messages. This allows a Filipino in say, Hong Kong, to send $100 to his sister in Cebu. She gets a text message on her cell phone notifying her that she now has $100 in her electronic wallet. She goes to a McDonald's restaurant, keys in the store's ID number in a text message, and a McDonald's cashier hands her cash from the till. Vodafone, the largest wireless telephone carrier on earth, is implementing a similar system in Kenya. Rather than targeting behemoth chains like McDonald's, Vodafone's M-Pesa microfranchise is available to established local merchants such as pharmacists and grocers. One person in every three on the planet currently carries a mobile phone. In just a few years, that number will increase to one person in every two. The possibilities for financial service microfranchises in every corner of the globe are practically limitless.

Business Format

This is the classic business structure most people think of when they hear the word "franchise." It is also the most common microfranchise business model.[16] Business formats are all about control with limited local adaptation. Franchisors create an operating system that often dictates not only the brand name, logo, and uniform, but also site selection criteria, pricing structure, and operating hours. These are cookie cutter replications of a nearly identical business format in a different neighborhood or another town. With nearly 10 000 locations in only ten years, Gary Heavin's Curves for Women is the fastest-growing business format franchise in history. Most Curves franchises are located in suburban strip malls with identical fitness equipment, the same exercise routines, similar decor and even the same music playing in background. Why do franchisees put up with this mind-numbing standardization? Because proven concepts make money, are relatively easy to manage, and this extreme predictability helps a franchisee acquire a second and then a third location. A new business format franchise opens somewhere in the United States every eight minutes and Australia has even more business format franchise locations per capita than North America.

Three thousand four hundred Farmacias de Similares generic drug stores dot Mexico and eight other Latin American countries. Aptech computer-based training centers began in India and now boast 2700 locations in over 30 nations. The 56 HealthStores generic pharmacies in Kenya, the 5000 Vodacom phone centers in South Africa, and the 33 Cellular City mobile phone shops in the Philippines are all business format microfranchises.

RECAP

This list of 14 microfranchise and microfranchise-like business models is neither definitive nor exhaustive. These are simply models that have worked, are currently working, or could plausibly work in the developing world. Some microfranchises will employ two or more of the models in various combinations. Bundled microfranchises will also develop. In the United States, many gas stations have a fast-food restaurant on the premises. In India, some pedi-cab and moto-taxi drivers carry an insulated cooler and sell Amul ice cream treats for pennies to children in the neighborhoods they transit.

An important business model distinction divides commercial microfranchises from social franchises. Commercial microfranchises are for-profit business entities, albeit on a small scale, whose owners expect a return on their investment. Successful microfranchises are capable of operating self-sufficiency through profitability. Social franchises, on the other hand, require eternal subsidies. They aim to deliver the greatest possible social good to the largest number of people. Education, health care, protected public lands, and the arts are seldom delivered profitably anywhere on earth. Public subsidies are almost always necessary in order for these social goods to be widely available in a society.

Regardless of the particular business model a microfranchise network adopts, I expect a great deal of creative financial engineering that will include innovative equity arrangements for the microfranchisees. Rather than taking out a bank loan and acquiring a franchise like entrepreneurs do in the Organisation for Economic Co-operation and Development (OECD) countries, many microfranchisees will acquire their location over time through an earn-out. One location may have ownership shared among two or more entrepreneurs. International financial institutions may buy down the risk of a venture, thereby paving the way for local bank participation. Debt plus equity financing models will develop that aggregate small business commercial paper into syndicated bundles that can be securitized on world capital markets.

Unfortunately, in the least developed countries, franchising is practically non-existent. The microfranchise movement will improve that grim picture as a productive plethora of franchised products and business formats designed for low-income entrepreneurs emerges. Understanding these different models will help would-be microfranchisors build their organizations more effectively because they will better understand the "nature of the beast" and have relevant examples to emulate.

I have attempted to articulate a variety of business models so NGOs, MFIs, MNCs, DCs and IFs have templates and ideas to help them organize effective microfranchise projects. The franchise business model is a powerful tool for individual empowerment and economic development in both wealthy and low-income economies. Microfranchises are small franchised businesses adapted to the stark reality on the ground in the developing world. The salient characteristics of a franchise: local ownership, nurturing institution, brand, mentoring, operating system, replication, and win/win orientation, are all present in a well-managed microfranchise. Microfranchising then adds the altruistic dimension of global poverty alleviation. Microfranchising is an idea whose time has come. It is capable of creating millions of small, locally-owned, successful businesses to energize under-performing economies worldwide. Political will can speed its progress. All humankind will benefit.

NOTES

1. "Institutions, Not Resources Matter Most," "US foreign aid: meeting the challenges of the twenty-first century," USAID white paper, Bureau for Policy and Program Coordination, January 2004.
2. See Magleby, K. (2006), *MicroFranchises as a Solution to Global Poverty*, Salt Lake City, UT: Ascend, a Humanitarian Alliance.
3. www.worldvision.org.
4. On a business trip to San Francisco in December 2004, one of my taxi drivers was a former WV Area Development Project (ADP) manager from Ethiopia. He reported that most of the people he used to work with, after they had even a modicum of training, migrated out of the area.
5. Personal communication with Tim Layton who serves with me on the board of Ascend, a Humanitarian Alliance, www.ascendalliance.org. In April 2006 Tim visited Ascend's project areas outside of Arsi Negelle, Ethiopia.
6. Personal communication with Scott Hillstrom, founder of Franchise Labs, May 2005.
7. It is widely noted in the international development literature that one million people lift themselves out of poverty in China each month.
8. The foundational work on the BOP is C.K. Prahalad (2004), *The Fortune at the Bottom of the Pyramid: Eradicating Poverty Through Profits*, Upper Saddle River, NJ: Wharton School Publishing. A rich source of contemporary BOP information is www.nextbillion. net sponsored by World Resources Institute (WRI).
9. The *Wall Street Journal*, 30 June 2006.
10. Magleby, K. (2006), Microfranchises as a Solution to World Poverty.
11. The five million neighborhoods currently served by MFIs are a good place to start.
12. In Kenya, these well-connected "strongmen" are called "Wabenzi," literally, "the tribe of the Mercedes Benz."
13. For decades, the Cajas Populares in Mexico, local savings and credit cooperatives, were only marginally successful because malfeasance was so rampant.
14. Personal communication with Chad Fugate, veteran of many medical missions to Peru, April 2006.
15. My son Rock is currently in India helping ICICI, the first Indian company listed on the New York Stock Exchange, refine its "credit franchise" model.
16. I have previously published a list of 69 microfranchised businesses originating in 22 different countries. Thirty-one of the 69 are business format franchises. See Magleby, K. (2006), *Microfranchises as a Solution to Global Poverty*.

8. Honey Care Africa[1]

Farouk Jiwa

According to the Poverty Reduction Strategy Paper (PRSP) published by the Government of Kenya in June 2001, over the period 1994–97, rural poverty increased in all but one of Kenya's seven rural provinces. The PRSP also states that one in every two Kenyans (50 percent of the population of the country) lived below the poverty line defined as just 1239 Kenyan shillings (Ksh) per month (or less than US$0.50 per day).[2]

Further, there is a lack of income opportunities for smallholder farmers and rural populations, where many have been frustrated by government control over the marketing of tea, coffee, cotton, and other cash crops. The PRSP states that "Low agricultural activity and poor marketing was cited by many communities as the major source of poverty." It continues:

> Mismanagement and collapse of agricultural institutions such as the Agricultural Finance Corporation, irrigation schemes, agricultural development corporations, National Cereals & Produce Board and Kenya Cooperative Creameries have contributed to poor marketing and low incomes ... this has acted as a disincentive for farmers and has further impoverished many households.

In addition, many large and state-run agro-enterprises have closed. In many parts of the country, this problem is acute, with sugar companies, a national molasses plant, cashew nut factories and cotton ginneries all closing down over the last decade. These closures not only eliminated employment opportunities in rural communities, but also affected the production of the cash crops that supplied those same industries, reducing the income of farmers who once grew them.

FOUNDING AND STRUCTURE OF HONEY CARE AFRICA

Honey Care Africa was established in 2000 as an innovative private sector social enterprise to promote sustainable community-based beekeeping in Eastern Africa. It was set up with an explicit triple bottom-line agenda,

149

with an emphasis on generating economic, social, and environmental value simultaneously through its activities.

In many ways, Honey Care was set up as a bold and daring experiment to redefine the traditional role of the private sector and redefine it as a key driver for development in the South, and to radically reconfigure the dynamics between the private sector, the development sector, and rural communities. This led to the evolution of Honey Care's innovative "Tripartite Model," which seeks to develop a synergistic "win-win-win" partnership between these three key actors, drawing on the core competencies of each as well as their complementary roles.

In partnership with a number of local NGOs and international development and financial institutions, including the World Bank Group, International Finance Corporation, European Union, Danish International Development Agency, Department of International Development (DFID-UK), Africa Now, UNDP, Aga Khan Foundation, German Agro-Action, Swiss Development Cooperation, Swiss Foundation for Technical Cooperation, CARD, K-Rep Development Agency and SNV Netherlands, as well as the Governments of Kenya and Tanzania, Honey Care undertakes village-level demonstrations, provides microfinance to smallholder farmers and offers training and community-based extension services.

Honey Care also provides a guaranteed market for the honey produced by smallholder farmers at fair trade prices (it is a member of the International Fair Trade Association), which it collects at the farm gate and pays for on the spot. It then processes, packs, and sells the honey for a profit through supermarket chains and other industrial clients. Its "Honey Care Africa" and "Beekeeper's Delight" brands are very well known in the East Africa region and have captured a significant market share.

Today Honey Care Africa employs close to 50 staff and has helped over 9000 small-scale beekeepers (representing over 38 000 direct beneficiaries) earn a supplementary income of US$180–250 per annum. For many, the income earned from honey production often makes the difference between living below or above the poverty line. Honey Care Africa is the largest producer of high-quality honey in East Africa and among the largest exporters of beeswax in the region.

Honey Care has tried to develop partnerships and find synergies whenever and wherever it is strategically important for the company. The network of community-based organizations (CBOs) and self-help groups that Honey Care has developed a working relationship with has significantly reduced the need for Honey Care to employ a large number of field staff and has allowed Honey Care to expand rapidly across Kenya.

One of the most innovative strategic partnerships that Honey Care has developed to its advantage is with Africa Now, a British NGO. Given that

Honey Care is a private company, it is not eligible to apply for direct funding from various donor agencies and international development organizations even though the work it is doing has clear and demonstrable social benefits for rural communities and the environment. Therefore, it has forged a partnership with Africa Now, and submits proposals jointly with it.

In part, the impetus for the development of this tripartite model arose from recognition of the need for a more proactive engagement of the private sector in development in Kenya. It was felt that the private sector had a number of inherent skills and valuable experience that had never been properly tapped in an integrated manner to drive forward development in Kenya. While at the same time, Honey Care recognized that this set of knowledge and skills that the private sector was endowed with was nicely complemented by the skill set of the development sector organizations. Therefore, at its center, Honey Care Africa's tripartite model sought to develop a synergistic partnership between the private sector, the development sector, and rural communities. By virtue of their different backgrounds, it was reasoned, each of the parties had a specific and complementary role to play.

The private sector organization injects a degree of economic reality into the project and ensures that the project operates within realistic market conditions at all times and is sensitive to supply–demand dynamics. This had been missing in numerous other development and income-generating projects where the development sector organization also tried to act as the link institution to the market or created a subsidized artificial market environment for the produce.

In this model, the private sector organization has a pivotal role to play. Honey Care guarantees to purchase every kilogram of honey a beekeeper can produce at a fair and fixed price, and pay in cash on the day of collection. Honey Care then processes and packs this honey and sells it for a profit. Honey Care also provides the necessary and requisite training for the rural communities.

Wherever economically viable, Honey Care also provides extension support for the farmers, and where it is not viable, alternative structures and models are developed and established to ensure that the farmers have the required technical advisory support that they need to take care of their hives and maximize honey production.

According to this model, the development sector organization (NGO, donor agency, or international development organization) should have the experience in working with rural communities and should have an extensive outreach into the rural areas, thereby making them the ideal conduit through which individuals in community groups and the private sector organization can communicate with each other initially. The development sector organization also plays an important role in acting as the primary arbitrator and mediator in this system, and therefore in the event of any misunderstanding between the private sector organization and the rural communities or any complaint from either party, the development sector organization can step in to help resolve the matter.

This system of checks and balances (where each party is held accountable to the other two parties in the model through an enforceable contract – for example, the private sector organization is accountable to both the development sector organization and the rural communities) also allows the development sector organization to ensure that an exploitative relationship does not develop between the private sector organization and the farmers. In some instances, the development sector organization also acts as the initial financier of the project, in this particular instance providing loans to farmers to acquire beehives, buy beekeeping equipment, and receive training. These loans are then recoverable at the time when the honey is ready for sale to Honey Care, which makes agreed-upon deductions from the honey as a loan repayment for the hives and makes the agreed-upon remittances to the development sector organization. These point-of-payment deductions made by Honey Care, apart from being far more efficient and cost-effective than previous mechanisms of loan recovery, also set up a "revolving fund" system where the funds injected by a development sector organization into a community-based income generation project are recoverable after a period of time, and can then be re-allocated for other projects.

The third partner in this symbiotic model are the rural communities and small-scale/subsistence farmers who are the honey producers and one of the key beneficiaries of the entire initiative. This model creates a favorable environment for them in which to start beekeeping. This is achieved through a combination of adequate training and easy access to loans to acquire beehives and other equipment, easy repayment terms, extension and advisory support, a guaranteed market for their produce at a mutually acceptable price, and cash-on-the-spot payments.

BUSINESS MODEL

The overall objective of the company is to produce and market high-quality honey that will successfully compete with honey products from elsewhere on the world market. To achieve this objective the company has opted to work with the rural community groups in an out-grower model whereby it has introduced modern beekeeping methods using the Langstroth hives. In this approach, the company closely monitors the production process to ensure the quality of honey produced by the contracted out-growers.

Honey Care makes a profit on reselling the honey produced by the farmers, while providing them with a fair price (Honey Care is a member of the International Fair Trade Association – IFAT). While this is its main source of income, it also makes some profit on the beekeeping equipment and hives that are sold to the farmers.

Honey Care primarily uses Langstroth hives and will only buy honey produced in Langstroth hives as it has found that honey from other hives is of inferior quality. Langstroth hives also produce more honey and attract bees faster than traditional hives and are superior to what has been in use in Kenya. However, more recently it has been working with beekeepers with traditional hives in order to train them on better harvesting practices and post-harvest handling. This has yielded encouraging results and an improvement in the quality of honey produced.

Initially, Honey Care Africa signed a distributor agreement with Premier Food Industries Limited (PFIL), one of East Africa's largest food product manufacturers affiliated with the Aga Khan Fund for Economic Development (AKFED), to distribute Honey Care's products across East Africa. This decision was prompted by the recognition within Honey Care that it did not have the resources to distribute its honey products to the various supermarkets and outlets and collect the payments on its own. The decision to select Premier Foods as the distributor was based on the lower distributor fee (15 percent) it offered to charge Honey Care. This was because it was impressed by the social component of Honey Care's work. Premier Foods' strong market position (it has over 65 listed processed food products on the market and its products are sold across East Africa), as well as the option of buying jars and other packing materials jointly at the discounted prices Premier Foods enjoyed, was also another reason for deciding to work with them. Further, the opportunity for joint product development like Honey Garlic Barbecue Sauce, Honey and Mustard Sauces – something it had expressed an interest in and have the food technicians on its staff to begin product development trials for – was another reason to select it as Honey Care distributor. Currently, Honey Care no longer uses Premier Foods but does its own distribution, as it has found this to be more effective and efficient.

FRANCHISEE BUSINESS MODEL

By assisting small-scale rural farmers – many of whom were earning less than US$1 per day and living below the poverty line – to get involved in beekeeping by providing them with access to loans, training, extension services, a guaranteed market, and cash on-the-spot payments for their honey,

Honey Care has been able to provide these individuals with a much-needed source of income.

Further, beekeeping has proven to be an ideal enterprise for small-scale farmers in many parts of rural Kenya because it complements existing farming systems; it is simple and relatively cheap to start, and it requires a very low level of inputs (land, labor, capital, and knowledge).

With just four beehives and 30 minutes of labor every two weeks, small-holder farmers can earn a reliable annual income between US$200–250 – an amount that is often enough to make the difference between living above or below the poverty line in Kenya. The cost to enter into the beekeeping business is around US$160 for purchasing the four hives and necessary equipment. A loan for most of this amount is often supplied by the donor agencies in the area, requiring the farmer to begin with very little initial investment of his or her own.[3] It should also be stressed that the revenue from beekeeping is supplementary income; beekeeping still gives the small-scale farmer plenty of time to tend to other responsibilities such as farming and other small enterprises that they may have.

One mandatory component is that farmers have to pay for the cost of their hives. This was mainly done through a loan system, where each farmer paid the NGO a deposit of at least 10 percent of the value of the hives, and then at least 25 percent of the proceeds of each kilogram of honey sale was deducted and remitted to the NGO as a loan repayment, until the entire loan had been repaid. Alternatively, the farmers had to pay for part of the cost of the hives (at least 25 percent of its value) upfront, with the NGO providing the rest. Honey Care does not like this latter option but has had to accept it due to pressure from the NGOs who have to spend their funds within a stipulated time period. But either way, Honey Care refuses to sell any hives to any donor agency or NGO that would then give out the hives to communities for free. This mandatory requirement that farmers who want to start beekeeping must pay for the cost of the hives was initially unpopular (especially in areas where they were used to handouts), but Honey Care insisted, and there has been a real sense of ownership that the farmers have developed over their hives. Its insistence that the hives are given out on a loan or cost-sharing basis and its refusal to work with any NGO or donor that wants to give out free hives has helped Honey Care to develop an excellent reputation among the NGOs and donor agencies in Kenya.

Further, Honey Care requires that the hives be owned individually, and not collectively. This appealed to the farmers because they would now get individual rewards for individual labor. Therefore, each hive has a serial number stamped on it, and each hive has an individual owner, regardless of whether the project is a community project or not. (The serial numbers have the added benefit of allowing Honey Care to trace all its honey back to the individual beekeeper and has enabled it to receive HACCP certification required for export.) Individual beekeepers could still collaborate and even share the beekeeping equipment (suits, smoker, hive tool, gloves, etc.), and were frequently encouraged to do so, but the hives have to be individually-owned and managed. This is mandatory.

Because of the manner in which Honey Care collects the honey (to be discussed below), it makes cash-on-the-spot payments to the farmers. This is done in a very open and transparent manner so that the farmers can see exactly how much honey they have produced (the difference in weight between the full super and the empty super after extraction).

At the time of paying the farmers, Honey Care makes the required loan repayment deductions (generally 25 percent of the value of the honey) before paying the farmers. These point-of-payment deductions are far more efficient and it ensures that farmers cannot default on their loan repayments (as opposed to a system where the farmers get paid 100 percent of the value of their produce and then pay back their loans if they want to).

The money deducted as loan repayments is then remitted to the donor agency or NGO at the end of the month, along with a list of the farmers from whom the loans have been recovered. Honey Care has gone even further with some donors and NGOs by recommending that these recovered loan repayments be used to establish a revolving fund, so that the money recovered can then be used for other development projects (or even more hives) in the future. For Honey Care, making these deductions and keeping the records is a simple and easy accounting step and adds little on a cost to its operations. However, this "full-service" approach has made Honey Care an attractive partner for donor agencies and NGOs to work with.

Again, because of the mode of payment and the loan deductions it makes, Honey Care tells its NGO partners and other donor agencies that it "takes the bank to the farmers" rather than the other way around. It tells the farmers that Honey Care has a no-nonsense "Money for Honey" policy, where they will be paid cash-on-the-spot for their honey. It has used this operational requirement to its advantage to gain publicity and make its approach even more appealing for farmers and their donors.

TRAINING

In the Honey Care model it is not the small-scale rural farmers who pay for the training but rather the NGOs and donor agencies (who can afford it) who pay for the farmers to be trained, or wealthier private farmers who can afford to pay for the cost of training.

When poor small-scale farmers approach Honey Care directly (not through a donor agency, NGO, or a self-help group, a group of retired teachers for example) about training, the training fee is generally waived. Sometimes it even pays half their food and accommodation costs at the training center. This is the standard procedure at Honey Care, although those being trained without charge might have to wait a few weeks before training with a group being funded by an NGO.

Honey Care undertakes the responsibility of training the people selected by the project implementers to ensure that the hives are properly maintained and honey production is maximized. This curriculum is equivalent to Honey Care Africa's Apiarist Level I training. This training has the following key components:

- the ecology and biology of bees;
- how to make the hives productive;
- how to harvest the honey;
- how to solve problems related to the bees and honey production.

Honey Care Africa provides the requisite written material for the trainees as well as basic pictorial reference material that succinctly summarizes some of the key aspects of the training for all trainees. It also provides its own hives and other teaching aids for the training sessions. Given the large number of trainees and the logistics of organizing the training, once it has a group of 25 people it commences training. Each training session lasts three days. However, a training schedule can be arranged to meet individual requirements within its existing courses or Honey Care can tailor a course to suit specific needs. Given the low literacy level of many farmers, Honey Care has also adapted its training approach so as to make it more hands-on, with an emphasis on practical skills development, as well as providing training in the local dialect of the farmers (in addition to the standard courses in English and Kiswahili).

Honey Care Africa offers some of the most experienced training instructors in the region. They are graduates in microbiology/environmental science, and have considerable hands-on experience as beekeepers. The course normally costs Ksh3500 (US$46). Ksh2000 (US$26) is for food and accommodation, where the rest Ksh1500 (US$20) is the tuition fee. Otherwise day scholars are charged only the Ksh1500 tuition fee.

LOCATION

Before commencement of any beekeeping project, Honey Care conducts a preliminary site evaluation of the proposed project site to assess the viability of financing each venture. Particular attention is paid to the geographical, climatic, and agro-ecological conditions of the proposed areas, as well as other logistical considerations and local conditions. Suitable sites for placing the hives are also selected once it has been verified that the initiative will be viable in that particular area. These assessment exercises primarily focus on whether the proposed area will be suitable for beekeeping using Langstroth hives, and whether the project will be economically, environmentally, and socially sustainable in the long run. Honey Care Africa then issues its recommendations to the financier or development partner on its findings and informs them whether the project will be adopted or not.

Honey Care has tried to establish projects across the country, in every area that is appropriate for beekeeping. It has hives set up in seven out of Kenya's eight provinces – they are not in North Eastern Province because it is extremely dry all year round. This strategy has diversified the risk and allowed Honey Care to produce honey around the year. As a result, Honey Care produces about 27 different flavors of honey that it then blends into the four flavors that it sells.

PRODUCT

Honey Care claims that the quality of its honey is superior to any honey that has been produced from East Africa to date, and that its unique natural flavors and blends are among the finest in the world. Its Highland Blend, Acacia, Wild Comb, and African Blossom honey have been well received and proven to be popular in the market. Honey Care is already supplying major retail outlets, hotels, and industries in Kenya with its organic honey and other related bee products. In response to consumer requirements, it also launched a range of flavor-infused honey (ginger, cinnamon, and soon mint), which is sold under the "Beekeeper's Delight" brand name.

In an effort to reach the bottom-of-the-pyramid (BOP) market, Honey Care is currently working on packaging its honey in smaller quantities in sachets, which it plans to retail through the thousands of kiosks and small shops found all over both the rural and urban areas of Kenya. Such kiosks and shops already carry soap, washing powder, and spices in smaller packages so that it is more accessible and affordable to lower-income groups in the country.

Honey Care's research on developing better beekeeping technology as well as finding methods to extract other high-quality products like pollen, beeswax, propolis, royal jelly, and bee venom is ongoing, and these improved methods will eventually be introduced through strategically selected beekeepers and community groups across the country.

DISTRIBUTION

Honey Care does not have any field offices. Its project officers are supplied with mobile phones, which its office in Nairobi uses to communicate with them. In addition, due to the good relationship it has built with its NGO and CBO partners, as well as the Local Government offices, the project officers can use their offices to send faxes and the like. Honey Care has developed a mobile extraction unit – a simple tent made of shade netting, a weighing scale, and a manually-operated centrifuge machine – which can be set up when required to collect and extract the honey from the farmers. A farmer comes in with his or her super boxes full of honey on a designated day. The super boxes are weighed, the honey is extracted, and the farmers are paid the requisite amount according to the weight of the honey. The farmers then return to their farms with their empty super boxes and continue with their beekeeping. Meanwhile, Honey Care fills the liquid and semi-processed honey (filtering is done on the spot) in 20-liter plastic containers, folds up the tent, and returns to Nairobi with the honey. The farmers are delighted with this process because Honey Care's extraction unit can be set up close to their homes for a day or two where their honey can be extracted. They don't have to travel long distances to deliver their produce to a fixed location.

For Honey Care, this method of produce collection is far cheaper and more effective; it has a "mobile factory" that can be set up whenever and wherever required in less than an hour, can extract and collect the honey, then pack everything up, and go. It tells its NGO partners and other donor agencies that Honey Care takes the factory to the farmers rather than the other way around (as is the case with all other agro-production companies in Kenya). It has used this operational requirement to its advantage to gain publicity and make its approach even more appealing for farmers and their donors.

PRICE

The price that most other buyers offer for honey is generally in the range of between KSh45 (US$0.55) and Ksh90 (US$1.125), depending on supply and demand and other factors. The price is not guaranteed and may fluctuate dramatically from one month to the next. Further, these buyers will only take what they require or force the price down as a condition to buy the entire quantity of honey from the beekeeper. In addition, using one beekeeper against another to drive the price of honey lower is a very common bargaining tactic, and the beekeeper always loses. Payments are rarely made on the spot, and there have been numerous anecdotal incidents of beekeepers being swindled by con artists.

The 2005 international price for honey is below KSh100 (US$1.20) per kilogram including freight and duty to Europe. This price has been brought down due to the increased production capacity of China, the United States, Germany, and other countries who now have the capacity to mass-produce honey on a very large scale.

On average, Honey Care's buying price ranges between KSh80 (US$1) and KSh150 (US$1.80) per kilogram of honey, depending on whether the beekeepers will deliver the honey to its factory, how long the beekeeper has been with Honey Care, the average production of the beekeeper, and other similar factors. This price is guaranteed for all the honey the beekeeper can produce, and for the entire period of the forward contract (generally two to three years), regardless of any fluctuations in the market. This guarantee to buy all the honey allows the beekeeper to rest at ease knowing that there is a ready and stable market for all his/her honey, while the price guarantee allows the beekeeper to plan ahead and forecast his/her income. In addition, Honey Care makes all payments to the beekeepers promptly, directly (no intermediaries), and always in cash. This ensures that the beekeeper's payments are never delayed and there is absolutely no room for any misappropriation of monies whatsoever – unlike what generally happens in other agricultural sectors. This instant cash payment boosts the beekeeper's morale and provides an added incentive to work harder and produce more honey.

Honey Care understands that the only way it can develop strong and sustainable partnerships in the long run is by being honest, responsible, and accountable. Honey Care is striving to operate as an ethical organization and believes in the principles of fair trade; it believes in paying a fair price and a fair wage to all those involved in the entire chain of honey production.

DIFFICULTIES

With respect to the involvement of local government people, Honey Care has had to straddle a very fine line between engaging with them and getting them too involved in the beekeeping activities. Honey Care has always made an effort to meet with the District Officers, Chiefs, Sub-Chiefs, as well as other members of the local government in the areas where it operates. Honey Care strives to develop a warm and cordial relationship with them, making courtesy calls at their offices, inviting its members to events in the area, and keeping them in the loop about any developments.

With respect to the District Beekeeping Officers (DBOs), Honey Care has followed the same approach. It has encouraged them to play a more facilitative and non-intrusive role, partly because the DBOs did not have experience with Langstroth hives. However, in some areas like Taita-Taveta and Kwale Districts, Honey Care has encouraged them to play a more direct role in providing extension services to the farmers.

Initially Honey Care didn't have the money or the resources to provide a follow-up extension service to the farmers. This created a problem because if the farmers had any trouble with their hives, they had no one to turn to. The DBOs had not seen the Langstroth hives before and were therefore not able to assist the farmers. Besides, the Ministry of Agriculture and Rural Development was severely underfunded and its field staff (like DBOs) didn't have the resources (motorbikes, bicycles) or the money (for fuel, allowances) to visit these farmers.

Honey Care decided to make use of the staff of the NGOs, CBOs and self-help groups instead. It trained them in beekeeping and provided them with additional technical skills in order to ensure that they would be able to help the farmers if they had any problems. Apart from their other ongoing responsibilities with their own organizations, in exchange for a small cash bonus from Honey Care, these staff members also informed the Honey Care office when the honey was ready for collection and the like. Honey Care still uses the staff of these partner organizations for most of its smaller projects – generally anything less than 500 hives in an area. This is because it is not economically viable to place one of its own staff members on the ground for a small number of hives. In some cases it has used some of the more skilled beekeepers in an area to help their fellow beekeepers, by implementing a small cash bonus incentive plan.

KEY SUCCESS FACTORS

Some of the keys to Honey Care's success are as follows:

- tripartite model – using NGOs to access not-for-profit funds, to fund the hives and training, and to help with some of the legwork in finding farmers;
- understanding of the marketplace, beekeeping, and the country;
- working carefully with the government's District Beekeeping Officers;
- introducing a better method of honey production to Kenya;
- maintaining quality standards and product traceability right to the farm gate in accordance with HACCP standards;

- requiring the purchase of the hives by the farmers to build a sense of ownership and self-reliance;
- long-term contracts to guarantee supply and attract more farmers;
- mobile collection and payment methods.

Franchisees' Advantage

Some of the advantages that come to a Honey Care Africa franchisee are as follows:

- training in improved apiary methods;
- very limited travel;
- purchasing contracts that guarantee a stable market;
- open and flexible contract negotiation;
- same-day payment;
- access to loans;
- extension support;
- very little time involvement;
- sense of ownership.

Further Success Factors

Before Honey Care got involved, beekeeping was exclusively an activity for men. This was because the traditional log hives were placed high on trees and therefore women could not do beekeeping. However, the Langstroth hive has a number of benefits over the traditional hives, one being that the hive is placed at the ground level and can be kept relatively close to a home. Another advantage is that harvesting is made much simpler due to the design of the hives, resulting in much less disturbance of bees during harvesting. These factors have opened up the activity to women. For its part, Honey Care has consciously tried to encourage women to take up the activity at demonstrations in the villages and by providing additional incentives and bonuses to women beekeepers. All of this has led to a positive reaction to the activity by women. This is especially important given the important role women play in the household and their general economic marginalization. Based on Honey Care's existing projects in both Kwale and Kitui Districts, it is now estimated that about 43 percent of the beekeepers are women. In Kwale District for example, over the last two years, the best beekeeper has been a woman.

Beekeeping is one of the best examples of an economic activity that uses natural resources and biodiversity in a sustainable manner. By getting more people in Kenya involved in beekeeping, Honey Care has tried to develop an environmentally sustainable economic sector, which had not been properly developed previously.

Honey Care has been able to get close to 9000 small-scale farmers involved in beekeeping, each with an average of four hives per individual. That amounts to an estimated projection of approximately US$1.5 million per annum in income that Honey Care will be helping these rural communities earn when all the hives are in full production and the farmers' loans have been paid off.

GROWTH PATTERN

By 2005, Honey Care has helped establish over 20 000 Langstroth hives across Kenya, and as a result are enabling close to 9000 rural households to earn supplementary incomes from beekeeping. In 2004, Honey Care expanded south of the border into Tanzania with the support of Swisscontact, the Swiss Development Corporation (SDC), the IFC World Bank and SNV Netherlands to engage traditional honey producers in the central and northern corridors of Tanzania. In 2005, a similar venture was begun for traditional honey producers in the Northern Rift regions of Kenya with the assistance of SNV Netherlands Kenya, the Community Development Trust Fund, and several community-based organizations.

CONCLUSION

Honey Care Africa has taken a novel approach to the problems of poverty facing farmers in Kenya. It has found a product that is in demand, that the farmers can produce with minimal training and time, and introduced the Langstroth hives to the region. It has developed relationships with NGOs and other donor agencies to leverage its funds and to extend the benefit to more farmers. Honey Care's innovative model has proven successful in a region where failures are common. Through Honey Care's efforts, the farmers, the environment, and the region are being benefited and Honey Care is growing its revenue and profits.

Honey Care Africa and its founders have received numerous international awards for its work, including the "Equator Initiative Prize" at the World Summit on Sustainable Development (2002), the "International Development Marketplace Innovation Award" in partnership with Africa Now from the World Bank and Soros Open Societies Institute (2002), and the "World Business Award" from the Prince of Wales International Business Leaders Forum and UNDP (2004). Honey Care also received the coveted "Kenya Quality Award" in the Small and Medium Enterprise Category from the Kenya Bureau of Standards (2004). Honey Care was recently named the "Top Small to Medium Sized Business in Africa" for 2005–06 at the SMME Awards in South Africa. It also received "First Prize in the Renewable Energy and Environment Category" at the same event.

NOTES .

1. Most of this text comes directly from honeycareafrica.com; it has been edited and changed from first to third person.
2. Exchange rate that calculations are based on is 80 Kenyan shillings per US$.
3. Gibson, S. and Fairbourne, J. (2005), *Where There Are No Jobs*, vol. 4, Provo, UT: Academy for Creating Enterprise.

9. Franchising health care for Kenya: the HealthStore Foundation model[1]

Michelle Fertig and Herc Tzaras

COMPANY PROFILE

While there are many providers of basic medication in Kenya in higher density areas, millions of Kenyans live hours away from the nearest reliable supply of quality medicine. Where providers do exist, pharmaceuticals are frequently overpriced, suffer from quality issues, are often not in stock, or are inaccessible to the local population. The non-profit HealthStore Foundation (formerly Sustainable Healthcare Enterprise Foundation) was founded to address some of these issues and operates as the franchisor of for-profit Child and Family Wellness shops and clinics (CFWshops) in three main regions of Kenya – Embu, Nairobi, and Western Kenya. HF[2] is incorporated in both the United States and Kenya (as HealthStore Kenya) and provides financial, marketing, procurement, and other support services to its franchise locations.

HF's overall mission is "To improve access to essential drugs, basic health care, and prevention services for children and families in the developing world using business models that are scaleable, maintain standards, and achieve economies of scale." To this end, the first CFWshops were established in Kenya, in 2000, to provide affordable medical care for easily treatable conditions such as malaria and diarrhea. HF's franchise model attempts to address these issues head on by offering standard prices; compelling owners to purchase quality pharmaceuticals; and by building a trusted brand, recognizable to consumers. HF ensures compliance with its standards through regular monitoring of individual locations and a threat of closure significant enough to minimize franchisees' incentives to cheat.

As of 2005, the CFWshops network includes 42 shops (owned by community health workers) and 22 clinics (owned by nurses) that serve roughly 400 000 patients per year on a run-rate basis. On average, individual franchises have reached a point of self-sustainability and the net donor funding required for HF's central operations is less than US$1 million annually. The three-year goal is to expand from 64 locations serving 400 000 patients per year to over 200 locations serving over 1.5 million patients per year.

Apart from the obvious impact of providing affordable, accessible, and high-quality pharmaceuticals and preventative products to the population of Kenya, CFWshops locations create two important secondary benefits. When a CFWshop enters a market, competitors are forced to improve prices, availability, and quality to compete. At the same time, health workers and nurses are provided with a living income. Community Health Workers earn an average annual income of US$600–800; nurses earn an average salary of US$1000–1400, with variance based on individual franchise sales.[3]

The principal benefit of the franchise model is that it provides effective incentives for outlet owners and thereby delivers a higher quality of care and social return on investment than is typically realized in other rural health care models. The franchise model is scaleable, self-sustaining at the outlet level, and with reliable start-up capital, replicable in other countries.

HF continues to improve its operational strategy and the performance of the individual franchises. Charles Slaughter, former president, was instrumental in implementing the appropriate business practices to improve individual shop performance before opening additional outlets. Slaughter's guidance and CFWshops' central team's efforts have paid off: as a result of a series of highly successful promotional campaigns, outlets reported serving 344 505 patients through September 2005, more than three times the number served in the same period of 2004. Patient visits per outlet increased 162 percent over the same period. The increase in patient visits drives better financial results: sales per outlet more than doubled year to date over 2004, as of September 2005, and seasonally adjusted sales per outlet hit all-time highs in five consecutive months starting May 2005.

Despite the typical operational challenges that many small and growing companies have to address, the dominant impression of CFWshops is one of solid progress. Shop-level compliance is dramatically improved and marketing efforts are clearly paying dividends. In 2004–05, HF received grants, donations, and pledges surpassing two million dollars, a major financial commitment to the HealthStore Foundation.[4] The HealthStore Foundation uses donor money to expand CFWshops' in-service franchisee training and to support network services such as compliance, delivery, evaluation, and promotion. One of the key pillars of the HealthStore Foundation's vision is to promote and support the replication of its franchising model, which organizations across Africa, India, and South America have expressed interest in adapting. To this end, HealthStore Foundation representatives have presented at numerous conferences, including the Bill and Melinda Gates

Foundation-funded SEAM Conference in Ghana (Strategies for Enhancing Access to Essential Medicines).[5] In the future, the HealthStore Foundation intends to put CFWshops and its Kenyan parent company on a path to greater independence. Meanwhile, the HealthStore Foundation is advising business leaders in India and Ghana who plan to launch new franchise health networks. These new networks are inspired by the example of CFWshops in Kenya, and will have their own local boards of directors, executives, staff, and brand names. The HealthStore Foundation is also considering developing the necessary materials to enter into master franchise agreements with business leaders in the developing world. Such agreements, common to the world of commercial franchising, would allow the HealthStore Foundation to spread the CFWshops brand throughout the developing world with necessary mechanisms in place to control the use of the CFWshops brand.

COMPANY ORIGINS

In a well-publicized story, Scott Hillstrom, then managing partner of a US-based commercial law firm, founded Cry for the World Foundation (now the HealthStore Foundation) in 1997 after being involved in a serious car crash in New Zealand. While lying on the side of the road waiting for help, Hillstrom made a commitment to dedicate his life to helping others. Immediately before the crash, Hillstrom had read about the number of preventable child deaths in Africa caused by poor drug distribution; to fulfill his personal commitment, he dedicated himself to helping reverse this trend. After meeting with Eva Ombaka, a pharmaceutical advisor to the World Council of Churches in Kenya, Hillstrom and Ombaka formed Cry, modeled on the principles of a franchise system. Cry was founded as a non-profit organization, while the individual franchise locations (CFWshops) operated (and still do) as for-profit enterprises. The foundation formally changed its name to Sustainable Healthcare Enterprise Foundation and then, in 2005, to the HealthStore Foundation (HF) as part of an effort to simplify and consolidate its brand.

OVERALL ORGANIZATIONAL STRUCTURE AND BUSINESS MODEL

The HealthStore Foundation is a US 501(c)(3) not-for-profit corporation. The HealthStore Foundation currently supports a Kenyan non-profit NGO, Sustainable Healthcare Foundation, which acts as a franchisor and runs the branded CFWshops franchise network in Kenya. Currently, the bulk of the fundraising and strategy work occur in the United States while the day-to-day management of operations occurs in Kenya.[6]

Business Model – Overview

HF loans new franchisees up to 88 percent of the start-up capital (approximately US$1700) required for inventory purchases to open a new store. Franchisees make a cash investment of US$200, and are given three to five years at below market interest rates to repay a US$500 working capital loan. Another US$1000 no-interest fixed capital loan is provided for store fixtures, signage, and tenant improvements to franchisees in good standing.

CFWshops owners receive an established brand and strong central support, making them better prepared to turn around and re-pay the franchisor. Franchisees agree to maintain company standards regarding inventory availability, procurement, signage, and customer service.

CFWshops' parent company is deeply engaged in franchises' operations, monitoring each for policy compliance and providing ongoing support, which includes training, streamlined procurement, product logistics, product formularies, and financing and marketing. CFWshops outlets that do not comply with standards have their franchise licenses revoked and the store is either closed down or placed under new management. HF's long-term goal is to achieve a self-sustaining model where at least 70 percent of shops are profitable to the point of providing the owner with "a reasonable living income."

Business Model – Revenue Model

When the CFWshops first opened, their parent company collected its franchise fee as a percentage of total sales. They soon discovered widespread under-reporting among franchisees, whose incentive to under-report sales trumped the risk of getting caught. As a result, CFWshops' parent company now builds its franchise fee into the wholesale price of drugs provided to each shop. Shop owners are obligated to purchase drugs from their parent company (who in turn purchase from MEDS)[7] with 5 percent of added margin built into the price to cover franchise costs. CFWshops' parent company then ensures compliance with the procurement policy through site visits (both announced and unannounced). CFWshops outlets that do not comply with standards have their franchise licenses revoked and the store is either closed down or placed under new management.

Financing franchisees' start-up costs is not merely intended as a revenue generator for CFWshops' parent company; without this assistance, many franchisees would be without recourse. It took CFWshops' parent company some time however, to find the right balance between financial support and overburdening franchisees with interest payments. In the late 1990s, shop owners could borrow up to 80 percent of the required capital (to cover inventory, fixed assets, initial salary costs). That loan was repaid at a rate of 18 percent. However, interest payments often consumed all of the shops' profits, leading to operational distress among the owners, and, in turn, delinquent accounts. As part of an overall plan to improve store performance, CFWshops' parent company restructured many loans, in some cases writing off as much as US$600 per shop. Now, CFWshops' parent company provides a loan of up to US$500 for working capital while requiring owners to put up a US$100–200 investment. CFWshops' parent company also owns the fixed assets of new locations through a no-interest US$1000 loan, simplifying transfers of ownership that result from non-compliance or poor performance.

While individual CFWshops are sustainable, profitable businesses, core support from the non-profit HealthStore Foundation will cost about US$1 million annually to manage a full deployment of approximately 200 outlets. Estimated income from financing and franchise fees will only account for US$150 000 per year in the long term. Despite this shortfall, the HealthStore Foundation is capable of raising necessary capital through grants and private donations – as a non-profit, it is uniquely positioned to raise development funds in order to support a network of for-profit enterprises. At a net cost of less than US$1 per patient served, this represents a cost-effective model for providing life-saving treatment – and one that provides a living income for franchisees.[8]

Business Model – HealthStore Outlet Level Models

At its inception, CFWshops' parent company managed two broad classes of outlet-level business models: a nurse-operated clinic and a community health-worker (CHW)-operated shop. There are key distinctions between the models:

1. Product formulary. Nurse-operated clinics are able (by law) to offer a wider variety of products. A typical CHW-operated shop is confined primarily to malaria, diarrhea, and amoebasis (stomach worms) drugs in addition to related health products such as mosquito nets and water treatment products. Nurse-operated clinics, however, can expand upon these offerings to include a range of antibiotics.
2. Services provided. Nurses are able to provide more services to their clientele. Legally, they are able to consult on a broader range of health

issues, which enable nurses to make more diagnoses and charge for these consultations.
3. Level of "living income". Nurses typically have higher opportunity costs than their community health worker counterparts. Nurses are educated and certified to work in any health-related field, and are therefore more employable. As such, nurses require a more profitable store to provide a comparable salary to what they would receive elsewhere.

As a result of these distinctions, nurse-operated clinics generally serve 50–80 percent more patients than health-worker-operated shops. The subsequent difference in financial performance is significant, with nurse-operated clinics generating an estimated annual net profit of US$1000–1400 compared with only US$600–800 for a CHW-operated shop.

As a result of the financial performance and greater impact on public health offered by nurse-operated clinics, HF is focusing primarily on these clinics as it moves forward. From a financial and performance perspective, such a decision makes sense, but is subject to the greater challenge of recruiting nurses who are capable of owning and operating a shop.

Franchisees' Advantage

The CFWshops franchise is attractive to practicing community health workers, nurses, and pharmacists for a variety of reasons:

- *Standardization.* Every CFWshops outlet has a consistent aesthetic, uses standard marketing materials, and operates under standardized franchise regulations.
- *Business and clinical training.* Owners undergo a four-week training program, which is critical as many do not have basic business skills.
- *Reports and analyses.* CFW shops and clinics receive cumulative quarterly reports from which owners are able to benchmark against other locations, along with interpretation and support from the field officers.
- *Strategic outlook and direction.* CFWshops has a dedicated central management team and guidance from the HealthStore Foundation's international Board of Directors that bring significant strategic capabilities to guide overall direction, growth, and performance strategy.
- *Ready-made, proven promotions.* CFWshops' parent company pre-tests promotions using a sample of its shops and clinics before rolling out to the broader network, ensuring that unsuccessful promotion campaigns are weeded out before broad implementation.

- *Consistent, regional support.* Field officers visit shops and clinics periodically to help owners and employees comply with CFWshops standards, interpret management reports from the home office and also conduct ongoing training.
- *Community trust.* CFWshops have built brand name recognition within the communities they serve. While national and international brand recognition will take time to develop, franchise owners report that trust in their shops develop best when they highlight their membership in a larger organization.
- *Lower cost structure.* In addition to discounted medication provided by MEDS, CFWshops and clinics do not have to worry about many of the marketing, training, and operational functions performed by the central franchisor. Also, dealing with regulators is simplified as government officials are referred directly to CFWshops' parent company.

SOCIAL IMPACT

Sixty-four CFWshops locations have served a combined total of over 750 000 patients since inception and, on a combined run-rate basis, serve approximately 400 000 patients per year. A network of 200+ locations, to be built by 2008, will serve between 1.5 and 2 million patients per year.[9]

While the number of patients served provides an objective measure of societal impact, it is not necessarily the metric to which HF assigns the most weight. As its stated mission is to improve access to quality health care, HF favors locations where access to health care was previously limited or non-existent; however these areas have lower anticipated patient volumes than areas of higher population where competition, and therefore access to health care, already exists.

HF is currently planning a controlled, academically rigorous study to examine the impact of CFWshops on public health outcomes over time.

Access

First and foremost, CFWshops and clinics provide access to quality health care for the communities in which they operate. Simply put, they provide affordable, effective, in-stock medicines, and pride themselves on quality service and accurate diagnoses and prescriptions.

To ensure quality of service and transparency throughout the network, CFWshops' parent company regularly monitors its locations for compliance with the franchise agreement. Drug prices are fixed and must be visibly displayed, and essential medicines must always be in stock. Franchisees must purchase their medicines through their franchisor, thereby guaranteeing wholesale-priced drugs that are approved, effective, tested, and not expired. Regular monitoring ensures uniform quality throughout the CFWshops brand, which is critical for a franchise operation with a nationwide marketing strategy.

CFWshops and clinics operate in urban, peri-rural, and rural areas (with populations of at least 5000) where there are few or no *quality* pharmacies and clinics available. For HF, one component of increasing "access" to health care is treating patients that might otherwise have gone without treatment. As such, clinics are no more than an hour's walk away for the population they are intended to serve, thereby lowering transportation costs that might otherwise be a disincentive for patients seeking treatment.

Customers that frequent CFWshops and clinics are attracted not only by proximity, affordable prices, and product variety, but also by high-quality customer service. Even if there are comparable pharmacies in the community, customers return to CFWshops and clinics because of owners' relationships with their community. Customers trust CFWshops owners and know that they will receive attention, unlike other pharmacies or clinics that either want to push sales or are overcrowded. CFWshop and clinic owners are specially trained in customer service and taught to develop long-term relationships and encourage repeat visits. Customers who have access to this exceptional service often return for all their medical needs, knowing that the treatment will be effective, even if a certain drug can be found for less at a competitor's shop.

Health Education

Communities benefit from the shops' outreach efforts. During school screening promotions, for example, children and parents are educated in basic health care, including topics that extend beyond the scope of the CFWshops' product line. In addition to school screenings, CFWshops' parent company also organizes "awareness days" to mobilize community health efforts and educate parents about common diseases.[10]

Such investigations provide more comprehensive assessments of children's health, and franchise owners are trained to help families with basic health and hygiene.[11] As a result of community outreach, franchise owners are regarded as health experts rather than simply medical shop clerks. Working alongside government and education officials further enhances the credibility and the perceived competence of the owners and CFWshops employees. Community outreach campaigns are developed and tested by CFWshops' parent company and executed by CFWshops franchisees. They go beyond product demonstrations by providing community support for disease prevention, identification, and treatment.

Price Convergence

The average price of anti-malarial medicine varies significantly, even within the same class of generic drug. For example, within the city of Kitengala, prices for treatment of malaria using generics range between 60–100 Ksh (US$0.80–1.30). Non-CFW pharmacies rarely display prices, and competitors often charge different amounts to different people for the same medication. In more remote locations where there is only one provider, monopolistic practices exploit community members.

By offering high-quality anti-malarial drugs at below-market prices, CFWshops create two price impacts. A first-order effect is that consumers pay less by purchasing from CFWshops as opposed to purchasing from pharmacies, hospitals, and other competitors. Second, the introduction of CFWshops often catalyzes competitors to reduce prices, also resulting in consumer savings – even if they never visit a CFWshop.

Availability

As a measure of compliance with the franchise agreement, CFWshops' parent company regularly monitors CFWshops locations for inventory levels. One of the HealthStore Foundation's primary missions is to have drugs available when needed. Similar to price and quality issues, availability in CFWshops may increase availability in competitor locations; however, the effect is almost impossible to quantify.

Franchise Owners' Income

Apart from the health benefits provided to society, there are also benefits in terms of providing income for nurses and community health workers. A nurse can expect to earn roughly US$754 in a government hospital,[12] but owning a CFW clinic brings in an average annual net cash salary of US$600–1400.[13] Some nurses migrate to other countries in order to advance their careers in the form of higher salaries, lower occupational risk (e.g., lack of protective equipment afforded by Kenyan hospitals), more efficient health systems, and welfare and/or Social Security benefits. Many of these nurses would rather not leave their nursing careers in Kenya.[14] The costs of emigration are too high for many qualified nurses to leave the country; many do not want to leave behind family and cultural roots for the promise of a strange life in a foreign country. CFW clinics are an alternative for nurses: owning a franchise provides career advancement, a sustainable income, fewer occupational risks (i.e., franchises stock essential medicines and preventative care products, and don't treat trauma patients), and fewer bureaucratic headaches.[15] Clinic owners not only treat patients and operate their own businesses, but also earn a sustainable income by serving their own communities.

HF's strategy for maximizing impact is to open new franchises only in areas with significant barriers preventing access to essential medicines. However, from the above analysis, it is likely that there is a positive impact on society regardless of the shops' location. Furthermore, urban CFWshops tend to have higher sales and profits than their rural counterparts and as such, are useful in terms of funding CFWshops' expansion into under-serviced rural regions.

SHOP-LEVEL PERFORMANCE

Financial Performance Indicators

Historically, there have been two types of CFW outlets: clinics and shops. Compared with the shops, the nurse-owned clinics average 59 percent more gross drug sales and 56 percent greater profit (before loan payments to CFWshops' parent company), despite the increased inventory costs and payroll expenses. Clinics have a higher bottom line because nurses are certified to sell additional drugs and are able to diagnose additional illnesses, earning them additional consultation fees. In the past, CFWshops' parent company has had difficulty regulating consultation fees charged by individual franchises, leaving it to the discretion of store owners. CFWshops' parent company plans to begin posting and tracking a fixed price list of consulting fees in its franchises.

In addition to increased sales, clinics perform better than the shops on other measures. Outlets are evaluated monthly on various performance metrics, such as drug management, patient care, financial management, and community awareness. The performance levers that affect sales include the following:

1. franchisee entrepreneurship and initiative;
2. effective promotion and marketing (including community networking);
3. being in stock on all essential items; having outlets that appear "full" of merchandise;
4. actual and perceived quality of service, care and diagnosis;
5. high traffic location.

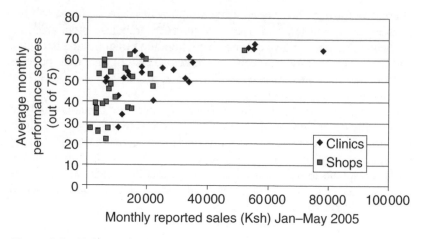

Figure 9.1 Relationship between HS performance levels and monthly sales

Figure 9.1 depicts the positive, linear relationship between average monthly scores on these performance levers and average monthly sales. These data were collected for 23 clinics and 27 shops in the Embu region during 2005. Figure 9.1 clearly shows that better scores on the evaluation rubric are correlated with profitability. Owners that take good care of their shops, inventory, customers, and community tend to sell more medicine and preventative products.[16]

The outlets that performed the best in this sample had the following characteristics:

- clean environments in and around the outlet;
- available (in-stock) HF-approved drugs;
- attractive arrangements of pre-packaged products;
- excellent customer care, including providing appropriate counseling and diagnoses, and first-rate customer service; and
- effective promotional and community outreach activities.

It is not surprising that the clinics scored better than shops on patient care: clinics averaged a 13 (out of 15) in the patient care performance lever; shops' average was 8. Field officers measure patient care based on customer service (e.g., appropriate prescription and counseling, medicines properly and hygienically handled, language used is understandable and clear to clients) and infection control standards. All outlet owners are given in-depth training in patient care, but registered nurses in clinic settings are setting the clear standard in this category.

One interesting discovery was that the CFWshops and clinics, on average, performed about the same in terms of the community awareness performance lever. The shops scored an average of 2.5 out of 5, and the clinics scored 2.4. While community awareness stands to be improved, shops and clinics continue to participate in organizational promotions. In addition to patient care, this community awareness is highly correlated to outlet sales and continues to develop and improve through ongoing promotions.

It is evident that CFW clinics perform better than shops both financially and operationally. HF has recognized this pattern and will focus primarily on clinics either owned by or employing a registered nurse as the network continues to expand.

MARKETING

Core marketing activities are largely handled by the CFWshops' central office; however individual locations have the opportunity to develop their own marketing plans in coordination with a local field officer, so long as they are complementary with brand-wide strategy.

Testing Marketing Campaigns

Marketing campaigns may involve price reductions, community outreach efforts, or new product introductions. In the past, money from the Acumen Fund[17] supported testing of marketing and promotional campaigns in a limited number of locations before franchise-wide implementation. While this partnership is not continuing into the future, HF plans to repeat the most successful of these tested promotions in 2006.

Product

The core product strategy is centrally controlled. CFWshops' parent company has an agreement with MEDS (a non-profit wholesaler of generic pharmaceuticals) to provide the primary pharmaceutical line. Related products (e.g., mosquito nets) are also centrally purchased by CFWshops' parent company and distributed to the individual locations.[18]

In order to maintain product quality standards and allow CFWshops' parent company to collect its royalties, individual shops and clinics must purchase products from CFWshops' parent company. CFWshops' parent company also uses its sole-provider status to audit sales and profitability (through inventory reconciliation) throughout the franchise network.

Product offerings differ between shops and clinics. Traditional shops (that did not employ a nurse) offered a narrower list of medications. Clinics offer the standard medications – approximately 150 products – as well as antibiotics and basic lab/diagnostic services. With most CFW franchises moving to a clinic model, the product offered throughout the system will be standardized.

Pricing

Pricing is also set centrally by CFWshops' parent company. Signs are provided to each location that clearly state standard prices, and franchise regulations mandate they be prominently displayed. Consistent pricing throughout the CFWshops network is critical to maintaining brand image and in achieving the HealthStore Foundation's mission. Effective implementation of a standard pricing scheme has proven difficult.

In visits to four CFWshops locations in mid-2005, none of the clinics displayed the standard price list. Even though the franchisees are consistently penalized in the Supervisory Checklist, they choose not to display the price list. The incentive for franchisees to inflate prices is strong. An owner's decision not to post the standard prices often stems from their desire to charge a rate that is more in line with what they feel the market will bear. Other times, owners wish to retain flexibility in charging consultation fees, which they selectively bury in the price of their products. In dealing with the latter case, CFWshops' parent company is standardizing consultation fees across the network. Nevertheless, the remaining uncertainty in actual prices being charged poses problems for CFWshops' parent company in evaluating success in terms of revenue and profit.

Stemming franchisees' non-compliance in pricing practices requires continued (or increased) vigilance by the field officers and stricter penalties for non-compliance. Beyond the current practice of field officer price display checks, further approaches to ensure compliance include customer interviews and secret shoppers. CFWshops' parent company plans to implement both approaches on a sample basis.

A key element of the HealthStore Foundation model is consistent pricing throughout the network, regardless of location. Other retailers often charge more for medication in remote areas and justify those higher prices on the basis of transportation costs. However, these rural areas typically have a lower per-capita income, exaggerating the gap between consumers' ability to pay and the retail price. The HealthStore Foundation is currently in the preliminary stages of designing a third-party payment administrative system that would allow franchisees to be reimbursed the full cost of drugs and services provided to customers who cannot afford the full cost. While most customers can afford the treatment they need, some cannot, and treating such customers creates a drain on franchisees. A third-party payment administrative mechanism in which donor funds could be placed in a pool to reimburse franchisees for services rendered to poorer customers would fulfill HF's mission while retaining the integrity of the business model.

Promotion

CFWshops' parent company emphasizes promotional campaigns on a franchise-wide level and supports these promotions through a CFWshops central staff team that works with individual franchisees on implementation. Campaigns are tested in a sample group of shops to ensure effectiveness before wider implementation.[19]

Measuring the success of marketing campaigns is inherently difficult, given the challenge of identifying the portion of sales increase directly attributable to the campaign. However, CFWshops' parent company has noted that same-store sales typically plateau after 6–12 months, fluctuating within a narrow ±20 percent range, if no interventions are taken. A clear picture of this volatility aids CFWshops' parent company in discerning the impact of campaigns on sales.

CFWshops' most successful marketing campaigns focus on community outreach. Price promotions on preventative products, like bed nets, have also been extremely successful, as customers regularly stock these products in their homes. Contrarily, price promotions on treatment products, such as Amodiaquine, a common anti-malaria medicine, have met with unexpectedly low success. Customers do not commonly stock such products in their homes, opting instead to seek them out when the need arises.

Local promotional activities include distributing promotional flyers at local markets or bus stops, providing free house calls, setting up tables after church services, and placing sandwich boards at busy locations.

TRAINING

The high success rate of franchise businesses stems from the use of a proven business model, in concert with the management and administrative systems provided by the franchisor.[20] CFWshops' parent company provides management and administrative support through upfront and ongoing business and clinical training. In fact, training is a part of compliance.

Before franchisees can open their outlets, they undergo four cumulative weeks of training. Training classes include between 10–20 new franchisees and provide a full range of relevant training from business management to medical skills.

Training does not end after the first four weeks; CFWshops' parent company emphasizes ongoing franchisee support. After an outlet has been open for three months, franchisees receive one day of "continuing information" training from central staff. In addition, each month, field officers provide support days, during which they talk to each franchisee and provide necessary business or medical support (for example, reviewing inventory management techniques). During the franchisees' monthly evaluations, they are asked to request specific training needs; given sufficient demand, a trainer from CFWshops headquarters will provide a training course at the closest regional field office.

One difficulty with the provision of ongoing training is that franchisees frequently request topic sessions that relate to drug usage and medical diagnostics, with the goal of increasing revenues from consultations. While a valuable skill, increased medical knowledge does not address the primary issue of increasing business acumen. Often, the skills that are most needed – inventory and cash flow management skills – are not as valuable from the franchisees' point of view and therefore not requested.

Another issue with the ongoing training involves the CFWshops manual. All franchisees are given business and clinical reference manuals to help answer questions that may arise after the initial training. Like most reference manuals in most organizations, these manuals are rarely read or referred to when a franchisee has a question. The HealthStore Foundation recognizes that disregard of the manual, which embodies the standard operating procedures of CFW outlets, will lead to failure to maintain clinical standards once the network scales to hundreds of outlets. Thus, the HealthStore Foundation is planning to engage a high-level franchise consultant to rework the CFWshops manual so that franchisees will use it regularly. Furthermore, important training support occurs after initial training, during monthly, one-on-one meetings between local field officers and franchise owners.

CFWshops' parent company distributes monthly newsletters, which highlight selected owners' successes and provide refreshers on franchise policy or new reporting techniques. Annually, all franchisees reunite at CFWshops headquarters in Nairobi to discuss the past year's financial results and social impact, and to share lessons learned and best practices.

PROCUREMENT

CFWshops' parent company obtains all of its products from MEDS, a non-profit supplier of generic medications. As a non-profit, MEDS is able to provide medication at prices 10–15 percent lower than other wholesalers. However, to qualify, the purchasing entity must also have non-profit status. The non-profit status of CFWshops' central operations enable it to pass on low prices to franchisees even after building a 5 percent mark-up into the price.

Originally, MEDS provided more logistical support than it does today, delivering medication directly to the individual CFWshops, regardless of order size. Today, CFWshops' parent company operates a distribution center and MEDS no longer performs this function.

PARTNERSHIP STRATEGY

HealthStore has three classes of partners:

1. Government. CFWshops' parent company works with representatives from the Kenyan government. Apart from seeking approvals for new locations, CFWshops' parent company partners with the government at all levels to shape policy in a way that is favorable to the delivery of health care in Kenya. CFWshops' parent company also works with local governments to ensure the presence of CFWshops' representatives at school screenings and other community outreach programs that lend credibility to the individual shop/clinic's marketing and promotion efforts.
2. Foreign Donors. While opening and operating a clinic costs very little, it still requires some capital to leverage an equity investment by the owner. Approximately US$1 000 000 is raised annually from various donors, including corporations, foundations, and private donors.
3. Suppliers. MEDS (Mission for Essential Drugs and Services) has been absolutely critical to CFWshops' and clinics' operation by providing low-cost medication. While CFWshops was scaling its operation, MEDS shipped medication directly to the individual locations. As the CFWshops network grew, direct delivery was no longer possible, but by then it had sufficient scale to support the franchise locations with an internal distribution and logistics network.

POLITICAL AND REGULATORY ASSESSMENT

The political and regulatory environment in Kenya is a challenging one in which to operate, particularly in the health care industry. Requirements for the establishment of new pharmacies, shops, or clinics are not clear, and the actual application of these regulations differs from region to region based on the whims of local health officials.[21] CFWshops' parent company, however, is able to deal effectively with these complexities through strategic relationships, thus removing a major burden from the franchise owners and also influencing or forecasting future regulatory decisions.

From a franchisee's point of view, CFWshops' parent company provides valuable support when dealing with the Ministry of Health (MoH) along two key dimensions. CFWshops' parent company handles all regulatory work related to establishing a franchise and obtains approval to open a new clinic. Owners also refer MoH officials directly to CFWshops' parent company whenever there is an issue with ongoing operations. While both of these services are invaluable to franchise owners, the former is of particular importance given the lack of a clear approval process for a new clinic.

CFWshops' parent company's Deputy Director, Julius Ombogo, provides key support with regard to the regulatory environment. As a member of the Pharmacy and Poisons Board (a regulatory agency for trade in pharmaceuticals) he is knowledgeable and experienced with government bureaucracy. Also, since Julius is involved with both CFWshops and the regulatory agency, his contribution in shaping government policy facilitates the expansion of CFWshops in Kenya. These connections have facilitated the establishment of CFWshops in Kenya since Julius joined the organization in 2004.

CONCLUSION

Ambitious mission statements are often written off by critics as overly optimistic. "To improve access to essential drugs, basic health care, and prevention services for children and families in the developing world using business models that are scaleable, maintain standards, and achieve economies of scale" – the HealthStore Foundation's mission statement – might be so criticized. Yet by supporting their ambition with a creative business model, anchored by proven principles like brand trust, franchisee buy-in, ongoing training, and community outreach, the HealthStore Foundation has given critics a source of hope.

It is possible to treat malaria, diarrhea, tuberculosis, and hundreds of other diseases that kill millions each year in developing countries. The medications exist. And by adding value to health care service delivery, the HealthStore Foundation demonstrates that it is possible to provide these medications cheaply and effectively. Delivery systems are often an impediment to access, but the HealthStore Foundation has leveraged local talent to provide treatment where it is most needed, while supporting a local business ecosystem by keeping profits in franchisees' hands. In 2005 alone, the CFWshops network treated over 400 000 patients for an average cost of less than US$1 per treatment.

What remains to be seen is whether the HealthStore Foundation can replicate its success to scale in Kenya and throughout low-income countries around the world. But it is apparent that such ambitious social missions, frequently considered optimistic, can at once be realistic, when tempered by the business discipline of the private sector.

NOTES

1. In the summer of 2005, Michelle Fertig and Herc Tzaras traveled to Kenya to assess the effectiveness of the HealthStore Foundation franchise model. The following is an abbreviated version of their report, with the full version available on the World Resources Institute (WRI) website: www.nextbillion.net/HealthStore-Case-Study. Further information about the HealthStore Foundation can be found at www.cfwshops.org. The authors would like to thank WRI for organizing and supporting this study.
2. HF acronym used for brevity within text.
3. Payroll calculated as average from HealthStore Consolidated Income Statements, January through September 2005 and interviews with franchise owners and CFWshops management. By comparison, the average salary for a trained Kenyan nurse is US$754, according to data from SalaryExpert.com, a leading provider of online salary data. Available at http://www.salaryexpert.com. Accessed 1 November, 2005.
4. The HealthStore Foundation recently received a $20 000 grant from the Donner Foundation, $50 000 from the Mulago Foundation, and the first US$350 000 of a three-year, US$1 million commitment from the Oswald family. In the last two months, eight people have committed $4700 each to sponsor CFWshops outlets. Additional key supporters include the Rockefeller Foundation, Bill and Melinda Gates Foundation, and forthcoming support from USAID.
5. Details, including full conference proceedings, are available at http://www.msh.org/seam/conference2005.
6. The HealthStore Foundation is also advising business leaders in India and Ghana to launch independent franchise networks, and is considering developing the materials necessary to begin offering master franchise agreements to business leaders in developing countries.
7. Mission for Essential Drugs and Supplies (MEDS) is an ecumenical organization headquartered in Kenya to support church health facilities and other non-profit health care providers. MEDS provides approved, tested, high-quality generic drugs and medical supplies at affordable prices through non-profit re-sale.
8. Net cost per patient is the quoted average patient transaction cost per the HealthStore Shops Consolidated Income Statements, January through September 2005.
9. The most common diseases treated by CFWshops are respiratory infections (30 percent), malaria (23 percent), worms (11 percent) and pain/inflammation (10 percent). Franchises also sell a variety of preventative products such as mosquito nets, condoms, and soap.
10. Mbeere District Malaria Day, for instance, brought 2000 people from the Mbeere District together to obtain information on the prevention and treatment for malaria. Franchise owners are also encouraged to make home visits in their community and screen the communities' children.

11. Basic health assessments include weighing and measuring children, maintaining immunization records, and promoting the use of anti-mosquito bed nets.

12. The average salary for a trained Kenyan nurse is US$754, according to data from SalaryExpert.com, a leading provider of online salary data. Available at http://www.salaryexpert.com.

13. Net cash income for nurses per HealthStore Consolidated Income Statement January through September 2005, interviews with franchise owners and HS management.

14. www.academyhealth.org.

15. CFWshops executive staff act as intermediaries between franchisees and government officials – thereby reducing nurses' exposure to tedious bureaucracy.

16. Out of 75 possible performance points for these levers, the clinics' average performance score was 54 with a minimum score of 28; whereas, the shops' average performance was 45 with a minimum score of 22. The average reported monthly sales for clinics were 26 506 Ksh (US$345), and the average monthly reported sales for shops were 10 665 Ksh (US$138).

17. Acumen Fund is a non-profit global venture fund that uses entrepreneurial approaches to solve the problems of global poverty. Available at http://www.acumenfund.org.

18. The three basic product categories that CFWshops stock are: required medications (e.g., anti-malarials), non-required medications (e.g., antibiotics) and peripheral health products (e.g., toothpaste, condoms).

19. For example, in January and February of 2005, CFWshops offered the following promotions: 1. anti-malaria campaign: a 50 percent discount on bed nets and Amodiaquine; 2. water treatment campaign: free treated water up to 5 liters per family per week at the HealthStore shop; 3. free consultation, de-worming, and growth check for children under the age of five; 4. school screening programs.

20. According to the Small Business Administration, less than 5 percent of all franchise units fail each year compared with 30–35 percent of small businesses that fail within the first year of operation (www.franchise.com).

21. Details on Kenya's regulatory environment and how it relates to starting and running a business can be found in the 2006 edition of *Doing Business*, published by the World Bank Group. Available: www.doingbusiness.org.

10. Vodacom Community Services: rural telephone access for South Africa[1]

Lisa Jones Christensen, Jennifer (Reck) Van Kirk and Brad Wood

Cell phones have become a prime example of a technology that benefits many different user groups – minimally, the individuals who use the phones as well as those who sell the phone services. Additionally, the benefits mobile phones bring at a local level can even be extended to a country as a whole. A 2005 study by the Centre for Economic Policy Research found higher rates of economic growth in developing countries with high mobile phone penetration. According to the study, a developing country that has an average of ten more mobile phones per 100 people (between 1996 and 2003), would have enjoyed per capita GDP growth that was 0.59 percent higher than an otherwise identical country.[2] The survey also found a number of other benefits from mobile phone usage and ownership including:

- Mobiles save people living in rural communities the financial costs and time involved with travel. As a result, 85 percent of people in Tanzania and 79 percent in South Africa said they had greater contact and improved relationships with families and friends as a result of mobile phones.
- Sixty-two percent of small businesses in South Africa and 59 percent in Egypt said they had increased their profits as a result of mobile phones, in spite of increased call costs.
- Over 85 percent of small businesses run by black individuals in South Africa rely solely on a mobile phone for telecommunications. This suggests that growth in the African telecom market will continue to benefit African economies.[3]

Such findings suggest that there can be great value to introducing cellular phone services (and other related services, such as Internet connectivity) to developing communities. Vodacom, a joint venture between Vodafone and

Telkom SA, has developed a unique program to accomplish this task and to address the need for rural connectivity and local business development in developing economies.

VODACOM AND SOUTH AFRICA'S RURAL MARKET

Specifically, Vodacom's "Community Services" program offers telecommunications services in townships and other disadvantaged communities provided at government-mandated prices set below commercial rates. The Community Services business model stipulates that local entrepreneurs (from within the disadvantaged communities) should own and operate the phone shop franchises. At a cost of about 26 000 rands (ZAR) (US$3450),[4] prospective owners can start a franchise to operate five cellular lines in a preapproved location. These franchises, commonly called "phone shops" and usually operated from converted shipping containers, offer phone service on a per-use basis to the surrounding community. Vodacom launched the Community Services program in late 1994, and over time the program has demonstrated how a technology company can operate profitably in low-income, rural areas by helping local entrepreneurs become franchise operators. Community Services is also an example of how business, communities, and government work together to achieve significant social and economic goals.

CREATION AND STRUCTURE OF VODACOM COMMUNITY SERVICES

In 1993, Vodacom was granted one of only two government licenses to build and operate a cellular network in South Africa. In 1994, the new post-apartheid government in South Africa revised the terms of the license; these revisions included a requirement to provide affordable cellular communications to under-serviced areas. Specifically, Vodacom was to have 22 000 lines in operation within five years.[5] Vodacom also committed ZAR1 billion (US$132 million) to the new government's Joint Economic Development Program. MTN, the only other cellular company granted a network license at that time, was similarly obligated to provide specialized services to disadvantaged communities.

The government's business regulating body, the Industrial Commission Authority of South Africa (ICASA), was appointed to ensure that Vodacom met its specific targets in a way that achieved the original goals of the agreement. Vodacom was to have the phone lines in operation by 30

June, 1999 (within five years) or face licensing penalties. Aside from this simple mandate, Vodacom was permitted to use its own discretion in how it carried out its newly formed Community Services program.

From the beginning, Vodacom was confident that it could not only meet its government obligations, but exceed them. While Vodacom's main business focus was to provide cellular services to middle and top market segments, the company recognized that a majority of South Africa's population lived in low-income communities and that it would need to embrace these groups if it wanted to become and remain the country's leading cellular company. As such, the company committed significant resources to its Community Services program to ensure that Vodacom was helping to truly "democratize telecommunications in South Africa." The program was launched with an ZAR5 million (US$660 000) budget and a newly-hired team committed to its success.[6] The team members share a diversity of backgrounds, which enabled the group to engage quickly with communities in order to co-determine how Vodacom could best address their needs. This partnership approach was critical to ensuring the new businesses would be accepted within South Africa's close-knit communities and contributed to helping the company meet its target of having 22 000 active Community Services lines in operation in March 1999 – three months before the specified target deadline. Currently, Vodacom has approximately 30 000 active Community Services lines and demand continues to grow.

BUSINESS MODEL

Vodacom operates the Community Services phone shops as franchises, setting standards and pricing and usually also providing the physical facility (the refurbished shipping container), but allowing the shops to succeed or fail under the management of their entrepreneur-owners. The phone shops themselves operate with a shared-access business model that aggregates demand, serving many customers with (typically) five (but up to ten) cellular phone lines. Pricing is set at levels mandated by the government regulatory authority and currently is less than one-third of normal cellular rates. Entrepreneurs retain one-third of phone shop calling profit, or gross margin. Operators are expected to pay for operating expenses and taxes from the one-third profits they retain.

New owners selected for the program are responsible for an initial investment of ZAR26 000 (US$3450) to cover the cost of equipment for five phone lines (each phone comes with ZAR750 [US$100] of free airtime), as well as the cost of transporting the container to their location, paid directly to the transportation company. Owners are also responsible for identifying the proposed location of their phone shop. As the location is an important factor in the phone shop's future success, Vodacom representatives work closely with prospective owners to evaluate the feasibility of a site. Owners also need to provide Vodacom with a rental agreement or a municipal permit for the land. Shops that plan to use electricity need to provide Vodacom with a Certificate of Compliance (COC) stating that the required electrical work has met national regulatory standards.

Prospective business owners learn about the Community Services program in various ways. The most common way is through word of mouth. Many owners have friends or family who started a successful franchise somewhere in the country, and this encouraged them to take advantage of the same entrepreneurial opportunity. Vodacom also produces marketing material targeting prospective owners and explaining the process for application and approval.

When Vodacom is approached by prospective entrepreneurs for a franchise license, Vodacom representatives are assigned to assess the candidacy of the applicant and the feasibility of the site using the following criteria. A prospective phone shop owner must:

- be South African;
- be at least 21 years of age;
- convey business acumen and entrepreneurial spirit;
- have sufficient funds to cover start-up costs; and
- propose a feasible site.

While race is not a predetermination in becoming a phone shop owner, it is sometimes a factor in assessing the feasibility of locating the phone shop in a certain area. In the past, disadvantaged communities have resisted attempts by white owners to locate shops in their area, even resorting to vandalism and robbery of the containers. Currently, there are many more individuals applying for Community Services franchises than Vodacom has the resources to make possible.

RATES AND AFFORDABILITY

The Community Services per-minute rate is determined by the government's ICASA and is set significantly below regular cellular rates. Community Services rates are ZAR0.85 (US$0.11) per minute versus Vodacom's commercial "Vodago" pre-paid rates of ZAR2.75 (US$0.36). All phone shop owners are required to offer the mandated per-minute rate to consumers. As the largest provider of Community Services phones in South Africa, Vodacom works closely with ICASA to set and periodically evaluate the rate used by Vodacom and MTN within their programs.

Phone shop profit margins are fixed, with owners earning 33 percent of the ZAR0.85 (US$0.11) per-minute fee. Despite these relatively low margins and the low per capita income in rural and disadvantaged townships in South Africa, aggregate buying power of a community provides sufficient revenue to support the operating costs of Vodacom and the shop owner, who is able to maintain a relatively high cash flow. The shared-access model, providing telephone connectivity for entire communities at an affordable cost per use, is quite profitable. For example, a phone shop located in a central location of a typical township can generate average revenues of approximately ZAR9000 (US$1190) per month for the owner, and twice that for Vodacom.[7]

The Community Services per-minute rate applies to calls anywhere within South Africa. International calls to neighboring countries of Lesotho, Swaziland, Botswana, Zimbabwe, and Mozambique are charged at ZAR3 (US$0.40) per minute. ICASA regulations currently do not allow international calls outside of this coverage area; pending regulatory approvals will relax these restrictions. Similar to the emergency use of 911 in the United States, Vodacom provides free calls to emergency access numbers.

Perhaps the most important factor of Community Services' affordability is that its services are offered on pre-paid cash basis (pay-as-you-go), which allows users to purchase precisely the amount of call time that they want or can afford. This method is far preferred over calling services that require the purchase of a calling card, such as required at some public phones, because it prevents consumers from having to come up with the initial calling card investment and eliminates the risk of card theft.

However, pricing risks for consumers still exist within these communities. Thousands of unofficial phone shops throughout the country claim low "per-unit" pricing. Consumers are often easily fooled into spending over ZAR2 (US$0.26) per minute for units that last only 15 seconds. There is little that can be done to put a stop to these deceptive variable-cost services, but the marketing practices and the increased accessibility of the Vodacom phone shops help combat these risks.

ACCESSIBILITY

Vodacom follows specific criteria to determine the feasibility of site locations and ensure that a community's needs are met. Site locations must:

- meet specific demographic and population criteria (i.e., be located in relatively densely populated, disadvantaged communities);
- have a high profile (be along a major road, near a taxi rank, or inside a store, etc.);
- be located an acceptable distance from existing phone shops;
- have authorized access to electricity (or be willing to purchase a large operating battery as an alternative).

The "acceptable distance" from another phone shop is determined on a case-by-case basis. The previously mentioned unofficial phone shops are small and informal structures, offering consumers variable-rate access to one individual's mobile phone. These phone shops typically warrant less competitive concern for Vodacom phone shop owners, because they are unpredictable, they offer varying rates and they tend to move locations to suit the preferences of the phone owner. Conversely, MTN phone shops offer consumers access to the same community service rates through simi-larly-modeled, permanently-located phone shops that even operate out of modified shipping containers. ICASA works with Vodacom and MTN to define and mandate appropriate distances between phone shops to meet the needs of a community. Locations of competing phone shops are taken into serious consideration; business impropriety such as infringement upon another's territory has resulted in "turf wars" and violent retributions.

TECHNOLOGY

The technology behind Vodacom Community Services also helps to make the program successful. Owners buy from Vodacom phones that are uniquely designed to suit the needs of a phone shop. These units are known as SIGIs and were originally manufactured by Siemens. In recent years, Vodacom has sourced phones from a national supplier, which allows the company to work closely with the supplier to evolve the phones to meet the changing needs of owners. For example, recent models of phones allow easier programming of call time and access to visual displays, which alert users as to how much time is left. Modifications are also in progress to make the phones fax- and data-friendly to support future user needs. Owners pre-pay for phone time from Vodacom, which gets credited directly to their phones. Phones are pre-programmed to charge at a certain rate. The phones resemble traditional landline phones, consisting of a simple handset, cradle, and number pad, which enables users to dial to their desired location; attached is a small device that tracks the amount of time users have left for their call. Wires connect each phone to units at the attendant's service counter, where he/she programs in the amount of money collected for each call. Wires usually run from the units behind the service counter up the wall of the container to small antennas, which facilitate transmission for each phone. Phones, as well as lights within the containers, run off grid electricity or large batteries. Transmission is conducted through Vodacom's cellular network, though the phones used are not mobile handsets.

PHONE SHOP PHYSICAL STRUCTURE, MARKETING, AND MAINTENANCE

The physical structure of the phone shop is a key distinction for Vodacom. When Vodacom first launched its Community Services program, the company knew it needed to facilitate owners' access to structures in which they could operate. While some owners identified retail space in traditional shopping centers, most high-traffic locations within the community required some sort of new structure. However, the widely available building materials in disadvantaged communities, which consist of plywood and sheet metal, would leave structures highly susceptible to theft. In response, Vodacom began providing owners with refurbished shipping containers.

Vodacom's refurbished shipping containers are 18 feet long, and are remodeled to suit the unique requirements of the phone shop. Each container has been modified to fit a service counter at one end, where the phone shop control units are located and where employees are stationed to collect money and program phone time into the control units. Each container also contains at least five phones (with a maximum of ten) located within phone stalls along the walls of the container. Insulation and ventilation are also added to containers during the modification process. Before a container is shipped to owners for use, Vodacom paints the container a distinctive "Vodacom green" and attaches branding signs and functional promotional materials throughout. Vodacom works with six container dealers located throughout South Africa to supply containers to new owners, and in some cases replace existing damaged containers. Each container costs about ZAR 30 000 (US$3950) to purchase and modify. Dealers buy used containers from shipping lines after five-to-eight years of active use, and then modify them to suit the needs of various clients.

Since the outset of the program, the container modification has evolved to ensure better quality, functionality, and usability of containers. Originally, service counters and phone stalls were made out of steel, container insulation was minimal, and ventilators were located on the roof. Branding was also minimal and inconsistent. Furthermore, the container design left the phone shops vulnerable to theft. Criminals learned that a small-framed person could enter through early containers' rooftop ventilators, for example. In some areas, gunpoint hold-ups were common. To address these challenges, Vodacom worked with owners to identify solutions. Some of these solutions include: wooden service counters and phone stalls, industrial strength flooring, thicker insulation, and a white wood-paneled interior. Side ventilators enable more natural movement of air, and make break-ins via ventilation units impossible. Bulletproof glass, which seals employees who collect money from customers, is sometimes installed to protect employees in higher crime areas. Highly visible and consistent branding is attached to the exterior, while "no smoking" signs and additional branding is added to the interior. A small cage protects the outside padlock used to lock the container after hours. While many of the above modifications are now standard with new containers, owners with older units must pay for the installation of additional, upgraded features.

Vodacom was one of the first companies in South Africa to utilize shipping containers for business purposes, but the method has gained widespread popularity in recent years to address a number of client needs. The shipping costs can range anywhere from ZAR200 (US$26.50) to ZAR1000 (US$132) depending on the distance to the site; owners are responsible for the cost of transporting a new container to its final site. It takes approximately one month from the time a container is ordered to the time of delivery to the phone shop site. A container is delivered to operation sites by a transport crane truck. Because phone shop owners do not own the containers, it is difficult for Vodacom to persuade owners to spend time and resources for container upkeep. As a result, many are in a state of disrepair and need replacing. Vodacom assumes all responsibility and cost of maintaining the containers. Unfortunately, all containers requiring servicing must be returned to the container dealer via the same transport trucks. Because of crime and safety concerns, container dealers are unwilling to service containers on-site.

PHONE SHOP STAFFING AND OPERATIONS

There are over 1800 owners and over 4400 phone shops nationwide, and each owner is empowered to staff and operate phone shops according to their own needs and preferences. Most owners operate only one or two shops while a few operate as many as ten. Regardless of the size of their operations, owners may or may not be involved with the actual operations of their shops. Most oversee their own operations, but some opt to hire middle management. Hiring of middle management and staff is virtually always done based in the communities where shops are located.

One entrepreneur, Mr Mncedisi Zungula, operates ten phone shops in the Umtata area of the Transkei region. Mr Zungula has hired three full-time middle managers to work from an office based in Umtata to oversee operations at all of his shops. This staff includes a schedule manager who hires all shop employees and sets their schedules, a phone manager who loads the phones with credit each morning and who does all necessary accounting, and a field manager who visits shops on an ongoing basis, collecting money and assessing service and technical needs. Most phone shops require at least two on-site employees to work as phone clerks at the counter. For shops with ten lines, it is common to have two employees working during the same shift, but most shops with fewer lines require only one employee per shift. These employees, each working in shifts up to eight hours, collect money, assign customers a phone, and program the phone units. They ensure that the phone shop is kept clean, and report any damages to the owner or manager. Shop employees also show customers how to use the telephones and make calls to various parts of the country.

However, as the Community Services program has been in place for several years now, most customers require little training. Neither Vodacom nor ICASA set regulations for the level of compensation that owners offer staff; it is up to the owner's discretion. In addition to an hourly wage, some employers offer staff various incentives and perquisites. For example, many owners allow employees to sell candy at the counter and retain profits from this venture. Some owners even offer staff the profits from a specific telephone line. Of course, this is done on the assumption that profits on that line are consistent with that of the other lines and that employees are not directing more customer traffic to the phone line for which they share profits.

COMMUNITY SERVICES STAFFING AND OPERATIONS

Staffing in Vodacom's Community Services occurs at two levels: national and regional. However, individual owners are empowered to determine and arrange their own staffing needs on a local basis. At the national level, Community Services is directed from Vodacom's headquarters near Johannesburg. The Community Services Division Head administers the program, developing operational procedures and policies, in addition to strategic planning responsibilities.

At the regional level, there are six offices that oversee areas closely aligned with South Africa's nine provinces. Regional managers oversee all operations within the regions and report to the Regional Executive. Each office enlists one or two business consultants to assist new owners through business development and franchising. Offices also utilize one or two support technicians to address all technical issues for new and existing owners. In addition, offices enlist administrative support according to their individual needs and the size of operations in their region. No formal training is conducted by the regional offices, though informal training often occurs as business consultants work with prospective and new owners.

PHONE SHOP REPORTING AND RECORD-KEEPING

Vodacom places great responsibility on each of its six regional offices to meet monthly goals and quotas for the Community Services program. The head office sets goals of how many additional lines each region must bring into service. Every month, each region must submit a report to the head office detailing the number of owners, lines, and calls sold (as well as any theft data). Regional offices have sole discretion in selling franchises and determining who qualifies for ownership. Because Vodacom is able to track Community Services line usage patterns and because owners pre-pay for phone time, owners are not responsible for providing specific reports to Vodacom on a regular basis. Owners thus have great flexibility in determining how they run their business. At a minimum, most phone shops track the amount of money collected and the number of minutes used on each phone. Owners who operate multiple phone shops often require more extensive reports. For example, one owner who operates ten phone shops requires the following from every shop, monthly: a payment schedule, a profit and loss statement, a loan report, an equipment stock list, and a general report highlighting problems encountered during the month along with suggestions on how to address those problems. These reports are usually generated by a middle manager who is hired by the owner to oversee staff in multiple phone shops.

FRANCHISE OWNER TRAINING AND EDUCATION PROGRAMS

As virtually all owners come from disadvantaged backgrounds and have limited financial and/or business operations experience, training is an important component of Vodacom's phone shop strategy. Vodacom works in conjunction with the privately-owned training company, Running Business Today, to provide training to owners. Company trainers, together with Vodacom representatives, travel throughout the country and meet with groups of owners to develop business competency. Owners are exposed to business training covering goal setting, profit maximization, financial statement development, staff salaries and expenses, and human resources management. Vodacom provides training and resources to new owners, but does not "spoon-feed" them along the way. Rather, owners are empowered to operate the businesses on their own accord, assuming all risk and financial liability. Vodacom is available to offer advice, insight, and lessons learned, but there are few mandates that owners must meet. To facilitate owner learning, Vodacom publishes a quarterly newsletter, *Ringers*, which is mailed to owners and shares the experiences of owners throughout the country. This publication features helpful articles about business ownership, customer relations, crime prevention, and taxes. It provides nationwide news and updates from Community Services and often includes a profile of a phone shop owner who gives back to the community through income generated from successful business operations.

COMMUNITY SERVICES' COMPETITIVE CHALLENGES

Vodacom's main competitors within the Community Services area are also its competitors in the commercial area. MTN launched its cellular services in the same month as Vodacom in 1994, and was subject to the same licensing obligations as Vodacom. However, whereas Vodacom was expected to provide 22 000 cellular pay phones in underserved communities within five years, MTN was expected to provide only 7500 within the same timeframe. Cell-C is the newest competitor in South Africa's wireless market, launching its services in November 2001. Cell-C is government-obligated to roll out 52 000 community phones within seven years. Cell-C's sizable community phone commitment is influenced by the company's partial ownership by CellSaf, an empowerment consortium of 33 black groups; and by its focus on the low- and mid-level markets. Cell-C has a 15-year roaming agreement with Vodacom, allowing Cell-C to use its competitor's lines until its own network is developed.

As the country's incumbent telephone operator, Telkom has struggled over the years to install and maintain fixed-line services. Currently, South Africa's mobile operators serve 14 million cellular customers, while Telkom oversees just five million fixed-line connections. Telkom is the sole provider of South Africa's traditional pay phones, available throughout the country. Telkom's pay phones operate at ZAR0.60 (US$0.08) per minute, cheaper than the Community Services phone rate, but more expensive for long-distance calls. However, theft and vandalism plague Telkom's phones, particularly in urban and disadvantaged areas, rendering the pay phones inoperable most of the time. Telkom maintains some influence with mobile operators though, as network usage fees generate almost ZAR2 billion (US$264 million) of Telkom's annual revenue.

OTHER CHALLENGES AND OPPORTUNITIES

Despite it success over the last decade, many challenges remain for Vodacom's Community Services program as it strives to ensure efficient, profitable operations. Some of those problems include the need for increased services (such as fax and data services, including Internet access), and issues with infrastructure (while the network currently reaches 93 percent of the population and Vodacom is still required to further develop its presence in disadvantaged, commonly rural, areas). Other concerns relate to equipment maintenance, as owners have little incentive to maintain the containers. Since they do retain full responsibility for their own telephone equipment, they do tend to take considerable care of phones to ensure the upkeep of their investments. Owners assume all liability for any replacement costs of lost, stolen, or damaged equipment. Maintenance is critical because the equipment ordering process can take considerable time and often induces a greater loss than the value of the equipment itself. For example, once a phone set is ordered, Vodacom reports that it takes anywhere from one month to three months for the set to be delivered to Vodacom, and an additional three days to two weeks to be delivered to the phone shop. The loss of just one phone can be enough to result in high revenue losses over the course of several months. While this challenge looks unlikely to be resolved soon, Vodacom is working with its suppliers to reduce the wait time.

As mentioned above, the containers are the responsibility of Vodacom. While this has not been a serious challenge to date, many containers are beginning to exhibit signs of wear and the need for maintenance. Owners have little incentive to maintain the containers because they pay no part of the initial or ongoing costs. It is anticipated that in a few years the maintenance cost of the fleet of containers currently in the field will become very expensive. Vodacom is committed to maintaining container ownership as a way to ensure brand consistency and identification. Potentially, requiring owners to pay the maintenance costs, or a predetermined percentage of the maintenance costs, would encourage owners to take better care of their containers and external branding.

Lastly, Vodacom faces societal and capital challenges within the communities where they operate. Theft, robbery, vandalism, and violent crime are significant concerns for owners throughout South Africa. Collectively, these social problems serve as Vodacom's greatest challenge in providing Community Services. In the Western Cape region alone, phone shop owners lost over ZAR40 000 (US$5250) to theft in 2002. Every owner contends with the real possibility of crime against the phone shop. In a few rare cases, employees have been killed during armed robberies. A number of steps have been taken to minimize these threats:

1. Each phone has a pin code that only the operator knows, and is required for the phone to work. Without this code, stolen phones are useless.
2. Owners are encouraged to collect money and deposit it in the bank on a regular basis. Owners are advised that it is important not to collect the money at regular times each day, in order to minimize the risk of someone observing the routine and making plans to rob the collector during the daily bank deposit.
3. In areas prone to violent crime, bulletproof screens are installed in phone shops to separate the staff from customers.
4. Large antennas located outside the container, at risk of vandalism, are being replaced by smaller antennas inside the container.
5. Cages are installed around the exterior padlock, making it more difficult to cut locks.

Regarding financial issues, access to finance is very difficult in South Africa. Banks offer limited financing options for the average customer, especially the type of prospective entrepreneurs Vodacom hopes to develop. Finding prospective owners able to invest ZAR26 000 (US$3450) was a challenge, particularly at the beginning of the program. As a result, Vodacom began providing its own financing options to increase interest and help entrepreneurs get their businesses started. The financing program helped many prospective owners get started, and ensured that the overall program succeeded. Community Services no longer provides these financing options and now requires all payments upfront. The phone shop program is so successful that there are more qualified franchise candidates with the available money to invest than there are available franchises. This goes against the nature of the program somewhat, as only those who are already established or who can access financing can afford to buy the phones to set up a phone shop. Early in the program's history, Vodacom issued credit to phone shop owners for airtime. Intended to help new businesses get established, this practice has since stopped as a result of abuse. All phone time must now be pre-paid by the owners. It is up to the discretion of individual owners to issue credit to customers for phone calls; however, as airtime is already pre-paid, this is entirely at the owner's own risk and responsibility.

MEASURES OF SUCCESS

Standard of Living Improvements and Local Empowerment

Vodacom found that each mobile phone shop spawned five new jobs and unquantifiable spin-off economic gains.[8] A local phone shop can be an invaluable convenience to a South African. One only needs to sit within a Vodacom phone shop for a few minutes to observe the myriad reasons why people use the community phones. Affordable access to a phone allows families separated for mobility or migrant employment reasons to keep in touch and manage family needs (and funds) more effectively. Some individuals use phone shops to pay bills and order personal effects. Professionals within the community rely on phone shops to conduct businesses more efficiently. Delivery drivers use the phones to keep in touch with headquarters or to report problems on their route. Consistent access to basic services such as electricity, sanitation, and water remains a problem within townships, and phone shops allow individuals to report service outages and emergencies. The phones ultimately contribute to the empowerment of individuals in South African townships when individuals gain access to widespread and consistent services that enable them to manage their lives more easily.

Phone shops also provide individuals with access to a range of social services, which can also contribute to an improved standard of living. For example, people can call a doctor or seek medical advice by phone. Ultimately, increased access to communications technology that enables customers to address family, professional, and individual needs also contributes to a more functional community.

Economic Empowerment for Local Communities

An essential measurement of Vodacom Community Services' success has been the development of a cadre of phone shop entrepreneurs who have invested in starting a Community Services franchise and then received business support from Vodacom via training and access to phone shop containers. The revenue generated by the phone shops suggests how powerful such a franchise approach can be. The phone shop owners and staff become empowered as they earn income and acquire key business skills.

Additional development benefits include enhanced productivity and social welfare as new sources of income within rural and disadvantaged communities. Indeed, an informal survey of phone shop staff showed that individuals are optimistic about their future employability and job opportunities. This optimism is significant as the development of professional skills, experience, and confidence will lead to increased future entrepreneurial ventures that can assist these communities even further. Program growth can also mean that owners can eventually provide more jobs for others too.

The provision of telephone connectivity to disadvantaged communities in South Africa has served two important purposes: promoting economic development by helping individuals and businesses gain efficiency through communications, and promoting social and economic empowerment for the individuals who own and/or operate the telephone enterprises.

Benefits to Vodacom

Vodacom has indeed found a business case for its Community Services model. Vodacom ultimately is investing in its future customer base as it provides subsidized services to disadvantaged communities. Current Community Services customers are familiar with the Vodacom brand and they trust its reliable services. As customers progress economically and determine that they are in a favorable position to buy a traditional cellular phone, they are most likely to purchase their plan from a trusted source, Vodacom.

CONCLUSION

The Community Services model is successful because it offers a basic and vital service to disadvantaged communities at affordable prices. It was built in collaboration with local communities, and it is based on a shared-use model that allows franchise owners to aggregate demand in order to capitalize on small margins with high volume. Concurrently, it creates entrepreneurial opportunities for thousands of prospective business owners, generating jobs and higher incomes. In fact, it is only through the entrepreneurial nature of the program that Vodacom is able to reach the three to four million customers who make close to 100 million calls a month. On its own, Vodacom would be challenged to operate and maintain the number of phone shops that now exist throughout the country. The wide geographical distribution and high number of local operations would make management costs prohibitive for Vodacom without the phone shop Community Services program. Additionally, phone shop owners are in a better position to assess the needs of local communities. The program has the potential to be replicated in other countries as well. Thus, the success of the Community Services program illustrates how cooperation between local entrepreneurs, government, local communities, and a technology company can address both business and social goals over the long term.

NOTES

1. Major portions of this chapter are excerpted from the "What Works" Vodacom case study and are reprinted with kind permission from World Resources Institute (www.wri.org). The complete "What Works" case study series is available online at www.nextbillion.net.
2. http://news.mongabay.com/2005/0712-rhett_butler.html, downloaded 1 June, 2006 and citing reports from the Centre for Economic Policy Research, MTN Uganda Ltd, International Telecommunication Union (ITU) and *The Economist*, 1 July, 2005.
3. Ibid.
4. Based on exchange rate of 0.1322 US$1 ZAR, 8 September, 2003. *Source*: Yahoo Finance, http://finance.yahoo.com/.
5. http://www.omidyar.net/group/poverty/file/0.98.11067702980/get/Vodafone%20Phone%20Shops.doc.
6. Vodacom Corporate Profile, Available on Vodacom's website: http://www.vodacom.com/about/corporate_profile/corporate_profile.asp.
7. Interview with Nobuhle Chonco, Senior Manager, Vodacom Community Services, May 2003.
8. http://www.omidyar.net/group/poverty/file/0.98.11067702980/get/Vodafone%20Phone%20Shops.doc.

11. Scojo Foundation[1]

Jordan Kassalow, Graham Macmillan and Neil Blumenthal

"Nearly one billion people living in the developing world need reading glasses, but less than 5 percent have access to affordable options."[2] "The invention of spectacles more than doubled the working life of skilled craftsmen, especially those who did fine jobs: scribes, instrument and toolmakers, clothes weavers, and metal workers."[3]

"Because the lens of the human eye hardens around the age of forty, it produces a condition similar to farsightedness (actually presbyopia). The eye can no longer focus on close objects. Eyeglasses solve that problem."[4] For tradesmen and tradeswomen whose work depends on seeing items up close, farsightedness can destroy their livelihood and make them dependent on others or force them to find other types of work. With a simple pair of reading glasses, weavers, tailors, farmers, and many others can effectively double their work life.

CREATION AND STRUCTURE OF SCOJO FOUNDATION

In 2001, Dr Jordan Kassalow and Scott Berrie, founders of Scojo Vision LLC, founded Scojo Foundation to address the need for affordable reading glasses in the developing world. Dr Kassalow, a trained optometrist and public health expert, had been exposed to sight problems in the Third World with various health organizations such as Helen Keller International and VOSH (Volunteer Optometric Services to Humanity). He had noticed, as he traveled giving eye care with these organizations, that "for [each person] who needed sophisticated eye care, there were 30 people who needed basic reading glasses. There was a huge market failure, and a huge market opportunity to sell cheap reading glasses."[5] In 2001, Scojo Foundation set up a six-month pilot program in India to test its theory and the following year entered El Salvador with the intent to:

- develop markets for reading glasses at the base of the economic pyramid;
- select, train, equip, and fund local entrepreneurs to establish new businesses that sell reading glasses;
- provide high-quality, affordable reading glasses for its programs;
- bring reading glasses and referral services directly to the customer at the village level; and
- conduct innovative and locally relevant social marketing campaigns to raise awareness about blurry, up-close vision.[6]

In order meet its obligation as a New York-registered non-profit organization, Scojo Foundation set up an office in New York to oversee operations and to raise funding. Scojo Vision LLC, which sells high-end reading glasses in such retailers as Neiman-Marcus and Saks 5th Avenue, pledged 5 percent of its pretax profits for the support of the Scojo Foundation. Scojo LLC had only been founded two years earlier and shares office space with the foundation.

After Scojo Foundation's initial entry into El Salvador, it launched fully-fledged programs in India and Guatemala, and just recently has expanded operations into Bangladesh. It is also exploring various distribution channels to scale operations at a reasonable cost. Two methods it is testing are: expanding the franchise model, set up in league with established partners, such as Hindustan Lever, Drishtee, BRAC, or other community-based providers; and to use the current Vision Entrepreneurs (VEs) to find and manage future VEs. Both of these methods will be discussed below.

The director of Scojo Foundation and director of programs are based in New York. The director oversees the Foundation's global operations while the director of programs oversees country programs. Within each country there is a country director with responsibility for that specific country. Below the country director the model differentiates somewhat. Scojo Foundation has two different distribution channels it is currently employing.

Distribution Channels

In the partnership distribution channel, Scojo Foundation finds a partner who has an existing distribution channel or delivery platform set up and licenses them as a Scojo franchise. This is done on both a macro and micro level. At the macro level, organizations receive technical assistance and guidance in large-scale program implementation while the micro level consist of an individual entrepreneur receiving a "business-in-a-box" to sell reading glasses. Scojo is pursuing macrofranchise opportunities with large, established companies/organizations that are already distributing and selling in the urban and rural areas such as Hindustan Lever and BRAC. The partnership channel is the primary channel in Bangladesh and Guatemala and is also frequently employed in India.

With the microfranchise, Scojo trains the franchisee in vision screening and business skills. At this point, the franchisee is responsible for all of the daily operations. A kit generally sells for around US$100 and is consigned to each Vision Entrepreneur so as to reduce the barriers to entry. Scojo replenishes stock when needed through the partner, which is the limit of Scojo's involvement. Often these franchisees carry other health products as is the case with BRAC. Scojo's product line makes a nice addition to the range of products that the community health workers generally carry for several reasons: they are complementary products that customers would buy in addition to other health products, the price point and margins on Scojo's reading glasses are higher than most of the products they currently carry, and it is inexpensive and fast to add. Furthermore, Scojo adds value to a Vision Entrepreneur by generating greater earnings per hour worked than most other rural occupations. Scojo is also pursuing further franchise opportunities with established companies that are already distributing and selling in the urban and rural areas.

The other distribution channel is called the Vision Entrepreneur channel. In this channel, Scojo is involved in all aspects of the value chain. Scojo recruits, trains, and sets up Vision Entrepreneurs (VEs) in designated areas. The VEs are the sales force of Scojo Foundation and work directly with Scojo's district and regional coordinators, who are full-time employees. The Vision Entrepreneur channel is Scojo Foundation's learning lab. This channel enables new ideas to be tested and refined before adoption by partners, organizations or macrofranchisees.

Scojo forms relationships with many different organizations in the various countries such as local NGOs, municipal entities, the Peace Corps and churches among others. These partners do various levels of work, such as recommend potential VE candidates, distribute merchandise and participate in training. Using partners allows Scojo better access to and knowledge of the areas that it enters. It also allows Scojo to employ fewer full-time staff and less money in accomplishing its mission.

Within the VE channel, there are regional (Latin America) or district (India) coordinators underneath the country director who manage up to 25 VEs in their assigned area, and also aid in the recruitment and setup of new VEs. The VE channel is the primary method of distribution in El Salvador. Both channels play an important role in India.

Another difference in Scojo's model in Guatemala is the use of the social enterprise incubator model as is the case with its partner, Community Enterprise Solutions:

Scojo Foundation and Community Enterprise Solutions have developed a small enterprise incubator where Scojo Vision Entrepreneurs and other entrepreneurs work together to leverage each other's strengths and share costs. Scojo Vision Entrepreneurs, wood burning stove makers and others operate from one office space and jointly advertise. Each incubator is assigned one Community Enterprise Solutions employee to help the entrepreneurs develop profitable businesses. There are generally 4–6 Vision Entrepreneurs per incubator.[7]

SCOJO BUSINESS MODEL

Scojo Foundation operates as a not-for-profit enterprise based in the United States, where it provides leadership in the operations of all countries as well as the future strategy. Its goal is for each country to be self-sustaining and not dependent on donor funds. In which case, the profits from operations in Guatemala, for example, would support all operations in Guatemala. At a headquarters level, the 5 percent donated by Scojo Vision LLC would support the small staff based there and reduce Scojo Foundation's needs to raise charitable investments. In the five years that Scojo Foundation has been growing its business it has needed additional capital to support its expansion. However, it is demonstrating success in generating revenue to cover costs. Guatemala became self-sustaining in 2006 and India is self-sustaining on a district level. The model is proving successful and profitability has increased overall.

Scojo distributes all of its glasses and products on a consignment basis to the VEs. It costs on average US$1 to manufacture a pair of reading glasses and nearly another US$1 to deliver the pair of glasses, giving each pair a cost of goods sold of about US$2. Scojo sets up each new Vision Entrepreneur with a kit enclosed in a backpack (the Scojo microfranchise). In the kit there are generally 20–30 pairs of reading glasses of differing strengths between +1.00 to +3.00 in steps of 0.50. Also included are banners, posters, instructional materials, sales tracking sheets, a shirt with the Scojo logo, and supplemental products, such as sunglasses, protective eyewear, and eye drops.

District or regional coordinators make rounds weekly or biweekly to replenish the stock so that each VE maintains a full product line. This is determined by the inventory that remains. At this time, the money is collected for the items that have been sold and the VE gets to keep their commission, which is between 30 and 50 percent. The average set of reading glasses sells for about US$5–7 a pair in Central America and for around US$2.50 in India.

ENTREPRENEURS' BUSINESS MODEL

The VEs, once selected and initially trained, receive on consignment their starting kits to set up business. They are encouraged to spread awareness in the community about vision problems and then to consult with those that come to their shop. Often with the help of partners, they will set up an event at a church or community center to raise awareness of age-related vision impairment. Awareness is an issue that takes considerable time and effort to develop in a community. People notice that they can no longer see up close, but they do not understand why, and they don't realize that an inexpensive set of reading glasses can correct their vision problems and allow them to carry on life as before and, in many cases, actually increase their productivity. Upon wearing the glasses, however, the customers realize instantaneously the benefits of improved vision.

Most of a VE's business comes through referrals rather than through general advertising. Once a VE has met a customer, that customer is then asked if they know someone in their family or a neighbor who might need glasses as well. The VE then visits the referral. This referral mechanism reduces barriers of awareness and hesitancy. If one family member or friend has purchased the glasses, the likelihood of a referral customer increases dramatically.

The process of screening and selling is rather simple. Scojo Vision Entrepreneurs give an eye exam to the customer, and either suggest reading glasses or refer them to the nearest eye clinic if the problem is something more serious that cannot be cleared up by reading glasses. They also sell related eye products such as sunglasses or eye drops, which have a higher margin and therefore a higher commission. Sunglasses are sold as a health product as well as a complementary product. Ultraviolet light causes significant damage to eyes. By wearing UV-protected sunglasses, customers are able to reduce the harmful impact of the sun's rays. As well, sunglasses, as a product, enable VEs to sell to a wider customer base. While reading glasses are for people of age 40 and older, sunglasses can be used by everybody.

In these countries, most of the VEs (90 percent) work part-time and the flexibility allows them to operate other businesses and manage housework or caring for children. The core idea is that the VEs will be able to supplement their family income by operating a Scojo franchise. A tremendous benefit of operating a Scojo franchise is the amount of money a VE can make in a short amount of time. Scojo VEs can work for three to four hours in the morning, make US$12–15, and then work somewhere else or take care of the family during the afternoon. The earnings per hour invested are significant and quite attractive to the VE.

CRITERIA FOR NEW ENTREPRENEURS

Scojo, when it first entered these developing countries, had a yearly turnover, among the VEs, of about 80 percent, which is comparatively normal in these markets, but Scojo wanted to reduce this number to cut costs. It changed the recruiting criteria and has reduced turnover to about 50 percent. This reduction in rate of attrition also can be attributed to converting from a loan program to the consignment model. Nonetheless, Scojo is still making changes to try and reduce the attrition rate.

Scojo Foundation found that choosing successful entrepreneurs was somewhat counterintuitive. The VEs with outgoing personalities were often quick to move onto the next big thing that came along and they would not commit to building the business over the long term. On the other hand, those who were more reserved often made for more stable VEs.

An important goal of Scojo is to empower women and give them the opportunity to earn money and respect in what is often a very male-centric society. To begin with, Scojo recruits women and therefore almost all of the VEs are female. They work out of their homes part-time, and this aspect of Scojo makes this type of business a very good fit for them. This aspect was carefully crafted by Scojo to allow women to be the primary recruits.

Scojo has often used partners, especially the Peace Corps in Central America, to recommend women who would make good VEs in many of the areas that Scojo enters. This again leaves Scojo free to focus on their strengths and to leverage their funds. Some of the VE success factors that Scojo has found along with those listed above are:

- connected with church community (especially mega churches);
- support from husbands and family;
- past experience with NGOs;
- sales experience;
- respect in the community; and
- most importantly, a friendly personality.

Among women in these small communities within developing nations, literacy has not always been a priority; in order to become a Vision Entrepreneur one must have a basic ability to record information so Scojo can gather data on sales, but high levels of literacy are not required.

Once enrolled and trained as a VE, one must have ten sales per month (this varies by country) to be considered active and "independent." Scojo is reviewing this requirement and may increase it so as to better leverage their kits and coordinators. Once a VE becomes inactive, the regional coordinator will pick up the merchandise in order to pass it on to someone else. They have recovered every kit from inactive VEs since they have moved to the consignment model. Early on, they tried to work on a loan model. The people are connected in the community and do not want to lose the respect or feel the embarrassment that not returning the kit would cause.

TRAINING

All potential VEs must attend a two- to three-day training session. The purpose is to train the Vision Entrepreneurs in testing vision and in running a small business. A Scojo employee conducts the training in both vision and business practices and covers the following points:

Vision
- how to do a vision screen (both far and close);
- how to identify other potential eye problems (glaucoma, cataracts, irritation caused by dust, etc.);
- how to determine the strength of reading glasses that the person will need; and
- if other products (eye drops, eye protection) can solve the problem or if the person should be referred to a clinic.

Sales
- inventory management and care;
- which models are the most successful;
- how to recommend supplemental and preventative products;
- data collection and how to fill out the forms; and
- how to conduct a marketing campaign.

Since Scojo works with women at the base of the pyramid, it tries to teach and build self-esteem and female empowerment. Many of these women have been marginalized by society and building their self-worth is essential to the whole process.

In the second part of the training, Scojo guides the VEs in building a business plan for their community. Together, they fill out a marketing plan and examine how they (the VEs) will attract clients. They also do a brief analysis of the market, asking questions such as: what is the size and demographics of their area and how does this translate into market potential? Based on the occupations that are common in the area, they can tailor their marketing approach to the type of eye problems their community may have.

Preparing this business/marketing plan requires time and energy, which weeds out some of the potential VEs who are less serious about the opportunity. Once they realize that it will require time, planning, and consistent effort, they often drop out. This also reduces the opportunity cost of having a trained VE be unproductive, which takes away the opportunity from another VE.

Scojo holds regional meetings twice a year in which the VEs from around the region or country get together and receive additional training. All results from all VEs are shown to the group and Scojo is working on developing a best practices portion of the meeting. Currently in some of the cultures, the VEs are not comfortable getting up in front of a group and talking about their success and methods so the VEs do not currently present in the meeting. The program directors and coordinators share success stories.

DISTRIBUTION

As mentioned previously, the regional coordinator comes around once every week or two to replenish the stock that has been sold. Since the regional coordinators also work with the VEs on their marketing plans and on the upcoming events that the VE is planning, they are generally aware when there will be an above-average demand on stock levels. The coordinators will prepare for the increased demand, either by leaving an increased amount of stock with the VE or actually coming to the event with stock to supplement the VE's supply.

PRODUCT

Scojo Foundation, because of its relationship with Scojo Vision LLC, has contacts in eyeglass manufacturing; it is able to source the reading glasses inexpensively, with the average being around US$1 dollar per pair. This also allows it to source the supplemental products such as sunglasses, eye drops, cords for the glasses, protective eyewear for working in dusty or dirty environments, and so forth. It includes these additional products in the vision kit so as to offer a full eyecare solution.

PRICE

In Latin America, the average price is about US$5–10 per pair of glasses (depending on the model); the cost of goods sold is almost US$2 after transportation has been added to the purchase price. The profit margin is split between the VE and Scojo, with the VE receiving roughly between 30 and 50 percent of the profit margin in commission. The commission is higher on the higher margin items, giving the VE an incentive to upsell and to sell additional supplementary products.

In India the average price is about US$3.50. Because of the larger population in India, the price has been lowered to increase turnover and to be competitive in the market. Therefore, Scojo relies on a volume-based model.

LOCATION

Scojo focuses on employing women as Vision Entrepreneurs because research shows that when women receive their own income, they use it to feed, clothe, and educate their families. This is an important social benefit to Scojo. These women live in small or mid-sized communities where accessibility to reading glasses has been negligible. Some of the partnership channels work differently, as they carry other lines of products and oftentimes have a small business establishment from which they work.

FRANCHISEES' ADVANTAGES

Being part of the Scojo VE program gives numerous advantages to the VEs, such as:

- Very little initial investment. Being part of the Scojo family allows the VE to set up business with almost no initial cost. The kit, a US$100 value, is given on consignment with no upfront costs (in India there is a 50 rupee deposit, about US$1, that is returned six months later if still active).
- Training. All VEs receive initial training that prepares them to check people's vision and either recommend one of their products or refer them to the nearest eye clinic. They also receive training in business skills, how to prepare and run a promotion, how to build a simple business plan, and how to manage inventory and finance issues. The ongoing training (which occurs during each visit by the regional or district coordinator) and the chance to meet and mingle with other VEs in the region also provides incentives and new ideas.
- Distribution. Scojo replenishes the VEs on a regular basis and makes provision to replenish more often when events are scheduled. In less populous areas, where the transportation is limited and the women's

ability to leave home for a day or even several hours is less feasible, a regular delivery is a large advantage.

- Price. The price advantage that Scojo gives the VEs allows them to sell at a more reasonable price, which makes Scojo products accessible to the masses.
- Scaling through partnerships. Utilizing the existing platforms of other providers increases the size and scope of Scojo's program, reduces overhead costs, and increases local ownership of the model.

With all of the advantages that the Scojo system provides, the VE is free to focus on the customers. Since all the sourcing and inventory issues are being taken care of by Scojo, the VEs can build awareness and relationships and spend their time interacting with and screening customers.

DIFFICULTIES

Scojo faces numerous difficulties, but they often differ by country such as:

- In Central America, the diversity of languages (many local dialects) poses a training and reporting problem since it must all be done in Spanish.
- Cost of transportation to these remote areas increases costs.
- The high turnover, and hence the increased training costs are also an issue that Scojo is addressing by developing better selection criteria.
- In India, the caste system poses a challenge. VEs from one caste cannot easily sell to those of another caste, which limits their market size.
- Simply empowering women and building their self-esteem in areas where women are often marginalized is a struggle.
- Scaling the operation is also difficult. Scojo has started using more partners to aid with this, as well as using current VEs to recruit the next generation of VEs and allowing the recruiter to share some of the profits of the new VE. This develops an intermediate level of VEs between the regional coordinators and the VEs on the village level. These women have the benefit of gaining more income and more experience and can also help in training the new recruits.

GROWTH PATTERN

Scojo Foundation entered India in 2001 through a pilot program and moved into El Salvador with a full-fledged program in 2002. It established operations, expanded, and learned several lessons that allowed it to refine its model. In 2003, it continued to expand in El Salvador, and then in 2004 it launched a full program in Guatemala. In India, it began in the state of Andhra Pradesh in 2005 but has recently expanded into four additional states. It has also experimented with other business models there, specifically the partnership model. Finally, in early 2006, Scojo moved into Bangladesh.

To date (mid-2006) it has trained over 500 Vision Entrepreneurs and franchisees. Over 33 000 pairs of reading glasses have been sold, and nearly 30 000 people have been referred for further testing at partner eye clinics. Below are the number of Vision Entrepreneurs they have trained in each country:

- El Salvador—120
- India—350
- Guatemala—75
- Bangladesh—11

Not all of these VEs are still active, but these numbers represent those that have begun the program.

SUCCESS

Success can be measured in several ways for a microfranchise foundation. Have they benefited the community in which they operate? Have they provided a living income for the microfranchisees? Have they earned enough to continue operations? On all of these accounts the answer is yes for Scojo Foundation.

The benefit to the community data is anecdotal at this point, and Scojo plans to undertake a more comprehensive study to verify the data. However, it is currently using the assumption that every pair of reading glasses sold gives the purchaser an additional two days of productivity a month. Focusing only on Guatemala for the next assumptions – if the person who purchased the reading glasses were making roughly US$2 per day, this adds an increase of US$4 per month to a person's income. It takes about one month's increase to purchase the glasses, so the yearly increase for each person who buys a pair of glasses is US$44. Since entry into Guatemala, Scojo's VEs have sold over 3000 pairs of reading glasses, adding around US$140 000 in increased earnings productivity in Guatemala alone.

Again focusing on Guatemala – the average male farmer makes about US$30 a month. In February 2006, the VEs in Guatemala sold 220 pairs of reading glasses. There were 27 active VEs during the month. Total revenue from glasses and supplemental products was US$2700, and US$630 was paid out in commission. That makes an average commission of US$23 per VE, all of which are female and over 90 percent are working part-time. This nearly doubles a family's income and empowers the women of the family.

By using partners and carefully watching costs, Scojo is able to minimize the funds that it needs to function. In 2005, it was able to make enough to break even on a country level in Guatemala. It is also breaking even on a district level in India, but due to the rapid expansion in this country, it is redeploying more funds than it is earning to continue the growth.

Key Success Factors

Some of the things Scojo has employed to continue to grow and to build upon its success are as follows:

- consignment method;
- capitalizing on a physiological need that gives an immediate benefit to the purchaser;
- no competitors in most markets;
- reduced cost, high-quality reading glasses;
- complementary products;
- continuous training and accountability;
- high use of established partners;
- adaptation between countries.

These success factors then translate into success factors for the franchisees and vision entrepreneurs, such as:

- no start-up costs, no barrier to entry;
- branded products;
- established distribution channels;
- supply-chain management;
- continuing training;
- time to focus on the customer.

If the VE or franchisee is successful, that, in turn, translates to continued and growing success for Scojo Foundation.

CONCLUSION

Scojo Foundation started with the idea of selling inexpensive reading glasses to the aging population at the base of the pyramid and at the same time providing jobs for women and empowering them. Over the last five years it has entered four countries and changed numerous lives through its efforts. It has encountered many difficulties that it is trying to overcome. Scojo continues to adapt and try new methods to serve these markets more effectively. As it continues to expand and refine its model it will undoubtedly make a difference to thousands of lives and allow parents to feed, clothe, and educate their children.

NOTES

1. Most information taken from scojofoundation.org, a personal interview with Scojo Foundation director Graham Macmillan and from an interview between Dr Kassalow and Ted London at the University of Michigan.
2. Scojofoundation.org.
3. Landes, David (1999), *The Wealth and Poverty of Nations*, New York: W.W. Norton, p. 46.
4. Op. cit.
5. *Entrepreneur Magazine*, August 2005.
6. Scojofoundation.org—this is their mission statement and is used as a guide in all markets entered.
7. Scojofoundation.org.

12. Microfranchise funding

Naoko Felder-Kuzu

Microfinance has attracted funding from both social and commercial investors in recent years. Investments in microfinance, though still a very small part within the world of socially responsible investments (SRIs), have been growing at an amazing pace. At the end of January 2006, Mixmarket (a major resource for microfinance funding information: www.mixmarket.org) listed a total of 74 microfinance funds.[1] Also noteworthy were two new large funds announced in November 2005: the Global Commercial Microfinance Consortium (US$75 million) and the Tufts-Omidyar Microfinance Fund (US$100 million). In December 2005, IFC announced its intent to invest EUR30 million for the European Fund for Southeast Europe (EFSE) with an expected final capitalization of EUR500 million. This fund is designed to spur lending to micro and small enterprises in the region. The Gates Foundation has also expanded its funding activities in 2005 to include microfinance. A broad range of funds are now catering to the whole spectrum of socially-oriented to commercially-oriented investors.

Microfinance has started to enter the sphere of mainstream financial markets. Commercial banks such as Citigroup, Dexia Bank, ABN Amro Bank, ICICI Bank, ING, Commerzbank, and Deutsche Bank are expanding their activities and investments in this area. Some outstanding microfinance institutions (MFIs), such as Compartamos, have been tapping directly the capital markets (both international and domestic) through the issuance of bonds. Not only are the funding sources in microfinance expanding but also new investment vehicles are surfacing such as collater-alized debt obligations (CDOs), securitization of microloans, and fund of funds. The acceleration in the growth of microfinance funds over the past few years was partly due to the public awareness raised by the UN, which proclaimed 2005 as the International Year of Microcredit.

The Consultative Group to Assist the Poor (CGAP) estimates that in recent years multilateral donors and development agencies have provided between US$0.5 to US$1 billion annually in grants and soft loans to microfinance. In addition to these donor funds, more than US$1.2 billion had been invested in about 500 MFIs by more commercially-oriented players between 2000 and mid-2004.[2]

BRIEF HISTORY

Funding in microfinance can be traced back to the late 1970s and early 1980s when entities in Brazil, Bangladesh, Bolivia, and Indonesia started to set up what are known today as microfinance institutions (MFIs). These institutions were mostly local NGOs providing microcredit to the poor. The encouraging results of these pioneering entities such as ACCION, Grameen Bank, and FINCA attracted the funding of non-profit organizations, private foundations, and developing agencies as a promising tool for poverty eradication and economic development. The financial and non-financial supports provided by these organizations were aimed to nurture, develop, and replicate these MFIs as well as to help them become self-sustainable.

Estimates of how many MFIs exist today vary widely. A total of 3164 MFIs reported to the 2005 Microcredit Summit Campaign,[3] and other industry estimates suggest the number of MFIs may be as high as 7000–10 000. Microcredits, or small loans to the poor, were initially the core service provided by many MFIs. Over the years, MFIs and supporters alike realized that the poor needed not only loans but secure saving facilities, insurance, pensions, and affordable money transfer services. Thus, the word microfinance was coined, encompassing all these financial services.

Funding in microfinance often refers to funding (investment, financial or non-financial support) the financial service providers or MFIs. Nevertheless, equally important is the funding for the infrastructure of the industry aiming to lower costs and enable transparency. The creation of services such as transfer and payment systems, credit bureaus, rating agencies, and auditors are just a few examples of infrastructure-related funding. This second type of funding is imperative in order to bring microfinance close to the mainstream financial systems. The rapid growth achieved in the area of microfinance in the past ten years would have not been possible without both types of funding.

The Evolution or Revolution of Microfinance

Entering the 1990s, the movement toward the commercialization of microfinance took off. Marguerite Robinson referred to this as "the microfinance revolution – the paradigm shift in progress in microfinance: from government- or donor-led subsidized credit delivery system to self-sufficient institutions providing commercial finance."[4] This paradigm shift was caused by the realization of the industry (donors, practitioners, MFIs) that unless MFIs become self-sustainable, they would perpetually struggle to survive as well as to increase their outreach. *The main obstacle was funding.*

If MFIs were solely dependent on donors funds, they would not only be vulnerable if the funding were cut or reduced but also struggle to reach the potential demand of funds for the people at the bottom of the pyramid. MFIs needed to be able to tap the unlimited commercial sources of funding; in order to achieve this objective, they have to become self-sustainable. The same applies to the clients of the MFIs or the economic active poor. Access to funding is indispensable for the poor as this allows them to start a trade or small businesses to generate or increase their income. There is a limit on subsidized credit provided by governments. Furthermore, if people start businesses based on subsidized funding, they incur the risk that their business will not achieve sustainability in the long run. The people at the bottom of the pyramid require access to funds on an ongoing basis, even if they have to pay commercial rates. The important point is for them to have access to financial services when they need it.

In June 1995, CGAP, the Consultative Group to Assist the Poor (www.cgap.org), was launched by nine donor agencies. This consortium was created with the objective to help create permanent financial services to the poor on a large scale. At the end of 2005, CGAP had 31 public and private developing agencies as members. CGAP has been building the framework of the industry by servicing four different groups: development agencies, financial institutions including MFIs, government policy-makers and regulators, and service providers such as auditors and rating agencies. CGAP provides to all these groups, advisory services, training, research and development, consensus-building on standards, and information dissemination. CGAP's role as a global resource center and coordinator between the different players has been and continues to be instrumental in supporting the development and the commercialization of the microfinance industry. CGAP aims to build inclusive financial systems, which it defines as "a world in which poor people are not viewed as marginal but legitimate clients of the countries' financial system."[5]

The commercialization of the microfinance industry is well under way. An attempt to illustrate this movement as well as the positioning of this industry is shown below in Figure 12.1.

It is possible to say that microfinance was born and nurtured in the social/non-profit world. Subsequently, in the past 25 years it has been growing dynamically while moving toward the commercial/for-profit world. This movement refers specifically to (1) the increase of regulated financial institutions[7] catering to the low-income or base-of-the-pyramid (BOP) people; (2) the ongoing infrastructure building of the industry (enabling policy frameworks, regulation, supervision, credit bureaus and ratings, information systems, promoting financial transparency, governance, and creating performance measurement tools); and (3) the

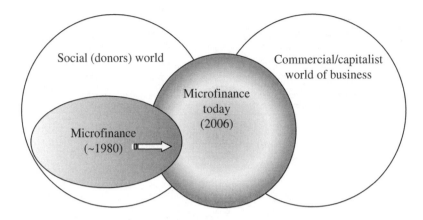

Source: Felder (2005).[6]

Figure 12.1 Microfinance today

emergence of investment vehicles to attract funding from commercial investors.

Nevertheless, it is unlikely to foresee the microfinance industry becoming fully incorporated into the commercial/for-profit world. Some MFIs and investment products will be targeting exclusively the commercial/for-profit world while new start-up MFIs and the ongoing infrastructure building of the industry will remain dependent on the support of the social/non-profit world. Microfinance is likely to remain part of both worlds and will continue to expand, creating a middle world of its own, a social-business world. The reason why such a diversity of players exists in the field of microfinance is due to this phenomenon that the industry is part of both worlds. The players come from the whole spectrum of social (NGOs, development agencies, private foundations, academia), socio-commercial, and commercial (private and institutional investors) organizations (see Figure 12.2). They fund the industry through different interventions (donations/non-financial support/investments). One of the areas where funding has seen especially rapid growth is through microfinance investment vehicles in the form of investment funds.

INVESTMENT VEHICLES

One important outcome of the commercialization of microfinance has been the emergence of investment vehicles to provide loans/equity/guarantees to self-sustainable MFIs or to MFIs working to become self-sufficient. In 1995

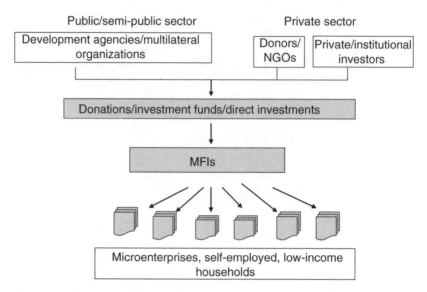

Source: ResponsAbility Ltd., NFK Felder Consulting.

Figure 12.2   Flow of funds

Table 12.1   Investment vehicles

	All Funds		Private Funds	
	(74)	%	(38)	%
Loans and debt	63	85.1	33	86.8
Equity	44	59.5	32	84.2
Grants	17	23	5	13.2
Guarantees	34	45.9	19	50
Technical Assistance	35	47.3	14	36.8

Source: Data from Mixmarket.

the first investment fund, Profund, was launched, backed by four non-profit organizations.[8] In 1998, Dexia Microcredit Fund, the first fund aimed at private and institutional investors, was registered in Luxembourg. Ten years after the emergence of the first fund, we have 74 investment funds, out of which 38 are private funds.[9] There is a great diversity of funds in terms of the objective of the funds (ranging from purely social to commercial) as well as in the instruments used. The table above shows the breakdown of the instruments used in these funds.

EXEMPLARY CASES OF FUNDING/INVESTMENT IN MICROFINANCE

Numerous outstanding organizations have played and continue to play important roles in the development of the microfinance industry. BRAC, Grameen Bank, Compartamos, BRI, and microfinance networks such as ACCION, FINCA, and Women's World Banking are all well known for their significant contributions. Some exemplary cases of institutions that created different types of funding/investment structures and partnerships to cater to the microentrepreneurs are featured below.

ProCredit Holding AG (PCH) – www.procredit-holding.com

ProCredit Holding (former name IMI AG) is a German development-oriented investment company that was founded in 1998 by the consulting firm IPC and IPC Invest. PCH's core business is the provision of formal credit and financial services to micro and small enterprises. PCH implemented its concept of establishing target-group-oriented fully licensed banks with public and private ownership. Its target group is micro and small enterprises and "ordinary people." Ninety-five percent of PCH's customers' deposits and loans are in amounts below EUR10000 and for 55 percent of borrowers and 90 percent of depositors the amounts are less than EUR1000.[10] According to C.-P. Zeitinger, Founder and Chairman of the ProCredit Group, "the ProCredit Banks have evolved from a network of microfinance banks originally supported by subsidies (technical assistance and soft credit lines) into a group operating at market terms and conditions."[11]

At the end of 2005, only seven years after its inception, PCH had set up 19 microfinance banks in Eastern Europe, Latin America, and Africa and employed 8000 people who served more than 1 million customers. The outstanding loan portfolio reached EUR1.4 billion and deposits amounted to EUR1.2 billion. PCH is an extraordinary case of a successful venture both in achieving sustainability and scale.

BlueOrchard Finance SA – www.blueorchard.com

BlueOrchard is a Swiss asset-management company that specializes in microfinance investment advisory services. The company has been linking microfinance to capital markets by launching investment products for the private sector. The company is the manager of the Dexia Microcredit Fund, the first private worldwide and fully commercial microfinance investment fund. The fund provides short-term to medium-term loans in hard currency to MFIs while offering to investors both a financial and social return. The fund aims to offer to investors a financial return higher than the six-month LIBOR and a social return by making available financial services to low-income people in emerging markets. At the end of January 2006, this fund had assets over US$77 million and was servicing loans to 57 MFIs spread over 23 countries.

BlueOrchard, in partnership with Development World Markets, LLC, also launched a long-term lending facility in collaboration with OPIC. The structured financial instrument, BlueOrchard Microfinance Securities I LLC, provides seven-year loans to the top MFIs worldwide. The total value of these loans is US$81.25 million.[12] In addition, the company is the fund adviser for one debt segment for responsAbility Global Microfinance Fund (rAGMF) sponsored by Credit Suisse and is the fund co-manager for Saint-Honoré Microfinance Fund sponsored by La Compagnie Financière Edmond de Rothschild Banque.

Calvert Social Investment Foundation – www.calvertfoundation.org

Calvert Foundation is an American non-profit organization focusing on community investment with the goal to help end poverty. The foundation provides a vast range of innovative products for investor participation ranging from donation to investments. The Calvert Community Investment Notes offered to the public allows the investor to choose the financial return[13] and the program (i.e., Oikocredit, Microvest, National Peace Corps Microenterprise Program, etc.). The minimum investment starts at US$1000 and enables many private investors and donors to participate. The foundation's loan portfolio at the end of 2005 reached US$83 million placed in 195 non-profit community development organizations and social enterprises. In 2005, nearly half of the disbursements of the foundation went to international microfinance efforts that primarily serve women entrepreneurs. In the past ten years Calvert has recycled more than US$300 million in investments that have helped create 127 000 jobs for low-income individuals, built or rehabilitated 7020 affordable homes, and financed 7398 non-profit facilities, including day-care centers, community health clinics, and schools.[14]

Oikocredit and Triodos Bank

These two outstanding Dutch institutions[15] have been supporting the development of the microfinance industry since its infancy. Oikocredit was established in Rotterdam in 1975. It is a worldwide cooperative society aiming to promote global justice by challenging people and churches to share their resources through socially responsible investments and by empowering disadvantaged people with credit. Individuals can participate by subscribing to buy shares in Oikocredit through Oikocredit's support associations worldwide. The shares are valued at US$200 or EUR200, and dividends are capped at a maximum of 2 percent. As of the end of 2004, more than 50 percent of the outstanding loans of Oikocredit amounting to EUR60 million were spread amongst 150 MFIs in four continents.[16]

Triodos Bank is a pioneer in sustainable banking. Triodos was initially set up as a foundation in 1971 and became a bank in 1980. Triodos Bank finances companies, institutions, and projects that add social, environmental, and cultural value with the support of depositors and investors who want to encourage the development of socially responsible and innovative business. Triodos has launched several social funds to achieve its mission. Three of these funds target the area of microfinance: Triodos-Doen Foundation, Hivos-Triodos Fund Foundation, and Triodos Fair Share Fund. The assets of these funds amounted to EUR32.5 million, EUR24 million and EUR12 million, respectively, at the end of 2005.[17] Both Oikocredit and Triodos Bank have been praised by the microfinance industry as being among the first to provide much-needed local currency loans to MFIs.

ICICI Bank

ICICI Bank is India's largest private bank with an asset base of US$45 billion.[18] The bank has been rapidly expanding on two fronts: on one hand building a global presence and on the other, covering the BOP through innovative ways such as partnerships with NGO MFIs across India. The bank's microfinance portfolio has increased from 10 000 clients to 2 million clients, and assets have risen from US$4.5 million to US$350 million in just five years (up to January 2006). ICICI has partnered with 72 MFIs and provides direct lending to self-help groups (SHGs). ICICI is also expanding rural outreach through low-cost networks. The bank is setting up Internet kiosks to be run by microentrepreneurs and kiosk network owners. ICICI Bank is a model of how a formal, large financial institution can make inroads to cover the BOP profitably by using new business models and technology.

Other Interesting Ventures

In addition to the five examples mentioned earlier, numerous innovative strategies and funding vehicles have been set up in recent years:

- Unitus (www.unitus.com) is a global microfinance accelerator that provides capital and capacity-building consulting to MFIs with high growth potential. Unitus is a non-profit institution that acts as a social venture capital investor for the microfinance industry. In 2006, Unitus launched the Unitus Equity Fund, which invests in MFIs with a high concentration in India.

- MicroCredit Enterprises LLC (www.mcenterprises.org) is a non-profit organization that sources and leverages guarantor-backed loan funds to finance the microbusinesses of impoverished families throughout the developing world.
- Kiva (www.kiva.org) is a non-profit organization that provides a "sponsor a business" service by linking private individuals to micro-entrepreneurs needing loans in developing countries. Kiva uses the Internet and Paypal for money transfers and works with MFIs for the selection and monitoring of microentrepreneurs.

MICROFINANCE VS. MICROFRANCHISE FUNDING

As seen in the previous section, funding in the area of microfinance has been growing rapidly due to a diversity of players, interventions, and products. The industry is likely to continue growing, benefiting from the infrastructure or framework (policy, regulatory, supervision, audit, rating, consensus-building on standards) that has been built over the past ten years. This section attempts to look into the following issues:

1. Can microfranchising make full use of the existing microfinance framework, funding mechanisms, and investment vehicles?
2. What kind of institutions or entities would be most effective in providing the funds and support to develop microfranchising operations?

Microfranchising, the replication of microenterprises by following proven operational concepts, is the next step or the next rung that follows micro-credit and microfinance on the economic development ladder.[19] Kirk Magleby, a strong proponent of the microfranchise movement, has identified five constituencies that are currently developing microfranchise networks.[20] These constituencies are indigenous franchisors, MNCs, domestic corporations, NGOs and social enterprises, and MFIs.

In order to start a microfranchising operation, the following steps need to be implemented:

1. set up or identify a microenterprise that is replicable (microfranchisor);
2. make this business into a franchisable format;
3. set up a few company-owned stores or pilot stores;
4. sell/provide this concept to microentrepreneurs (microfranchisee);

5. train the microfranchisees;
6. roll out the franchise;
7. replicate the franchise in other areas (villages, countries).

From the funding point of view, it is important to distinguish between two evolving models that differ depending on who the microfranchisor is. The first model has the microentrepreneur as the microfranchisor. The microentrepreneur is the originator of the potentially replicable enterprise. This model unleashes local entrepreneurship by creating both microfranchisors and microfranchisees at the base of the pyramid.

This model requires an entity that provides financial and non-financial support throughout the process of launching the franchise (Steps 2, 3, 5, 6 and 7). This entity could be an NGO, a social enterprise, an educational institution, or a social venture capitalist that can provide entrepreneurial training and business development support. If these entities choose to give grants, they could implement the whole process on their own; otherwise, they could partner with MFIs for funding and for finding potential microfranchisees.

The Academy for Creating Enterprise (the Academy) is an example of an NGO/educational institution involved in this type of microfranchising. The Academy selects replicable businesses from the microenterprises set up by its graduates and assists in converting these into microfranchise businesses. These microfranchise businesses launched by the Academy include Cellular City, which has expanded to more than 34 outlets; Majarlika Drugstores; Mr. Dreamburger; and USA Ink Patrol, an ink-jet refilling business.

The second microfranchise model has an established company/entity rather than an independent microentrepreneur as the microfranchisor. The entity ideally already has a proven business format and a line of products and services to bring to the market. MNCs, domestic companies, social enterprises, and large MFIs are well positioned to participate in microfranchising under this model, which concentrates on making microfranchisees.

The second model requires less involvement of external parties in launching the businesses because the microfranchisor is capable of creating the franchise format and providing the training (Steps 2, 3 and 5). They might opt to fund it themselves or might look for assistance for finding and funding the microfranchisees. Thus, this model is likely to be faster to launch and replicate compared with the first model. The CFWshops by the HealthStore Foundation, Scojo Vision, Honey Care Africa, HP Photo India, and Shell Solar are examples of this model. The Grameen Village Phones of Bangladesh is one of the most successful microfranchises existing today. The village phone project was started in Bangladesh by Grameen Bank and later was replicated in other countries through the Grameen Technology Center of Grameen Foundation USA. Many variations of potential partnerships exist for this model between the MNC/domestic company/social enterprise and an MFI.

Potential Key Players

The financial service providers operating at the base of the pyramid (MFIs and microbanks) are likely to become one of the key players in microfranchising as they are the most obvious funding source for the microfranchisees and local microfranchisors.[21] The targeted clientele (the low-income and economically active poor) for microfranchising is the same clientele as that of microcredit and microfinance. Like everyone else, this clientele needs access to financial services (microfinance) and funding (microcredit) to start an income-generating activity or business. This is the core business of MFIs. Some MFIs might opt to set up a separate department handling microfranchises (as in the case of SKS in India), some might not differentiate these businesses as it is the same as their core business, and some MFIs that have entrepreneurial training programs might choose to specialize in microfranchising.

Another reason for the MFIs to play an important role is due to the distribution network they have built over the years. The innovative partnership launched between BRAC and Scojo Vision is such an example. BRAC, which serves more than five million clients in Bangladesh, plans to sell Scojo Vision microfranchises to its clients. BRAC brings an established distribution network to the partnership, and Scojo Vision brings a much-needed product line. Similarly, other MFIs that enter into microfranchising partnerships with companies are likely to benefit by making use of established distribution networks.

In addition to MFIs, key players will include the providers of entrepreneurial skills, training, and business development services. In setting up, rolling out, and running a microfranchising operation, the microfranchisor and microfranchisees need entrepreneurial skills and business development training. This training is imperative for microfranchise models to succeed. MFIs, in most cases, do not possess this knowledge. Educational institutions, NGOs, social enterprises, development agencies, social venture capitalists, venture capitalists, consultants, MNCs, and domestic companies could enter this field by providing these crucial services.

Funding Sources

Funding for microfranchising is likely to follow a similar course taken by microfinance, albeit at an accelerated pace. Donor funds are likely to be the main source of funding at the early stages; thereafter, private investors and commercial investors will follow. The funding sources for the individual projects will depend on the entities involved.

Microfranchising will benefit from the existing infrastructure and the investment vehicles designed for MFIs because microfranchising is most likely to become part of MFIs' business operations. For example, it would be hard to imagine that ProCredit Holding's 19 microbanks catering to one million micro and small entrepreneurs would not be interested in offering or supporting microfranchise opportunities.

Microfranchising is likely to attract commercial capital (i.e., private equity) much faster than in the case of microfinance because many of these franchises will be operating in the formal sector. It will also attract donor funds because it will offer very high social returns. The probability is high that new investment funds dedicated to microfranchising will be launched both for social and commercial investors. SME funds and venture capital funds are also likely to enter this sector. Microfranchising is the rung that was missing in the economic development ladder between the small microentrepreneurs running family businesses and the SMEs.

CHALLENGES AND EXPECTATIONS

Challenges to the microfranchising movement are likely to be related to its enormous potential growth and popularity. Three areas of concern are: (1) regulatory framework; (2) imbalance of resources such as enough funds but a lack of trainers for capacity building; and (3) issues related to the diversity of players with different objectives (missions):

- Information dissemination and regulatory framework. Effective information dissemination and advocacy/marketing will be crucial for the smooth development of microfranchising. An urgent task is to market the concept of microfranchising to the microfinance industry and CGAP; this marketing effort would lead to the full use of the existing framework for microfinance. The role of MFIs will be very important not only as the funding source for microfranchisees but as networks delivering the goods and services.
- Funds and skills training (capacity-building). Funding from donors and private investors might be less of a problem or challenge for the industry. Funding is likely to appear when several successful microfranchising businesses start surfacing. The launching of these businesses will depend on the institutions that will engage in skills training and business development support. But questions remain:

are there enough institutions to provide these skill sets and are they willing to do it?

- Diversity of players. Some challenges are likely to surface depending on the format of who the microfranchisor would be (MNC, social enterprise, MFI, local company, or local microentrepreneur). For example, is there a risk that microfranchises with an MNC as the microfranchisor might limit the microentrepreneurs in developing countries from getting the full or fair benefit of the business, or might limit the potential of "unleashing entrepreneurship" in developing countries? Most likely this risk exists. Nevertheless, as there are four other formats it is highly likely that collaboration between parties such as MNCs with MFIs and/or social enterprises with MFIs or local microentrepreneurs would limit the risk of MNCs abusing the microentrepreneurs from getting their fair share. Microfranchising, similar to microfinance, will develop in an environment with the participation of players covering the whole spectrum from social to commercial, thus spurring healthy debates between the pro-poor and the commercial camp.

A major advantage that microfranchising has in its course of development is that it has just started. Information dissemination can be made quick and effective thanks to the existing technology and also due to the readiness of the people. The technology available today and the extent to which the world is connected are much more advanced than a few years ago and not at all comparable to ten years ago. Furthermore, the increasing awareness, acceptance, and interest in "social good" and "socially responsible investment" will make microfranchising an attractive proposition to people and organizations.

Microfranchising is a powerful tool and an accelerator to eradicate poverty. It creates not only wealth at the base of the pyramid but also employment. It is a simple and convincing concept that individuals and organizations will embrace fully. Thus, there will be entrants from all segments and industries (private and public sector, NGOs, for-profit and non-profit social enterprises, academia, financial institutions, etc.). New partnerships and many different formats of microfranchise will emerge. It is the most promising tool we have to empower the people at the base of the pyramid and to make poverty history.

NOTES

1. List of 74 funds can be found in the Appendix at the end of this chapter.
2. Gautam Ivatury and Julie Abrams (2005), CGAP Focus Note No. 30, The Market for Foreign Investment in Microfinance: Opportunities and Challenges, CGAP.
3. Sam Daley-Harris (2005), State of the Microcredit Summit Campaign Report.
4. Marguerite S. Robinson (2001), *The Microfinance Revolution: Sustainable Finance for the Poor*, p. 3.
5. http://www.cgap.org/strategic_priorities.html.
6. Naoko Felder (2005), *Introduction to Microfinance* (in Japanese language), p. 66.
7. These institutions are a result of (a) NGO MFIs transforming into regulated financial institutions, (b) commercial banks entering the microfinance field and (c) new micro and small banks created by public/private partnership as in the case of ProCredit Holding (formerly IMI AG).
8. Accion, Calmeadow, Fundes, and SIDI.
9. Data as of 31 January, 2006, www.mixmarket.org.
10. C.-P. Zeitinger (2006), *Procredit Holding News*, 6 January.
11. C.-P. Zeitinger (2006), *ProCredit Holding News*, 8 January.
12. This amount is the combined assets after two closings July 2004 and April 2005.
13. 0–2 percent for one to three-year notes and 0–3 percent for five, seven, ten-year notes.
14. www.calvertfoundation.org/mediacenter.
15. The Netherlands has been in the forefront in supporting microfinance amongst the industrialized countries. In 2003, 13 Dutch organizations formed Netherland's Platform of Microfinance (15 members at the end of 2005).
16. http://www.oikocredit.org/site/microcredit/doc.
17. http://www.triodos.com/com/about_triodos/?lang=.
18. Presentation by Sonjoy Chatterjee (2006), ICICI Bank in Micro-finance 3 February, Amsterdam.
19. Definition given by Jason Fairbourne and Stephen W. Gibson, BYU Center for Economic Self-Reliance.
20. Magleby, Kirk (2006), *Microfranchises as a Solution to Global Poverty*.
21. If it is the first model when the microentrepreneur is the microfranchisor.

FURTHER READING

Drake, Deborah and Elizabeth Rhyne, (eds) (2002), *The Commercialization of Microfinance*, Bloomfield, CT: Kumarian Press, p. 5.

Felder-Kuzu, Naoko (2004), *Making Sense: Microfinance and Microfinance Investments*, Hamburg: Murmann Verlag.

Felder Naoko (2005), *Nyumon Microfinance* [Introduction to Microfinance], Tokyo: Diamond Inc. (in Japanese).

Gibson, Stephen, W. and Jason Fairbourne, (2005), *Where There Are No Jobs: The MicroFranchise Handbook*, Provo, Utah: The Academy for Creating Enterprises.

Helms, Brigit (2006), *Access for All: Building Inclusive Financial Systems, Capturing 10 Years of CGAP Experience*, Washington DC: The International Bank for Reconstruction and Development/The World Bank.

Magleby, Kirk (2006), *MicroFranchises as a Solution to Global Poverty*, Salt Lake City: MicroFranchises.org.

Robinson, Marguerite S. (2001), *The Microfinance Revolution, Sustainable Finance for the Poor*, Washington DC: The World Bank and Open Society Institute, New York.

APPENDIX

Table A12.1 List of 74 funds (31 January, 2006)

Fund Name	Country of Incorporation	Fund Assets (US$)	% of Fund Assets Allocated to MF Investments	No. of Active MF Investments	Protected New Funds Allocated to MF Investments
1. Accion Gateway Fund	United States	5 100 000 (31/05/05)	100.00% (31/05/05)	9 (31/05/05)	0 (31/05/05)
2. ACCION Investments	Cayman Islands	12 969 985 (31/12/04)	96.47% (31/12/04)	5 (31/12/04)	5 000 000 (31/12/04)
3. AfriCap	Mauritius	13 300 000 (31/07/04)	24.06% (31/07/04)	3 (31/07/04)	– (31/07/04)
4. ALTERFIN	Belgium	11 084 244 (31/12/04)	32.74% (31/12/04)	26 (31/12/04)	1 488 729 (31/12/04)
5. ANF	Netherlands, The	28 421 190 (31/12/04)	33.33% (31/12/04)	16 (31/12/04)	11 503 815 (31/12/04)
6. AWF	Luxembourg	23 073 410 (15/09/04)	6.42% (15/09/04)	3 (15/09/04)	– (15/09/04)
7. Bellwether	India	5 000 000 (15/07/05)	100.00% (15/07/05)	6 (15/07/05)	5 000 000 (15/07/05)
8. BIO	Belgium	– (30/06/04)	n/a (30/06/04)	16 (30/06/04)	– (30/06/04)
9. CAF	Venezuela	–	n/a	26 (31/10/04)	–
10. Calvert Foundation	United States	80 000 000 (31/12/04)	25.00% (31/12/04)	40 (31/12/04)	4 000 000 (31/12/04)

11. Citigroup Foundation	United States	63 000 000 (01/01/02)	n/a (01/01/02)	42 (01/01/02)	2 400 000 (01/01/02)
12. CMI	Netherlands, The	3 000 000 (01/12/05)	100.00% (01/12/05)	0 (01/12/05)	12 000 000 (01/12/05)
13. Consorzio Etimos	Italy	16 079 805 (31/12/04)	28.00% (31/12/04)	30 (31/12/04)	5 068 446 (31/12/04)
14. CORDAID	Netherlands, The	63 473 991 (31/12/04)	54.58% (31/12/04)	90 (31/12/04)	9 473 730 (31/12/04)
15. CRESUD	Italy	2 483 480 (30/09/04)	60.00% (30/09/04)	8 (30/09/04)	2 235 132 (30/09/04)
16. CSF	Kyrgyzstan	50 000 (31/10/05)	50.00% (31/10/05)	7 (31/10/05)	500 000 (31/10/05)
17. DBMDF	United States	3 259 923 (31/05/05)	86.81% (31/05/05)	28 (31/05/05)	1 000 000 (31/05/05)
18. DEG	Germany	– (05/10/04)	n/a (05/10/04)	9 (05/10/04)	– (05/10/04)
19. Dexia Microcredit Fund	Luxembourg	51 669 512 (31/12/04)	89.67% (31/12/04)	49 (31/12/04)	50 000 000 (31/12/04)
20. DID Fonidi	Canada	3 816 870 (31/03/04)	10.30% (31/03/04)	1 (31/03/04)	2 061 110 (31/03/04)
21. DID GF	Canada	633 397 (30/06/04)	100.00% (30/06/04)	0 (30/06/04)	– (30/06/04)
22. DID PF	Canada	5 669 988 (30/06/04)	47.37% (30/06/04)	11 (30/06/04)	1 100 425 (30/06/04)
23. DOEN	Netherlands, The	64 674 337 (31/12/04)	95.25% (31/12/04)	13 (31/12/04)	20 300 850 (31/12/04)
24. ECLOF	Switzerland	n/a (31/12/04)	n/a (31/12/04)	n/a (31/12/04)	n/a (31/12/04)
25. FIG	Switzerland	3 481 771 (31/12/04)	72.08% (31/12/04)	17 (31/12/04)	– (31/12/04)

Table A12.1 (continued)

Fund Name	Country of Incorporation	Fund Assets (US$)	% of Fund Assets Allocated to MF Investments	No. of Active MF Investments	Protected New Funds Allocated to MF Investments
26. FMO	Netherlands, The	– (31/12/03)	n/a (31/12/03)	30 (31/12/03)	– (31/12/03)
27. FWWB	India	n/a (31/12/03)	n/a (31/12/03)	n/a (31/12/03)	n/a
28. Geisse Foundation	United States	14 000 000 (31/12/03)	2.14% (31/12/03)	3 (31/12/03)	100 000 (31/12/03)
29. Global Bridge Fund	United States	1 691 000 (31/05/05)	0.00% (31/05/05)	0 (31/05/05)	2 000 000 (31/05/05)
30. Global Partnerships	United States	2 000 000 (30/11/05)	100.00% (30/11/05)	9 (30/11/05)	5 000 000 (30/11/05)
31. Gray Ghost	United States	50 000 000 (10/01/05)	20.34% (10/01/05)	11 (10/01/05)	– (10/01/05)
32. Hivos	Netherlands, The	n/a	n/a	n/a	n/a
33. HTF	Netherlands, The	22 529 883 (31/12/04)	91.20% (31/12/04)	36 (31/12/04)	6 766 950 (31/12/04)
34. I&P Developpement	France	n/a (31/03/05)	n/a (31/03/05)	5 (31/03/05)	– (31/03/05)
35. ICCO	Netherlands, The	6 496 272 (31/12/04)	72.92% (31/12/04)	20 (31/12/04)	– (31/12/04)
36. IDF	United States	2 060 986 (31/12/01)	85.16% (31/12/01)	28 (31/12/01)	300 000 (31/12/01)
37. IFC	United States	– (30/09/04)	n/a (30/09/04)	52 (30/09/04)	– (30/09/04)

	Country				
38. Impulse (Incofin)	Belgium	15 413 875 (31/05/05)	100.00% (31/05/05)	6 (31/05/05)	15 413 875 (31/05/05)
39. INCOFIN	Belgium	5 600 000 (31/05/05)	80.36% (31/05/05)	13 (31/05/05)	500 000 (31/05/05)
40. KEF	South Africa	48 550 000 (31/12/01)	n/a (31/12/01)	– (31/12/01)	20 480 000 (31/12/01)
41. KFW	Germany	85 400 000 (31/12/01)	26.93% (31/12/01)	31 (31/12/01)	– (31/12/01)
42. Kolibri Kapital ASA	Norway	650 000 (31/12/04)	76.92% (31/12/04)	3 (31/12/04)	– (31/12/04)
43. LABF	United States	5 340 505 (31/05/05)	27.15% (31/05/05)	3 (31/05/05)	– (31/05/05)
44. LCCU	Lithuania	17 198 854 (01/09/05)	n/a (01/09/05)	16 364 312 (01/09/05)	– (01/09/05)
45. LFI	Luxembourg	18 022 620 (25/10/04)	100.00% (25/10/04)	0 (25/10/04)	– (25/10/04)
46. LFP	France	511 280 (25/10/04)	100.00% (25/10/04)	3 (25/10/04)	– (25/10/04)
47. Luxmint-ADA	Luxembourg	2 242 879 (30/06/05)	97.11% (30/06/05)	19 (30/06/05)	– (30/06/05)
48. MFDF	Mongolia	3 000 000 (05/03/04)	44.13% (05/03/04)	11 (05/03/04)	500 000 (05/03/04)
49. Microfinance Alliance Fund	Philippines	1 700 000 (31/12/01)	70.59% (31/12/01)	10 (31/12/01)	– (31/12/01)
50. MicroVest I	United States	14 400 000 (30/06/05)	93.75% (30/06/05)	16 (30/06/05)	20 000 000 (30/06/05)
51. MIF	United States	– (31/12/04)	n/a (31/12/04)	19 (31/12/04)	20 000 000 (31/12/04)

Table A12.1 (continued)

Fund Name	Country of Incorporation	Fund Assets (US$)	% of Fund Assets Allocated to MF Investments	No. of Active MF Investments	Protected New Funds Allocated to MF Investments
52. NOVIB	Netherlands, The	– (31/12/04)	n/a (31/12/04)	50 (31/12/04)	9 700 000 (31/12/04)
53. Oikocredit	Netherlands, The	304 662 000 (31/12/04)	26.51% (31/12/04)	169 (31/12/04)	39 125 000 (31/12/04)
54. Omidyar	United States	400 000 000 (12/05/05)	6.25% (12/05/05)	7 (12/05/05)	25 000 000 (12/05/05)
55. OTI	United States	13 500 000 (31/08/04)	143.70% (31/08/04)	13 (31/08/04)	5 000 000 (31/08/04)
56. Partners for the Common Good	United States	7 095 500 (30/09/04)	4.23% (30/09/04)	5 (30/09/04)	– (30/09/04)
57. PCH AG	Germany	110 918 700 (30/09/04)	80.40% (30/09/04)	19 (30/09/04)	– (30/09/04)
58. PKSF	Bangladesh	– (30/06/02)	n/a (30/06/02)	188 (30/06/02)	– (30/06/02)
59. PlaNet MicroFund	France	407 129 (14/11/05)	93.50% (14/11/05)	18 (14/11/05)	100 000 (14/11/05)
60. PROFUND	Costa Rica	11 404 098 (30/06/04)	141.84% (30/06/04)	10 (30/06/04)	– (30/06/04)
61. PT UKABIMA	Indonesia	3 901 625 (31/12/03)	57.99% (31/12/03)	41 (31/12/03)	3 125 000 (31/12/03)
62. Rabobank	Netherlands, The	12 180 900 (30/06/04)	78.20% (30/06/04)	89 (30/06/04)	– (30/06/04)

63. responsAbility Fund	Luxembourg	40 275 725	(30/11/05)	91.72%	(30/11/05)	77	(30/11/05)	30 000 000	(30/11/05)
64. RFC	Moldova	4 800 000	(31/12/01)	100.00%	(31/12/01)	200	(31/12/01)	–	(31/12/01)
65. Rockdale	United States	8 262 477	(31/12/02)	9.35%	(31/12/02)	7	(31/12/02)	760 000	(31/12/02)
66. SFD	Yemen	5 000 000	(31/12/01)	40.00%	(31/12/01)	8	(31/12/01)	1 500 000	(31/12/01)
67. SGIF	United States	5 500 000	(30/09/04)	39.23%	(30/09/04)	9	(30/09/04)	–	(30/09/04)
68. ShoreCap Intl.	United Kingdom	28 333 000	(24/11/05)	12.29%	(24/11/05)	4	(24/11/05)	3 000 000	(24/11/05)
69. SIDI	France	12 652 433	(31/12/03)	38.12%	(31/12/03)	37	(31/12/03)	–	(31/12/03)
70. TFSF	Netherlands, The	11 073 367	(31/12/04)	63.06%	(31/12/04)	11	(31/12/04)	6 766 950	(31/12/04)
71. Triodos-Doen Foundation	Netherlands, The	34 822 585	(31/12/04)	88.00%	(31/12/04)	64	(31/12/04)	3 383 475	(31/12/04)
72. UNCDF	United States	–	(31/12/03)	n/a	(31/12/03)	12	(31/12/03)	4 500 000	(31/12/03)
73. Unitus	United States	6 325 000	(31/08/04)	112.25%	(31/08/04)	3	(31/08/04)	200 000	(31/08/04)
74. USAID Credit Guarantees	United States	–	(30/09/04)	n/a	(30/09/04)	25	(30/09/04)	–	(30/09/04)

Source: Mixmarket.

PART III

Conclusion

13. The future of microfranchising: opportunities and challenges

W. Gibb Dyer, Jr

In this final chapter I will briefly summarize what we have learned from the authors of the preceding chapters and discuss what appear to be the major opportunities and advantages as well as some of the potential problems and challenges of microfranchising. I will also outline what we feel are the questions that need to be explored in the future regarding this approach to helping the poor and disadvantaged.

THE OPPORTUNITIES AND ADVANTAGES ASSOCIATED WITH MICROFRANCHISING

The authors of this volume have gone to considerable effort to describe the various advantages of microfranchising. The major advantages are summarized as follows:

1. A microfranchise has some unique advantages for microentrepreneurs. First, it provides them with products or services and a "recipe" for success – operations manual, advertising, etc. Thus, the microentrepreneur need not "reinvent the wheel" when it comes to starting up and managing a new business. Moreover, the franchisor may also provide a ready market for the entrepreneur, making the need for developing a marketing and selling strategy unnecessary. The franchisor may also provide training, access to capital, networks, and access to goods/products at discounted prices because of the buying power of the franchisor. This can give the microfranchisee a significant competitive advantage.
2. Since franchising in general has grown significantly worldwide in recent years, it is likely to become more and more accepted as the way to start a business. Thus, attracting potential microfranchisees will likely become easier in the future.
3. There are a variety of forms of microfranchises that allow franchisors some flexibility in choosing a franchise model that fits their specific

needs and situation. Some models are relatively simple – a "business-in-a-box" – while others are more complicated and function more like cooperatives or are operated by multi-national corporations ("top-down versus "bottom-up" models).

4. Microfranchises may reduce "moral hazard" problems by increasing trust and reducing risk. The franchisor essentially becomes a "collateral agent," thus allowing the franchisee easier access to critical resources. This may foster the development of more efficient markets in developing countries.

5. Microfranchises are likely to be much more scaleable than traditional, small businesses run by "cottage industry" entrepreneurs, and hence a franchisee may be able to provide employment for several people, possibly beyond the boundaries of his or her family.

6. The cases studies we have presented suggest that successful microfranchises tend to fill a broad social need as well (e.g., communications and health). The franchisors identified an important social need and then provided the goods and services to fill that need. Thus, microfranchising can lift people out of poverty and fulfill social needs as well.

7. A partnership between microfranchising and microfinance may lead to superior results. Franchisees need access to funds to acquire a franchise and pay fees, and microfinance institutions would like to find entrepreneurs who have a proven business idea and who are backed by a reputable franchisor who can provide support (training, etc.) for their borrowers. As John Hatch has suggested in Chapter 5, the synergy generated between microfinance institutions and those involved in microfranchising may be the wave of the future.

8. New methods and institutions are being developed to fund microfranchises. Thus, microfranchising will likely be able to grow even more rapidly in the future.

THE CHALLENGES FOR MICROFRANCHISING

The authors of the preceding chapters have also alerted us to the fact that microfranchising is not without some challenges and risks. Some of these are as follows:

1. Microfranchising will only be successful if there are a sufficient number of entrepreneurially-minded people in a given area who would be willing to become a franchisee and accept the risks of ownership. Without an entrepreneurial class of willing franchisees, a franchise concept wouldn't likely succeed. There is likely to be some basic level

of education, skill, and motivation that is needed for a franchisee to succeed.

2. The experience of several cases noted that franchisees did not want to supply accurate information to the franchisor to avoid paying franchise fees. This distrust can pose a significant problem for the franchisor. The challenge for franchisors is to develop mechanisms to enhance trust between them and their franchisees.

3. Training franchisees and supporting them is seen as a significant challenge given the franchisees' backgrounds and the logistics of meeting with them – particularly in rural areas.

4. Since a franchisor provides the franchisee with a business opportunity and the means to succeed, this raises the question: are franchisees less likely to work hard and blame failure on the franchisor when things don't go well? Franchisees have a built-in excuse for failure.

5. One potential problem for economic development may be the impact that a microfranchise might have on local markets. What happens if a basket-making microfranchise is so efficient that it drives the other basket-makers out of business? Have we robbed Peter to pay Paul? Thus, a microfranchise might prove to be highly disruptive to local markets. However, we might also find, as in the case of HealthStores, that increased competition may be beneficial to consumers and improve market performance.

6. Funding large-scale franchises is likely to be a challenge. While Naoko Felder-Kuzu in Chapter 12 suggests that there are new forms of funding becoming available, it still remains to be seen if microfranchisors will have access to enough capital to scale their businesses.

QUESTIONS FOR THE FUTURE

Even though the book has, in our opinion, provided some ground-breaking information about this relatively new method for helping the poor, we are still left with several questions unanswered:

1. Are microfranchises more successful than businesses started "from scratch?" Why have some microfranchises failed? We have highlighted a number of "success stories" in the various chapters, and we might do well to do more "post-mortems" on those microfranchises that have failed to better understand why they failed.

2. Which microfranchise models work best under what conditions (for example, type of national culture, availability of capital, societal needs, etc.)? This is a question that demands further investigation.

Microfranchisors will be reluctant to expand their franchises into different countries, economies, and cultures if they don't understand the factors that determine success in different contexts. What microfranchisors will be looking for are microfranchise models that have universal application.

3. Is there a profile of a successful franchisee? This too may be contingent on the type of franchise, the national or local culture where the franchise is embedded, or several other contextual factors. To the extent that we understand the "success profile" of a franchisee, microfranchisors will be more likely to pick those who will succeed in their businesses.

4. What are the advantages and disadvantages of the various models (for example, MNC-funded microfranchises versus NGO-funded, top-down versus bottom-up)? We need to know more about each of the various models and when and where those models will be more likely to succeed.

5. What kinds of microfranchises are scaleable and sustainable over the long term? This is a critical question. Are all microfranchises equally scaleable and sustainable? Probably not. Thus, we need to better understand what models will provide for sustainable growth and opportunities for those in poverty.

6. Will microfranchising reach the "poorest of the poor?" This is probably one of the most important questions that demands further attention. It is not clear that the poorest of the poor can gain access to even modest amounts of capital to own a franchise. Moreover, they may not have the necessary background and skills to run a successful franchise. To answer this question requires further research to ascertain who are actually becoming microfranchisees and determine what segments of society are benefiting from these new opportunities.

7. How will we measure the "success" of microfranchising? This question relates to the previous question. Are microfranchises truly helping to alleviate poverty and provide social benefits, or are they merely benefiting a rather narrow band of individuals in a given region or of a certain economic strata? Clearly more research needs to be done to see who is indeed benefiting from microfranchising.

CONCLUSION

Our purpose in putting this edited volume together was not to supply a definitive answer to the problem of poverty. However, we do see microfranchising as a promising approach to the alleviation of poverty, one that can be coupled with various approaches that have been used in the past such as microfinance. We hope the various ideas presented in the chapters will stimulate the reader to explore this concept further and for those who are planning to start a microfranchise, we hope the book will provide them with some wisdom to avoid some of the pitfalls and problems associated with microfranchises. For it is only through additional experience and research with the microfranchise concept that we can fully understand its impact in lifting the poor out of poverty.

Index